19.95

D0475507

Walking with the Great Apes

Walking with the Great Apes

*Jane Goodall,
Dian Fossey,
Biruté Galdikas*

Sy Montgomery

A Peter Davison Book

HOUGHTON MIFFLIN COMPANY

Boston 1991

For information about permission to reproduce selections from
this book, write to Permissions, Houghton Mifflin Company,
2 Park Street, Boston, Massachusetts 02108.

Library of Congress Cataloging-in-Publication Data

Montgomery, Sy.
Walking with the great apes : Jane Goodall, Dian Fossey,
Biruté Galdikas / Sy Montgomery.
p.   cm.
"A Peter Davison book."
Includes bibliographical references.
ISBN 0-395-51597-1
1. Goodall, Jane, date. 2. Fossey, Dian. 3. Galdikas,
Biruté Marija Filomena. 4. Apes—Behavior—Research. 5. Women
primatologists—Biography. 6. Primatologists—Biography.
I. Title.
QL26.M66 1991
599.88'092'2—dc20   90-48043
[B]   CIP

Printed in the United States of America

AGM 10 9 8 7 6 5 4 3 2 1

Portions of this book appeared first in *Lear's* and the *Boston Globe*
Magazine.

For Dr. A. B. Millmoss

ACKNOWLEDGMENTS

I am grateful to so many people whose information, insight, and inspiration contributed to this book. I list only a few of these here; to the rest, some of whom have requested anonymity, others too numerous to list, my private thanks must suffice.

While I was traveling overseas to research this book, I especially appreciated the hospitality of several individuals. Rosamond H. Carr shared with me her rich memories and the comforts of her beautiful home in Gisenyi, Rwanda; in Tanzania, Gombe staff researcher David Gilagiza introduced me to the chimpanzees, and was a wonderful host and instructor. Dr. Richard Estes provided me with many useful contacts in Nairobi, including Bob Campbell and his two delightful hyraxes. I am indebted to Dr. Biruté Galdikas and Pak Bohap bin Jalan for making me welcome at their home and study site in Tanjung Puting and Pasir Paganj in Borneo, and to the staff and orangutans at the Orangutan Project. A special thanks to Dianne Taylor-Snow particularly for caring for me in Singapore while

I recovered from whatever disease it was I picked up in the interior of Kalimantan.

Closer to home, I would like to thank Farley Mowat for his friendship and solicitude, as well as Geza Teleki and Heather McGiffen, the Schwartzel family, Mrs. Tita Caldwell, Ian Redmond, Richard Wrangham, Amy Vedder and Bill Weber, Elizabeth Marshall Thomas and Steve Thomas, Gretchen Vogel Poisson, and Bob Fleegal. My thanks to the Goodall family — Jane, Vanne, and Grub — for their kind help and for making me welcome in their home in Bournemouth, England.

My deepest thanks to my husband, Howard Mansfield, a better writer than I and the best editor I have ever had.

Several organizations and their staffs provided me with reference materials and personal recollections. Of these I would particularly like to thank the National Geographic Society, the L. S. B. Leakey Foundation, the Jane Goodall Institute, Earthwatch, the International Primate Protection League, and the African Wildlife Foundation in both Washington and Nairobi.

I thank the Money for Women/Barbara Deming Memorial Fund for the funds and moral support provided me during this project.

I am grateful to Dr. Pamela Parker and the Chicago Zoological Society for making possible my first field studies of wild animals.

I thank Sarah Jane Freymann and my editor, Peter Davison, for contributing their ideas and impetus to this book and bringing it to fruition.

And finally I would like to thank my father, Brigadier General A. J. Montgomery, whose idea it was that I make my first trips to Africa and Australia and in whose intrepid footsteps I falteringly follow.

CONTENTS

ILLUSTRATIONS

PREFACE

This is a book about African and Indonesian apes and the women who studied them. But the book began to take shape, for me, not in Africa or Indonesia but in Australia, and not with apes but with giant flightless birds.

I was squatting, alone, amid a dry sea of angry-looking *Bassia* on a wombat preserve in South Australia. It was July, the dead of Australian winter, and the most challenging part of my task that day was to keep my equipment from blowing away. I was assisting with a study, sponsored by the Chicago Zoological Society, of the nitrogen cycle in this area. My scientific equipment, besides a case knife and a meter-square metal measure, was a bunch of thrice-reused paper lunch bags. I was supposed to lop off the plants in the sampling area, stuff them into the bags, and label them with the species names; later the plants would be dried and weighed. I looked up from my work at one point and saw, twenty-five yards away, three birds, each nearly as tall as a man, staring at me. Emus.

Emus are an ancient, flightless species, ostrichlike, with eight-inch stumps for wings, long black necks topped with periscope heads and goose beaks, and powerful scaly legs that can carry them over the outback at forty miles per hour. The emu stands beside the kangaroo on Australia's coat of arms, a symbol of that otherworldly continent.

After a few minutes the three who had been watching me strolled away, lifting their backward-bending legs with careless grace. Once their brown-feathered haystack bodies had evaporated into the brown bush, I realized I was sweating heavily in the forty-degree cold. I was stricken. I thought them the most alarming, most painfully beautiful beings I had ever seen.

For the next six months, whenever I saw them, I followed these three birds, recording their behavior and diet. After a few weeks, I was able to locate them daily, and I could approach and follow them within fifteen feet. I learned to recognize the individuals, and I named them. I never knew their sexes—it is impossible to discern sex by appearance alone—but I knew they were subadults, for they lacked the turquoise neck patches that characterize the mature animals. They always traveled together. Probably all three had hatched from the same clutch of giant, greenish black eggs, incubated by their father.

During this time I thought often about Jane Goodall, the most famous of Louis Leakey's "ape ladies." In a way our studies could not have been more different: she was studying chimpanzees, animals so closely related to man that blood transfusions between the two species are possible. I was studying beings more closely related to dinosaurs than to humans. She worked in a jungle, I in a scrub desert. She has continued her study for three decades; I knew I had to return to the States in six months. Nonetheless, I modeled my approach on hers. I reminded myself that although I had no formal scientific training, neither did Jane when she began her study. I remembered how she acclimated the animals to her presence, and I did the same: each day I wore the same clothing—jeans, the shirt I slept in, my father's billowing green army jacket, and a red kerchief, so they could easily recognize me. Like Jane, I approached the animals only to a point where they were clearly comfortable; I never wanted them to feel I was pursuing them. I did not want to steal from them, not even glimpses; I asked only that they show me what they chose to. I would enter their lives on their terms.

In doing this, I began to think about the relationships that are possible between a human and a wild animal. A relationship with a wild animal is utterly different from the bond one shares with a domestic animal such as a dog or a cat or a horse. As Vicki Hearne writes in her wonderful book, *Adam's Task*, over the centuries that man has shared the company of domestic animals, we have worked out agreements, a sort of common language, with them. Whether we like it or not, our pets and livestock are dependent on us; we are the ones in control. Our agreement is that I, the "master," will provide X (food, water, shelter, and so on), and you, the animal, will provide Y (companionship, transportation, sentry duty, and so on). The animal does not have the choice to live without us.

But with a wild animal we have no such agreement. Several kinds of relationship are possible with a wild animal. One is adversarial, like the relationship modern man has had with the wolf. Another is the relationship in which the animal is "tamed" through the provisioning of food, as children do with squirrels in the woods. Again the human writes the contract. And there is the relationship, if you can call it that, that so often exists between a field worker and the animals studied. He observes the animals from a hidden location or drugs them and outfits them with radio collars so they can be followed with tracking devices. The animals do not come in contact with the human willingly. The relationship is forced upon them independent of their own will.

But the relationship that Jane Goodall has with the chimpanzees of Gombe—and that Dian Fossey had with the mountain gorillas she studied, and Biruté Galdikas has with the wild orangutans of Tanjung Puting—is different. There is a trust between human and animal, a privileged trust unlike any other. The contract for that trust is not written by the human: the animals are the authors of the agreement. The relationship is on the animals' terms.

The trust I came to share with the emus was no contract for my safety. This is not the kind of trust you have, for instance, with your dog: most medium-sized dogs could kill a person, but we have an agreement with dogs—one that we write and enforce with our food and care—that they will not kill us. I did not have this assurance with the emus, nor did Jane or Dian or Biruté with their huge, powerful apes. The emus' legs are strong enough to sever fencing wire with a single kick. They could have killed me if they chose. Though I knew this, I didn't fear them. My trust was simply this: being with them was worth a great price.

Dian Fossey and Biruté Galdikas modeled their approach on Jane Goodall's: they began their studies by relinquishing control. In the masculine world of Western science, where achievement is typically measured by mastery, theirs was an unusual approach. It was no accident that Louis Leakey, the paleoanthropologist who launched these long-term studies of the great apes, chose three women to lead the research. Although certain men have also learned how to relinquish control, the approach seems particularly feminine. This approach allows choice and the nurturing of a relationship on the Other's terms.

As I followed the three emus, I imagined myself walking in the footsteps of three women who had been my heroines. For six months, with joy indescribable, I simply recorded what the birds did all day: they rested, preened, grazed, browsed, played, traveled. They nearly always stayed within a hundred yards of one another, these three youngsters. When one wandered farther, it would look up, seem to suddenly realize the others were too far away for comfort, and jog nearer to the other two. I loved watching them preen; when their goose beaks combed roughly through the twin-shafted brown body feathers, it recalled for me those sunny, sofa-bound afternoons when my grandmother would brush my hair. I imagined this activity comforted them; it certainly comforted me.

Soon I could approach the birds within five feet, close enough to examine their massive toenails in detail, close enough to see the veins of the leaves they were eating. I could look them in the eye, pupils black as holes, irises mahogany; when our eyes locked I felt as if I was capable of staring directly into the sun. I collected a lot of data, but no scientific breakthroughs came out of my study. The revelations were private ones.

One revelation came when I was on a fossil dig I was committed to help with, which forced me to leave the birds for a week. Each night as I lay in a sleeping bag soaked with rain, I wondered what the birds were doing. Were they sleeping, their beaks tucked under their stumpy wings? Were they wandering in the moonlight? Would the volunteer I had trained to take data in my absence be able to follow them when I was not there with her? Each night I grew increasingly miserable. I left the fossil dig a day early, worried, I thought, about losing data.

My first evening back at the park, I found that my volunteer had filled more than a hundred sheets of data. I merely glanced at them before leaving camp at dusk to look for the emus. It was windy and raining, and they were jittery, as they often were in such weather. I always had trouble keeping up with them in the evening, and this night I lost them as they faded into the darkening bush. I broke my own rule and ran after them, desperate to stay with them. But they ran away. Soaked and miserable, I embedded myself in a *Gigera* bush as the rain turned to hail, and I wept. I realized it was not just data I wanted. I wanted to be with them — and they had run away from me.

Only a few days later I would have to leave Australia. On my

last day, of course, I went out again to the emus. They seemed
to be looking for me. I followed them all day, and toward evening
they stopped to graze on some wild mustard. Then I thought: I
wish I could tell you what you have given me. How could I
express to creatures whose experience of the world was so different from mine what they had allowed me to feel? I said aloud,
in a low voice: "You have eased in me a fear more gripping
than that you feel when you are separated from the others. You
have given me a comfort more soothing than the feel of your
feathers passing through your beaks under the warm sun. I can
never repay you, but I want you to feel my thanks."

This speech was one of those expressions like laying flowers
upon the graves of the unknowing dead. The recipient doesn't
know or care. But the human species is like this: we have to
utter our prayers, even if they go unheard. So while I sat with
them that night, deep in the bush, I whispered over and over:
"I love you. I love you."

Five years after I left the emus, I began the research for this
book. The relationships Jane, Dian, and Biruté have had with
the great apes they studied were far deeper than that I had with
the three birds I studied. Jane has studied generations of chimps
for thirty years; she has known many of them from birth to
death. Dian lived among the mountain gorillas for eighteen
years; Biruté will doubtless live with the orangutans even longer.

All were passionate about the apes. Before Dian's murder I
saw all three women together at a symposium in New York. I
was warmly amused at the way each one tried to outdo the
others in showing how *her* ape was the "most human" — trying
to win the audience over to favor her animal. Orangutans, Biruté
said, seemed the most human because of the whites of their eyes.
Dian insisted that her gorillas were most humanlike because of
their tight-knit family groupings. And Jane reminded us that
chimps are the apes most closely related to man, sharing 99

percent of our genetic material. I was reminded of kids who insist "my dad can beat up your dad," or of grandmothers comparing their grandchildren. None of the women would ever think of disparaging the others' work, but each is firmly convinced that the animals she loves are the best. For they do love them. It is a love as deep and passionate as the love one has for a child or a spouse or a lover; but it is a love unlike any other. The bonds between the women and the individual apes they studied are complex, subtle, and almost universally misunderstood.

Some scientists who specialize in animal behavior believe one should not be emotionally involved with one's study subjects. But the relationships that these women dared share with the apes were the crucible in which their achievements were formed: the relationships informed their science, inspired their commitment, and transformed their lives. It is through their relationships with these animals that the women have transformed our views of ape and human, of animal and man. And it is to illustrate and honor these relationships, their power and their outcome, that I have written this book.

May 1990
Hancock, New Hampshire

I *Nurturers*

1 *Biruté Galdikas and Supinah*

BIRUTÉ GALDIKAS sits cross-legged by the female orang-utan, Supinah, who is lying spread-eagled in the dirt. "Poor Supinah. Make you better, it will make you better," Biruté croons.

Though a circle of American volunteers stands by, and a tame gibbon spies on the scene from a tree, it is as if Supinah and Biruté are the only two beings on earth. Two large, powerful, rounded female forms. Both have auburn hair, though Supinah's is redder. Biruté's hooded gray eyes do not leave the orangutan's face, and she offers her high, light voice like cool water.

Supinah, a one-hundred-pound adult, has been anesthetized so that a young American radiologist can remove the maggots from the orangutan's infected vagina. "I got all the way through medical school without seeing a maggot on a bum's leg," Judy Weinstein murmurs into her white face mask, "and here I am fishing them out of an orangutan's vagina." The doctor scrapes another pale, squirming larva off her surgical tweezers, leaving it on the dirt.

Ants crawl to the blood-stained maggots and carry them away. Though it is only midmorning, the heat presses palpably, drawing beads of sweat to forehead and lip. Soon it will be 90 degrees in the shade, humidity 90 percent—hot enough to melt film in a camera, so humid that film and cassette tapes swell and jam. Biruté, forty-two, has lived here, among the orangutans and the heat, the fire ants and the leeches, the pit vipers and the sun bears, for seventeen years. Lithuanian by heritage, Biruté was born in Germany, grew up in Canada, and was educated in the United States. But Tanjung Puting National Park, a swamp jungle in southern Indonesian Borneo, is emphatically her home.

The doctor makes an incision with the scalpel, cutting away dead flesh. With infinite gentleness, Biruté runs the long red hair of Supinah's face through the teeth of an outsized, Day-Glo-green comb. "When people do bad things to Supinah, we comb her hair, and she feels better." Biruté says this less to the gathered crowd than to the unconscious orangutan.

When Supinah first came here to Camp Leakey in 1981, having been confiscated by the Indonesian government from an illegal owner, the orangutan immediately attached herself to Biruté. By then Biruté had been living here for ten years; though she had come to study wild orangutans, she had also mothered dozens of orphaned ex-captives like Supinah, nurturing them, teaching them, until they could be released into the rain forest. Biruté guessed that Supinah might be six years old; Biruté herself was then thirty-five.

During Supinah's first year in camp, her home range was confined to the few hundred feet between Biruté's small wooden house and the staff dining hall. "She wasn't particularly clingy," Biruté recalls, "she just wanted to be with me." She would wait for Biruté on the front step of her house, lurk under the pilings of the dining hall, or watch for her from the dining hall roof.

At first Supinah showed no interest in other orangutans. When one of the dozen or so ex-captives in camp attacked her, Supinah would run to Biruté, who would soothe her, combing her hair with the big green comb.

That was seven years before my visit. Soon after that first year Supinah grew livelier and more mischievous. She began to play with other orangutans, wrestling and cuddling. She would leave camp for weeks at a time, foraging for fruit in the forest. But her enjoyment of human company did not diminish. Eyes gleaming, she would lurk behind a tree and wait for a passerby, leap upon the unsuspecting visitor to grab camera gear or notebook, then retreat to a tree to examine the prize and mouth it. She would wait on the dock to wrestle with visitors, spreading her lips in a play-face as she took their pale hands in her long black fingers for a game Biruté calls "handsies."

Biruté judged Supinah to be particularly intelligent. The orangutan quickly worked out the social hierarchy among the ex-captives who roamed the camp and made peace with the dominant females. Supinah learned how to break into the dining hall to retrieve warm Cokes and how to remove the bottle tops with her teeth before drinking the sweet contents. Several times she broke into the generator and dismantled it in a few hours.

After Biruté's work had been made famous by *National Geographic* articles and TV specials, Western volunteers streamed into her camp. Earthwatch, an organization based in Watertown, Massachusetts, recruits teams of laypeople who pay to assist with scientific field projects; the Orangutan Project is one of its most popular two- or three-week expeditions. The Earthwatchers dubbed Supinah the camp mascot. Some wrote poems and myths and ascribed the words to her. One story, "as told to Mark Rosenthal by Supinah," went:

> In the beginning the Great Orangutan created the *rawa*, the primordial swamp of cabernet-colored water. And in the *rawa* he hid all things nasty and mucky and oozy and told them, "Be still and bide your time." And to his people, the forest-men, he gave great long arms of such power that they could swing freely from

the arches of the canopy so as to never dip their shiny red coats into the foul waters. But his people were without joy and went to the Great Orangutan and beseeched their lord, "Give us cause for laughter in our forest."

So, the myth continues, the Great Orangutan created

silly Americans with puny arms and stubby legs, and let them travel many days to the *rawa* to trip confusedly over hidden logs and into dark holes, and let them cover their bodies with rashes and bites. . . . And that is why orangutans have such wide mouths: so they can laugh at Earthwatch volunteers in the *rawa*.

Supinah seemed to enjoy a good joke. She frequently master-minded raids on the guest house, working holes in the chain-link mesh over the windows to steal volunteers' towels, malaria pills, sunscreen. Once she found a can of paint in a room she had broken into and poured it over a bed in another room. She was often the first orangutan to greet visitors as they arrived by sputtering wooden motorboat up the Sekoyner-Cannon River from Pangkalanbuun, five hours away. She would wait on the dock and rush to newcomers with her long hairy red arms upraised, or poke her head under their raincapes or up the skirt of a sarong.

But then one year, after Biruté returned from her annual trip to British Columbia to teach at Simon Fraser University, she found that Supinah's bright eyes had turned haunted. In Biruté's absence Supinah had given birth to her first infant. It had died within days, for Supinah had no milk. Biruté tried to comfort the orangutan, grooming her with the comb, but Supinah would simply turn away. She no longer played with other orangutans or with visitors. And one day, said Biruté, she recognized the look in Supinah's eyes: it was the same look she sometimes saw in the eyes of one of the American volunteers. This woman's eldest son, a teenager, had committed suicide. "All of a sudden I realized the look was the same," said Biruté: "just pain, pure pain."

Biruté knows that as orangutans age they, like many other animals, tend to become less playful; adult orangutans are the most solitary of the great apes. A young adult female will sometimes spend more than a month alone without seeking contact with other wild orangutans. "But I don't think it was just that; it just wasn't typical of Supinah.

"I think," said Biruté, "that she understood the death of her infant."

Once Biruté was following a wild mother orangutan whose infant was dying. "As soon as that infant died, I have never seen such tenderness," she recalls. The mother groomed the corpse. She ate the maggots off it. She sucked the eyeballs. She carried the corpse gently, clinging to it for such a long time that the eyeballs finally popped out. Only many days later did she lay aside the mummified baby, leaving it behind in the treetop nest where she had slept the night before.

Biruté knows, in a sense, what it is like to lose a child. Her first baby, Binti, was three years old when Biruté had to give him up to live with his father in Vancouver.

Rod Brindamour and Biruté had been married for two years when they first came to Indonesia in 1971; he was a young college student with dreams of becoming a helicopter pilot. Long-term use of an antimalarial drug was causing his retinas to detach. He realized that living in the jungle was doing nothing to advance his career. And besides, he had fallen in love with Binti's baby sitter, a young Indonesian named Yuni; Biruté formally thanked her for her help with the doctoral thesis she submitted to the University of California at Los Angeles in 1978. In the middle of the following year Rod flew home to Canada with Yuni. Binti joined them six months later.

Biruté didn't particularly blame Rod for leaving. For more than seven years, while Biruté was out observing wild orangutans, Rod was cutting trails through the sweltering, leech-infested swamps, or conferring with Indonesian officials. And

within months of their arrival, the couple began to use their camp as a rehabilitation center for the captive orangutan orphans confiscated by the Indonesian government. From then on Biruté and Rod shared their bed with up to five clinging, biting, screaming infant orangutans at a time. The orphans ripped up their mattress to search for edible seeds in the stuffing. They tore apart the thatched roof of the house. At the table the orangutans would cram their mouths with rice and, while the humans weren't looking, spit the bolus into their tea. They would drink the shampoo, eat the toothpaste, and suck fountain pens dry. When Rod left Biruté, he said she loved orangutans more than she loved him.

Biruté agreed that North America would be the best home for her blond son. The couple had constantly worried that Binti would be eaten by Bornean bearded pigs. His main playmates in camp were ex-captive orangutans. The child's facial expressions, posture, and sounds became increasingly orangutanlike; on occasion, Binti bit people. A visiting psychologist gave this advice: "You've got to get him out of here." But as Binti and his father boarded the plane that would carry them both away from her, Biruté stood on the runway with tears streaming down her face.

Biruté fell in love with a former employee, Pak Bohap bin Jalan, a man of the Dayak tribe seven years her junior. They married in 1981, and with him she had two more children: Frederick, born in 1982, and Jane, named after Jane Goodall, born in 1985. Biruté has joint custody of Binti with Rod, and every year she visits him when she teaches at Simon Fraser.

Now Biruté employs and houses thirty Indonesian helpers and their families; her children with Pak Bohap have human agemates to play with. Camp Leakey is now a thriving community, not merely an isolated jungle outpost. Biruté is deeply involved with people, but she remains bound to the lives of the orangutans; the rhythms of their lives are part of her own.

Biruté Galdikas and her first husband, Rod Brindamour, used to share their thatched hut with orphaned orangutans. *Rod Brindamour,* © *National Geographic*

Three weeks before Supinah's operation, the orangutan again gave birth, in a small glade near camp. Biruté was with her, so close that they were touching. Birth, she believes, can be painful for an orangutan; she was the first primatologist to witness the birth of a wild orangutan, which occurred high in a tree. The mother animal moved about in her nest in obvious discomfort during labor and sometimes clung to the trunk of a tree as if to stop the pain. Biruté herself has given birth twice without pain-killers; Binti and Frederick were born in Indonesian hospitals, where anesthetics aren't provided for laboring women. When she groaned in pain, the nurses hushed her angrily for making noise. An Indonesian woman, she says, gives birth in silence; in the hospital labor and delivery room you can tell a woman has delivered when the silence is broken by a long, loud sigh. Then you hear the baby cry.

Supinah's second birth seemed easy. Her labor appeared to last only minutes, and then the little female slid out all at once. The one-pound infant was premature. And again Supinah had no milk. After three days the infant became feverish and dehydrated and fell into a coma. Swaddled in towels, she was nursed around the clock by American volunteers and Indonesian assistants. Finally her fever broke and her appetite returned.

Now it is Supinah's life that is in danger. Biruté was hesitant to have the operation performed because the risk from anesthesia is so great. In zoos up to one in five sick orangutans may die from the immobilizing drug. None of Biruté's orangutans have died from anesthesia, perhaps because she uses it so rarely. She is very worried now, as Supinah lies in the numbing grip of the drug.

Biruté's face is usually as smooth as a calm lake; normally she does not give herself away. Perhaps she was easier to read when she was younger, more angular, when she first came to the forest of Tanjung Puting in 1971. Then she was a twenty-five-year-old newlywed on a great adventure. But now, when Biruté looks at the old photos of herself in *National Geographic*, she notes that

Biruté soothes Supinah during her operation.
Sy Montgomery

she was never smiling. She was supple and shapely, with the face and figure of an ingenue, but her heart-shaped face, framed with auburn hair, always bore a look of almost grim determination.

Today her hair is a bit gray at the temples. Her figure and features are rounded by childbirth and maturity. She radiates a Buddhalike serenity, seldom smiling or frowning, issuing words only. The words sound pleasant; the syllables are rounded with the open vowels of the Indonesian language, like stones worn smooth. Yet you can seldom tell what she is thinking.

Biruté is not a sentimental woman. She and Rod never celebrated their birthdays at Tanjung Puting, and she cannot remember the date of her marriage to Pak Bohap. But at this moment tiny dents burrow into her brow above her oversized plastic-rimmed glasses. This is not sentimentality; this is the expression you see in an emergency room when a mother holds a sick child's hand, when a wife wipes the brow of a pain-stricken husband. It is a deeply feminine expression; her own panic is subsumed by an overriding need to soothe.

Suddenly Supinah rouses. The doctor pauses cautiously — she should not be coming out of the anesthetic this early. Dianne Taylor-Snow, acting as surgical assistant, freezes. Supinah doesn't like Dianne; the orangutan once bit a chunk out of her knee for no apparent reason. Biruté is always quick to champion Supinah's good disposition, but she admits Supinah has "a thing" about Dianne. The circle of onlookers steps back as suddenly as a shudder. Orangutans Supinah's age and size can easily push over a dead tree and are capable of ripping off a human arm. Magnified by pain, her tremendous strength could turn against us. No one knows what she will do next.

Supinah draws her lips back in a wince and grits tartar-stained teeth. "It's all right, Supinah, make you better," Biruté says gently, still stroking her hair with the big green comb. The powerful animal lays her head back down. Her eyelids, vulnerably pink in a blackened face, close gently. The operation resumes.

*

By the end of the operation, more than a hundred maggots have been removed from Supinah's body. The infection was severe; this may have been why she delivered prematurely. Supinah, semiconscious, is carried by her arms and legs to a wire and wood quarantine cage to recover.

Her baby, SiDyDy, is carried in a sling by Mr. Merciman, the chief park ranger at Camp Leakey. People talk to SiDyDy, croon to her; a man offers a finger for her to grip, as people do with a human infant. And when her caretaker rests, in a hammock strung between two trees, she nestles on his chest and sleeps.

Few wild orphans are as pathetically vulnerable as a baby orangutan. In the wild an infant clings constantly to its mother's coarse orange fur for most of its first two years. It nurses until age eight. You cannot put an orangutan baby down as you would a human infant. A healthy infant orangutan hangs on so tight with its four-fisted grip that it leaves bruises on your flesh; any attempt to dislodge the infant from your body, even for a moment, brings high-pitched, pathetic screams until it begins to choke on its own terror.

Biruté's first infant was not her own Binti; it was Sugito. The year-old male orangutan arrived only days after she and Rod had set up camp. Sugito had been taken from his mother in the wild and had lived in a tiny wooden crate until he was found and confiscated by Indonesian government officials. Determined to mother him as a female orangutan would care for her baby, Biruté slept, ate, and bathed with the wide-eyed infant clinging to her side, legs, arms, or head. Only three times in the first year did she force him off her body.

Shortly thereafter followed Sinaga, Akmad, Siswoyo, Sobiarso, Gundul . . . Biruté has mothered more than eighty ex-captives. Most arrive worm-infested, stunted, diseased. Many have died in her arms. But those who survive their infancy are then free, like Supinah, to roam through camp and its outlying forests until they voluntarily leave for life in the wild.

Before Frederick and Jane were born, Biruté would often

trudge off to the swamp forest to study the wild orangutans with an infant orangutan clinging to her side. Once, carrying Sugito, Biruté was watching a wild orangutan mother and baby in the forest, high in a tree. Sugito tried to climb the tree just as the wild baby decided to venture down it. "There we were," remembers Biruté, "this female orangutan and I—both tugging at our baby orangutans!"

Biruté mimicked orangutan mothers; her human child imitated orangutans. And in turn the ex-captive orangutans began to mimic human behaviors.

"Sometimes," Biruté wrote in a *National Geographic* article in 1980, "I felt as though I were surrounded by wild, unruly children in orange suits who had not yet learned their manners."

Sugito would occasionally alarm Biruté and Rod by using a knife and fork at their table. He loved to blow out candles at night. Another orphan piled a mound of rice onto a large, concave piece of bark and then handed the "plate" to Biruté. Once, while I was visiting Camp Leakey and preparing to bathe in the river, a young orangutan sitting with me on the dock unzipped my cover-up, pulled it off my body, and slipped it on over her own head. Ex-captives in camp have even been observed wiping their backsides with leaves. They are imitating humans who thought they had been attending to nature's call unobserved.

Today Biruté discourages allowing orangutans in her house or dining hall. But the more than fifty ex-captives she has released into the wild, as well as the twenty-five or so still under her care, continue to define Camp Leakey. As you walk the neat dirt paths connecting the visitors' dormitory with the dock and dining hall, at any moment an orangutan may leap onto your back, grab for your camera, or gently take your hand in a hairy hand or foot and stroll beside you as casually as a lover.

To have an orangutan choose your company is an honor few humans can imagine. Shortly after the operation on Supinah, Dianne Taylor-Snow and a visiting veterinarian decided to sit

Biruté has served as surrogate mother for more than fifty orphaned orangutans. *Earthwatch* out a rainstorm on the dock. As they huddled beneath their shared raincape, Kusasi, a two-hundred-pound immature male ex-captive, and Tut, a large adult female, approached from the edge of the forest. Orangutans do not like rain; they are the only apes that make roofs over their treetop nests. The two orangutans lumbered over to the two women and ducked under the raincape. The four sat together silently, the orangutans' backs to the women's chests, for fifteen minutes, until the storm's end.

And yet, even in this seemingly Edenic community of ape and human, there are misunderstandings—seldom grave but often deep.

Mr. Merciman, now caring for SiDyDy, is exceptionally gentle with infants, and Biruté is delighted with the care he provides. But sometimes, she admits, he "goes overboard." The first orphan he cared for was an infant named Dianne, who arrived in 1986. He carried her everywhere with him. One day he took Dianne on a trip to the riverside town of Kumai for supplies. When he returned to camp, he brought tiny yellow dresses, little hats. To Biruté's horror, he had bought the baby clothes for Dianne to wear.

One Earthwatch volunteer spent much of her time with Siswoyo, who is the dominant female ex-captive. Whenever the woman saw her, she would throw her arms around the adult orangutan and begin to groom her fur. Then one day she saw Siswoyo on the dock. The woman went to hug the orangutan, and Siswoyo slammed her to the ground and bit her arm.

The woman, explained Biruté, did not know that Siswoyo was having a bad day. Her infant had been whiny; she had sat all morning on Biruté's doorstep waiting for a treat, and Biruté, busy writing, had pretended she wasn't in.

Of course these are circumstances in which two humans may find each other—one may simply be in a bad mood. But there is a social pact implicit between humans; it is a pact we begin to seal in infancy as we clothe ourselves with the garments and language and customs of human culture. These agreements, however, are different from the understanding negotiated between a human and a free-living orangutan.

One of Biruté's graduate students once came to her frustrated and hurt. He had been at Tanjung Puting only a few weeks and had grown fond of an ex-captive male called Richo. "You can't trust orangutans!" he complained to Biruté. "I thought Richo was my friend, and then when I turned my back on him, he stole my soap!" He was genuinely insulted.

"That isn't what it means to be friends with an orangutan," says Biruté. "Not at all."

Biruté grew up as a child of several cultures. Born in Wiesbaden, Germany, she was two when her Lithuanian parents, with her sister and two brothers, fled Europe after the Soviet occupation. She came with them as a small child to Ontario, where her father found work as a miner, a machinist, and a painting contractor; her mother worked as a nurse. Biruté's first language was Lithuanian; she remembers that on her first day of kindergarten, in Toronto, she could understand nothing that the teacher or children said. But before first grade she was fully bilingual. She was beginning to learn, as she knows now, that "there is more than one way of looking at the world"—a view that would later serve her well.

From the moment she could read, Biruté's interests were science and history. She remembers the first book she checked out of the Toronto Public Library in first grade: *Curious George*, about a monkey. She still reads it to her own children today. Biruté loved nature. As a child she would roam Toronto's enormous High Park, collecting tadpoles in Grenadier Pond, looking for salamanders under rocks. And in the evenings, while her mother bathed her, Biruté would listen to her describe the progression of human civilization.

"I was fascinated by prehistory," Biruté once said. "Not just the written history, but all of it. Human history and beyond . . . back. I remember thinking that if we understood our closest human relatives we'd understand our origins . . . maybe our own behavior."

Fifteen million years of evolution separate Biruté from Supinah, as the woman stands by the quarantine cage waiting for the orangutan's eyes to open and meet hers. It is the eyes that have always drawn Biruté to orangutans; unique among the eyes of apes, the irises are surrounded by white, like ours.

Fifteen million years ago orangutans and humans shared a common ancestor, a being whose experience of the universe we can only imagine. It probably loved and protected its young, lusted for the opposite sex, enjoyed a good meal; it may well have possessed a sense of humor, guarded its memories, mourned its dead.

The people of Malaysia and Indonesia recognize this kinship and honor the orangutan with its name, which is Malay for "person of the forest." Biruté pronounces the name with reverence: orong-oo-tahn. Never does she call one an "orang," which would mean "person."

People and orangutans have traveled separate evolutionary paths for fifteen million years. The path the orangutan took was arboreal, and it is in the leafy world between earth and sky that their social agreements have been worked out.

Once Biruté followed a wild female orangutan who was moving through the trees for thirty-one days. She met up with other orangutans only five times. Sometimes the female didn't even glance at them. The total time spent in association with other orangutans, besides her dependent offspring, was perhaps six hours in a month.

Harvard primatologist Peter Rodman, after completing a fifteen-month study of wild orangutans at Kutai in Borneo, commented that "orangutans are hardly more social than any mammal must be." Because orangutans eat mainly fruit, a resource widely scattered through the forest, the large, slow-moving adults do not travel in groups or bands like gorillas or chimpanzees or humans; a large group would quickly eat all the ripe fruit in a given area. Adult females usually travel with only their dependent young. Adult males seek company only to mate with a chosen consort. They will battle bloodily with invading males. They are solitary, serene in their aloneness, "their only company," their inner universe Biruté says. But she has found another side of orangutan life. She has discovered that subadult orangutans, particularly females, are quite social, sometimes spending days together foraging and traveling through the canopy.

One of the wild females Biruté has long studied is Fern, whom she first encountered as a juvenile traveling with her mother, Fran. Mother and daughter traveled together through Fern's first pregnancy. But after Fern gave birth, Biruté did not see her associate with her mother for ten and a half years.

Sometimes, though, the two orangutans would be in nearby treetops. "From the lack of interest each paid the other," Biruté wrote, "I would never have guessed, had I not known, that this was a mother and her grown-up daughter . . . just moving by each other with not so much as a blink of the eye to signal overt recognition."

This solitary life is the heritage for which Biruté prepares the orphans with whom she has slept and bathed, cuddled and fed. Unyuk, one of Biruté's favorite orphans, would scramble into her arms as to a mother. She used to give Biruté French kisses. And then one day Unyuk went into the forest and did not return for two years.

Biruté remembers the day Unyuk returned to visit camp. "The only sign she recognized me was, she just looked at me. She looked at me, and her eyes locked into mine. And then when I came real close to her she made a little squeak. And for an orangutan, that's a big thing. That's all there is for an orangutan. That's the nature of the animal, the nature of the being."

It is far more difficult to establish a relationship with a wild orangutan than to make friends with an ex-captive. Food is not in the equation; and they show no interest in our cameras or clothing or culture. Their world—leaves, bark, fruit, sky, earth, swamp—is complete without us.

Yet Biruté has forged a friendship with a wild adult male orangutan. She calls him Ralph. From the sides of his dark face swell two enormous, fleshy cheek-pads, each the size of half a dinner plate. A deflated air sac, used in producing the male's bone-chilling, soul-shattering, territorial long call, droops above his chest. His body is shaped like a sumo wrestler's. He weighs close to three hundred pounds. Each of his three-foot-long arms embodies the strength of perhaps five men. Biruté once saw him pluck a fair-sized tree from the ground.

When she first saw him in the forest, Ralph was an adult male in his prime. Sixteen years later he seems not to have aged; orangutans may live longer than sixty years. Ralph is not old yet, though he has known many battles. His cheek-pads are notched, his back bears vestiges of a circular wound, and several of his long fingers are stiffened from repeated injuries. As far as Biruté knows, he has never lost a fight.

Once when Biruté's daughter Jane was two, Biruté encountered Ralph unexpectedly near camp. Biruté was alone, holding Jane in her arms. Ralph stopped fifteen feet from her. He was on the ground between her and the trail to camp. He raised his jaw—a reverse nod, as if pushing her away with his chin. Biruté did not move. "It took your breath away, he was so close," Biruté remembers. But still she stood her ground. Ralph looked her in the eye, then turned his back.

"I was so elated—that really shows how deep our relationship is. It's so much deeper than it would be between human beings if that's all there was between them." For an adult male orangutan to turn away—to choose not to flee or attack—is a sign of deep trust, respect, and affinity. For Biruté it is as moving a gesture as an embrace between two humans.

The next time Biruté saw Ralph, she was walking in the forest, miles from camp. He was consorting with a female prior to mating. Both orangutans glanced down from the trees at her. "I knew I should be following them to observe their consortship," Biruté said. "But for once I did as wild orangutans so frequently do with each other. I returned Ralph the favor." She turned her back on him and walked away.

"When you have a relationship with a wild adult orangutan, it puts down the pompousness, it humbles you. I am in awe of Ralph and his power," says Biruté. "And we're friends—as much friends as a wild adult male orangutan can be with anybody who's not his consort. Of course it's different from a relationship with a human. Because they're not human, their expectations of the relationship are totally different. The relationship is on their terms, totally."

This is what it means to be friends with an orangutan. Friendship with an orangutan, not an incomplete version of something else.

One month after her operation, Supinah weakly tries to cradle her infant. SiDyDy's head is cornered haphazardly between her mother's arm and chest. Her eyes and nose are running. Her grasping feet flail about as she tries to suckle but fails. The baby's skin shows signs of dehydration, and Biruté is worried about SiDyDy's diarrhea. Supinah, still weak, is not lactating well.

Biruté kneels gently before Supinah and helps adjust the baby in her arms. The infant nuzzles and finds the nipple under Supinah's armpit. "There, Supinah, that's better," Biruté says.

Supinah's mothering skills are confused. She has been taking SiDyDy off her body and putting the infant on the ground. For the first six years of her life, before she came to Camp Leakey, she was somebody's pet, with only humans as role models— primates who breastfeed and then lay their babies down.

Yet Biruté is moved by Supinah's natural tenderness with SiDyDy. She remembers when Supinah used to play with Fred-

The ex-captive orangutans make gentle playmates for
Biruté's younger son, Frederick. *Earthwatch*

erick, her dark-haired son. Frederick would jump on her, hit her
with his fists, even bite her. Biruté has seen young orangutans
act like this in the wild. Sometimes a youngster throws a temper
tantrum while clinging to the mother's side, screeching and grappling and biting. Usually this happens when the youngster wants
something the mother is eating. The mother typically waits out
the tantrum, then hands the youngster a piece of fruit as though
nothing had happened. When Frederick hurled himself at Supinah, she would never fight back. She would simply tolerate
his outburst, showing him a play-face.

Supinah, so gentle with human children, still inept with this
infant of her own, waits, like Biruté, at the crossroads of two
worlds: the world of cups and saucers, clothes and houses, and
the world of rain forest, leaf and bark, fruit and sky.

Eventually, Biruté hopes, Supinah will return to the forest with her infant. SiDyDy, she hopes, will grow up as a wild orangutan. She looks at them and recalls other orangutans she has known: Unyuk, who left camp for two years and returned to greet her with only a look and a squeak. She thinks of Fern and Fran, who did not travel together or touch each other for ten and a half years. Biruté does not pretend to know what orangutans carry around in their heads. But she knows they have memories. In 1987 she saw Fern and Fran again in the forest canopy. After a decade of separation, mother and daughter embraced and then traveled for four days together.

2 Jane Goodall and Flo

FLO LAY on her back dangling her baby, Flint, above her in the sun. With one black-soled, thumbed foot she gently held her ten-week-old son's wrist; with her hand she reached up to tickle him in the groin and neck. The pink-faced baby waved his free arm and kicked his legs with the same unfocused, reflexive delight as a human infant. He opened his mouth in a toothless smile.

Flo was then very old for a wild chimpanzee, probably thirty-five. Even in the early morning sunshine, her coat looked faded, a dull brown; her ears were scarred and torn, her teeth worn to the gums. But as she gazed at her son, her brown eyes sparkled bright with playfulness.

Flo's five-year-old daughter, Fifi, stared at the infant, sometimes reaching out to touch him gently with the tips of her fingers. She craned her neck to observe her brother more closely. Nearby, Faben and Figan, Flo's older sons, chased and wrestled with each other. They pant-chuckled, chimpanzee laughter. To Flo and her family, Jane Goodall owes some of the richest portraits ever gathered of chimpanzee infant care and development and family relations.

Jane was then thirty years old and a new bride. Her husband, Hugo van Lawick, crouched beside her as she watched the chimps. Westerners usually crouch precariously on the balls of the feet; but Jane and Hugo crouched African style, soles flat on the ground. Jane, who as a young girl had practiced a full English curtsy, had perfected the African crouch after she began studying the chimps at Tanzania's Gombe Stream Reserve in 1960; not only is the stance stable, it allows you to rise instantly. Hugo, a Dutch baron born in Indonesia, had learned the crouch while working as a photographer and filmmaker in East Africa. It was this job that had brought him to Jane's camp to document her work for *National Geographic* in 1962. They had found that their lives blended easily: their love of animals and the outdoors, their commitment to their work. Hugo had proposed to Jane by cable—WILL YOU MARRY ME STOP LOVE STOP HUGO—and she had accepted instantly.

They were married on March 28, 1964, in London. Their wedding cake was topped not with a plastic bride and groom but with a clay chimpanzee. The walls of the reception hall were decorated with large color photographs that Hugo had taken of the chimpanzees: Flo and Fifi and Faben and Figan; the gentle adult male, David Graybeard, one of Jane's favorites; the powerful alpha male, Goliath.

Three weeks before the wedding Jane had received word from her camp cook, Dominic, that Flo had given birth. So the couple cut their honeymoon short—only three days—and rushed back to Gombe to see Flo's new baby.

By the time they arrived, Flint was seven weeks old. Jane will never forget the first time she saw him. "I can even recapture six years later the thrill of that first moment when Flo came close to us with Flint clinging beneath her," Jane wrote in her

1971 book, *In the Shadow of Man*. "As his mother sat, Flint looked around toward us. His small, pale wrinkled face was perfect, with brilliant dark eyes, round shell-pink ears, and slightly lopsided mouth, all framed by a cap of sleek black hair. He stretched out an arm and flexed the minute pink fingers, then grabbed Flo's hair again and turned to nuzzle and rootle with his mouth until he located a nipple." Flo cradled him beneath her, adjusting his position so he could nurse more easily. He suckled and then closed his eyes. Finally Flo got up, gently supporting her sleeping son with one hand under his back as he clung to her belly, and walked away carefully on three limbs.

Jane had first met Flo when Fifi, only two, was still riding jockey-style on Flo's back. Jane had watched Flo shelter her young daughter from the rain: Flo would hold Fifi close, folded in her great, hairy arms and feet; when the clouds cleared, Fifi would emerge from her mother's embrace perfectly dry.

Often Flo would share fruit with her young daughter; she would allow Fifi to take food from her lips or would hold out fruit to her with her callused black hand. Jane had seen them fishing for termites together: Fifi would watch intently as Flo inserted a grass probe into the mound, waiting for the termites to cling to it, to be withdrawn and eaten. Flo would then wait while Fifi inserted her own stem, imitating her mother, to fish for the juicy insects. Jane knew that Fifi slept with her mother in the leafy night nest Flo built each evening in the tall trees, comfortable, warm, nestled in her mother's arms.

And now, with her gold wedding band still gleaming new, Jane watched Flo, a mother half a decade Jane's senior, with her perfect new infant. Jane could imagine pink human fingernails, tiny and perfect, and blue eyes, and the joy of coaxing from her own child, one day, a smile.

Flo was among the first chimps Jane named at Gombe. In the early days the males were the boldest. David Graybeard would wait for Jane to catch up as she followed him through the forest, tripping over vines, ripping her clothing from the catch of thorns. But Flo, of all the female chimpanzees, tolerated Jane's presence best. With her deformed, bulbous nose, tattered ears, and lower lip that often drooped open, Flo seemed an ugly old matriarch; but when Jane looked into Flo's eyes she saw deep wisdom and calm.

Flo was confident and relaxed even in the company of the most dominant adult males, who would sometimes groom her. One female, the wobbly-lipped, long-faced Olly, was so fearful of adult males that she would nearly choke on hysterical pant-grunts if a dominant male approached her. Some female chimpanzees will flee from their own adult sons. Occasionally an adult male chimpanzee will become so caught up in a charging display, intent on showcasing his male vigor and power, that he will attack or drag anything in his path—even tiny infants, whom the males normally treat with tolerance and affection. Much later, when Flo's son Figan was about twenty years old, Jane would see him perform such charging displays: hair erect, hurling himself down a slope, running frenziedly as if propelled by some inner demon. One time Flo sat directly in his path. All the other chimps in the area scattered, but Flo stayed put. She simply ducked as her huge son leaped directly over her head.

Not all mothers would have been as calm and tolerant as this. Flo and her family sometimes traveled with timid Olly and Olly's young daughter Gilka. When Gilka begged for food, her mother usually ignored her requests; another mother, Passion, would just get up and walk away from her two-year-old, without waiting for her daughter to hop onto her back.

So Jane was astonished when calm, tolerant Flo attacked Olly's son, Evered. He had been playing with Flo's son Figan, and the two had begun to squabble. When Figan screeched, Flo rushed to her son's side, hair erect. Jane was stunned at the viciousness of the attack: furiously Flo slapped at Evered, rolling him over and over until, screaming hysterically, he escaped. For many years Jane did not understand this behavior. But Flo understood many things that Jane did not.

Flo, in her advanced age, embodied a sense of history: she had known decades of suffering, birth and death, triumph and grief that Jane could not yet imagine. The old chimp was battle scarred; her tattered ears hinted at past accidents and disease, fights won and lost. "Flo," Jane said admiringly, "was a survivor, tough as nails." She remembers wondering, what does Flo remember from her youth?

Jane was only twenty-six when she began her study. With her blond hair gathered into a girlish ponytail, her pale legs bared in shorts, Jane was an innocent in the Garden of Eden, a portrait of youth, new womanhood, and human vulnerability. She did not come here prepared by a Ph.D. or armed with theories; she came propelled by childhood dreams.

When Jane was eighteen months old, her mother gave her a toy she would cherish for the rest of her life: a stuffed chimp doll commemorating the first chimpanzee born in captivity at the London Zoo. Neighbors warned Jane's mother that a young girl would surely develop nightmares from sleeping with such a frightful toy; but Jane loved Jubilee, as the toy was named, and still has it.

Jane's father, Mortimer, was an engineer. Her mother, Vanne, was a writer and homemaker. For most of her childhood and adolescence, Jane lived with her parents, her younger sister, Judy, and her two aunts in a large old brick house called the Birches in Bournemouth, an English seacoast town.

Jane had always loved animals and nature. When she was two, her mother discovered with dismay that the child was sleeping with earthworms under her pillow. When she was four, she spent five hours crouching in a hen house, waiting for a hen to lay an egg. "I had always wondered where on a hen was an

opening big enough for an egg to come out," Jane remembers.
That day she made the discovery.

By the time she was seven, she had read *The Story of Dr.
Dolittle* seven times, as well as *The Jungle Book* and the *Tarzan*
series, and had firmly decided that she would one day study wild
animals in Africa. Her guidance counselor at school proclaimed,
"No girl can do that!" But Vanne, Jane remembers, "brought
us up never to take no for an answer." Once Jane, hiding in a
tree, overheard her mother telling her uncle about Jane's plans.
"She doesn't have the stamina," her uncle said. Jane had begun
to suffer migraines when she started school, but from that day
forward, Jane never again complained of migraines.

When Jane went to Gombe, her life was all future, all questions, all eagerness. In Flo, Jane found the wizened old wisewoman; Jane was her initiate. To Jane, as to no other human,
Flo would pass on her experience of sexuality, of motherhood,
of the wisdom that comes with maturity. As the orangutan Supinah learned from Biruté, a human, how to be an orangutan
mother, Jane learned from Flo, a chimpanzee, how to be a human
mother. And in turn, Jane's own unfolding life deepened her
understanding of Flo's life.

Jane learned much about chimpanzee sexuality when, early on,
Flo's receptivity resulted in a stunning exhibition. Never before
and seldom since has Jane seen adult male chimpanzees so excited by a female of any age. In response to Flo's large, pink
sexual swelling, nearly every male chimpanzee Jane had ever
seen at Gombe followed her into Jane's camp: old Mr. Mc-
Gregor, Goliath, the irascible J.B., David Graybeard, young
Mike, Leakey, Hugh, Humphrey . . . and one by one, Flo approached each of them to present her fabulous swelling.

Each male, squatting in an upright position, would mate with
Flo, sometimes with a hand laid gently on her back. Intercourse
was brief—the couple would remain joined for only ten to fif-

teen seconds — but quite obviously pleasant; sometimes Jane saw the chimps close their eyes in ecstasy.

Although no fighting erupted over access to Flo, all the males seemed almost frantic with fear that she might walk away and they would lose another opportunity to mate with her; they followed her every movement with eager, hungry eyes. For nearly six weeks she was followed everywhere by this retinue of up to fourteen males. One day Jane counted Flo copulating fifty times.

During these weeks Flo conceived Flint. Of course Jane would never know who Flint's father was, but almost certainly it was someone she knew.

Jane recognized their faces, some of which were as dear to her as her own family's: Mr. McGregor; scheming, round-faced Mike; David Graybeard, whose eyes she considered the most beautiful she had ever seen; ancient, wrinkled Mr. Worzle. The females were equally recognizable: long-faced Olly, tattered Flo, taut-faced, pointy-eared Passion.

When Jane first arrived, only three years earlier, all the chimps had simply looked like black spots in her borrowed binoculars, a thousand yards away. If excited or frightened, chimpanzees seem to move frenetically, like a film run at high speed. The baboons at Gombe move with a haughty elegance, holding the base of their tails erect, like a pinkie finger extended outward from a teacup; but chimpanzees seem at first to be mumbling their movements, careless, sloppy, compared to the stiff precision of human motion.

But when they move suddenly and powerfully, chimpanzees can be terrifying animals. Although a male chimp stands only four feet tall, he weighs nearly as much as a woman — 100 pounds — and his strength is greater than that of two men. Early in her study Jane once watched chimpanzees displaying during a thunderstorm. As the rain lashed, the chimps leaped into trees, swaying the branches, their black hair bristling with excitement. Like shamans drugged to superhuman frenzy, the black apes broke off branches in their hands, jumped to the ground, and ran, dragging the branches. To the booming thunder they added their voices, pulling back their lips to expose white teeth, pink gums: they screamed and called, drumming on trees with hands and feet. The vigor of their thrashing and swaying echoed the force of the lightning-split sky.

Jane watched this not with terror but with an almost religious awe. "With a display of strength and vigor such as this," Jane wrote, "primitive man himself might have challenged the elements." The chimps' rain dance recalled man's most ancient longing: to become one with the forces of the gods.

Comparisons of DNA now show that the chimpanzee is our closest living relative, sharing 99 percent of man's genetic material. In fact, chimpanzees are more closely related to humans than they are to either orangutans or gorillas. "Chimpanzees are so like us — intellectually and emotionally — in their needs, their expectations, their outlook on life," Jane points out. When two chimpanzees greet after a separation, they may bow or crouch, hold hands, kiss, embrace, or pat one another, much like two people meeting on a street. After two chimpanzees have fought, almost invariably one will return to embrace his opponent, to lay an arm on the victor's back, to offer a hand to be kissed — just like a couple who have fought and now must make up. The games of young chimpanzees are almost identical to those played by human children. Chimps will use round fruits as toy balls, and little ones will often pirouette around and around, spinning dizzily with arms out, just the way human children do; they will use sticks to probe imaginary termite mounds, much as children use cups and saucers for imaginary tea parties.

In the chimpanzees Jane saw the beginnings of what would make man define himself as human, those characteristics we hold so precious about ourselves: our imagination and playfulness and our connections to one another, forged by touch. In the lives of the chimpanzees at Gombe, Jane saw man's heritage,

Jane Goodall peers up at Goblin, a chimp she has
known since his birth in 1964. Goblin eventually
became the top-ranking male at Gombe, overturning
the rule of Flo's son, Figan, in 1979. *Ken Regan/
Camera 5*

saw deep into the past of our lineage. And in the mirror of Flo's
dark eyes, Jane would glimpse her own future.

Before he was five months old, Flint took his first tottering steps.
For several weeks Jane and Hugo had watched Flint standing
on three limbs, one hand clutching at Flo's hair. But one morning
Jane saw Flint suddenly let go of his mother and stand on four
legs by himself. "Then very deliberately," Jane recalls in *In the
Shadow of Man*, "he lifted one hand, moved it forward safely,
and paused. He lifted a foot off the ground, lurched sideways,
staggered, and fell on his nose with a whimper." Instantly Flo
reached out and gathered him into her arms.

Fifi watched Flint's progress with fascination. From the start she had found her baby brother irresistible. She tried to touch him with her hands, her feet, her lips. As Flo held him, Fifi would fondle his minute fingers. Once Fifi was nibbling at Flint's fingers while Flo was holding him in her arms; the infant issued a whimper of distress and Flo gently pushed her daughter's hand away. Fifi rocked back and forth, twisting her arms appealingly behind her head in frustrated surrender. She continued to stare petulantly at the baby, her lips in a humanlike pout.

Flint was thirteen weeks old when Fifi finally succeeded in stealing him away from their mother. Jane watched entranced as Fifi's plot unfolded. As Flo intently groomed Figan, Flint clung to Flo's hair. Seeing that her mother's attention was elsewhere, Fifi began to stealthily pull at the infant's foot. By inches, she slipped his body toward her, then suddenly pried him free. Fifi, on her back, cuddled Flint to her belly, wrapping her prize in her arms and legs. At first neither Flo nor Flint seemed to notice; but then, with a soft plaintive *hoo*, Flint called to his mother, who then took him to her breast.

After that success, Fifi would pull her baby brother away from her mother every day, sometimes carrying him up to ten yards away to play with him privately, grooming him, tickling him, carrying him in her arms as she walked upright, just like a child with a beloved doll.

As Flint grew more independent and vigorous, Flo seemed to regain some of her youth; once, while Flo was playing with her family, Jane saw the old mother actually turn a somersault with youthful glee.

Older chimps would walk by to greet the youngster; several times Jane saw the powerful Goliath approach Flint and gently chuck him under the chin. And just as Flo had gradually allowed her daughter to play with tiny Flint, now she permitted Jane, too, to touch him. Sometimes Jane would hold Flint's hand as he walked bipedally. He would reach out to Jane as he dangled from a low tree limb or as he tottered on the ground. Hugo took several photos of Jane and Flint together. In one, Jane crouches, making herself small. She extends her right arm, her wrist rotated so her thumb hangs down, her fingers curled like young leaves unfurling from a branch. Flint reaches forth his right arm, his hand open to grasp hers. Jane's expression is soft, her lips parted in awe.

Hugo and Jane recorded and documented every event in Flint's early life — his first attempts at riding on Flo's back as he graduated from clinging to her belly, his first climb up a tree, the first time Fifi held him — with the wonder of first-time parents.

"For Hugo and me," Jane wrote in *In the Shadow of Man*, "the privilege of being able to watch Flint's progress that year remains one of the most delightful of our experiences — comparable only to the joy we were to know much later as we watched our own son growing up."

When Jane became pregnant, she wrote, "I watched the chimpanzee mothers coping with their infants with a new perspective. From the start Hugo and I had been impressed with many of their techniques, and we made a deliberate resolve to apply these to the raising of our own child."

Flo, Jane had long since decided, was a model mother. Observing her with her offspring, Jane had seen the pattern unfolding. Throughout their childhood, Flo was always with her children, ready to rush to their side at the slightest whimper or call. She was endlessly patient and would try to distract her children, often with tickling, when they were about to get into mischief. Flo constantly held, cuddled, and groomed her children and always reassured them with caresses after the occasional disciplinary tug.

When Hugo and Jane's son, Hugo Eric Louis, was born in 1967, a time when most English women bottle-fed their infants, Jane breastfed her baby on demand for a year. She was with him almost constantly, cradling him, carrying him, caressing him. Until he was three, little Hugo, who by then had acquired the nickname Grub, was never away from his mother for a single night.

Jane and Hugo would rush to their son at his first cry of distress, as Flo had always reached out to Flint. In an album Jane and Hugo put together for their parents there is a sequence of photos showing Jane and Grub in almost exactly the same situation as Flo and Flint when he, taking his first steps, fell on his nose with a whimper. Grub, imitating the adults, is trying to pound a tent stake into the ground, using a mallet about half as large as he. Unable to control the immense tool, the little boy hits himself in the nose. His hand flies to his face and he begins to cry. Instantly Jane is beside him. Sitting in exactly the same posture as Flo, her knees drawn up in front of her, Jane gathers her son into her arms and presses her face to his. A vein in Jane's temple stands out. Her eyes close to kiss him, as if to black out the pain of his hurt with the sheer force of her love.

Jane first brought Grub to Gombe when he was only four months old. Sometimes the chimps would stare at the human baby through the windows of their house on the beach. On two occasions in the 1940s African babies had been seized by chimps in the area. One of the babies had been killed and partially eaten. The other baby was rescued by his six-year-old brother. The chimps had eaten part of the baby's face.

Once at Gombe two adult male chimps, hair bristling, shook the protective welded mesh of Jane and Hugo's windows and stared at the infant with tight-lipped ferocity. "There was not the slightest doubt in our minds," Jane wrote in a *National Geographic* article, "that had they been able to, they would have snatched little Hugo away for a meal."

For this reason Jane and Hugo built a special cage for their baby. They painted it light blue and hung colorful birds and bright stars from its ceiling. Their friends were horrified. Jane remembers that they predicted, "Surely he will have a complex for the rest of his life." Jane and Hugo explained that there really was no danger; Jane was constantly with Grub, and no harm could come to him. But still their friends were not satisfied. Baby books at the time counseled parents to foster independence in their children by sometimes leaving them to cry alone — "surely Grub will be a clingy, dependent child," they fretted.

But Grub was a cheerful, active, somewhat precocious child. He was able to crawl at five months — about the age when Flint had taken his first tottering steps — and by holding on to the wire mesh of his cage, he learned quickly to pull himself to his feet. Hugo and Jane used to joke that their son was determined to keep up with the baby chimps.

Grub quickly learned to walk and to swim. Frequently he ran about naked at Gombe. Some now worried that Jane was raising a "wild child." One American friend was horrified when, while Jane and Grub were visiting his Washington home, the diaperless toddler urinated on his couch. But at Gombe, with the air and water so warm, Grub needed few clothes, and Jane could revel in the touch of her baby's skin when she hugged him close to her.

Together they explored Gombe's streams and forests and beach, holding hands. If Grub reached out carelessly to grab a thorn or tried to wander beyond her reach, Jane would not scold or spank him; as Flo had done with Fifi and Flint, she would distract Grub with a new sight or a new game. When Grub grew old enough to understand, Jane would rebuke him for careless or thoughtless behavior, but then she would hold him close.

To stay beside her child, Jane gave up all-day follows of the chimps. "That was the sacrifice," she said years later. "I'd learned enough from the chimps to realize that the early years of my own child's life were very, very important, and if I didn't give him that time, I might as well not be studying chimps. What

Jane Goodall's first husband, Hugo van Lawick, with baby Flint . . . and Grub (below) *Jane Goodall*

point watching an animal and believing something you've seen is beneficial to humans, and then just doing the exact opposite, and saying in my case it's fine, I'll just leave my child aside and go on with my study? That's a nonsense. Then how can I stand up and say what I believe about the importance of the early mother-child relationship?"

"Now watch here how gently the mother fends off Fifi's hands," Jane tells her audience at the National Geographic Society. The audience is watching a film Hugo made of some of Fifi's first attempts to touch Flint. "I think many human mothers under these circumstances might hit their children," Jane tells the crowd, "but Flo only gently pushes her hands away."

During a time when women's liberation was an idea still new to Western consciousness, Jane chose to launch a crusade: in lectures in the United States and England, Jane, a woman who to so many was a symbol of women's independence and achievement, championed women's traditional role in human society: the gentle, supportive, full-time mother. "I never, ever, *ever* put my career before my child," Jane told a *New York Times* reporter. Jane considered delivering this message "my central mission."

Mothering, Jane believes, is the single most powerful force in chimpanzee society, not in terms of establishing a dominance hierarchy, but in terms of sculpting the outlook and experience of each chimpanzee infant. "I have come to appreciate the importance of early experience in the life of each chimpanzee," Jane told audiences and reporters over and over.

Jane observed that good chimpanzee mothers raised confident, socially adept, competent offspring. She often compared Flo's mothering styles with those of other Gombe mothers: look at Flo, Jane told her audiences, who would distract her offspring with play and grooming instead of cuffing them when they misbehaved, as Olly sometimes did with Gilka. Flo would always run to her sons or daughter at the slightest distress call, unlike Passion, who ignored daughter Pom's whimpering. And look at Flo's family: her older son Figan eventually became the alpha male of the community, and Fifi became an exceptionally efficient and loving mother. Olly's Gilka became a timid, sickly adult; Passion's Pom became a wildly aberrant female, an infant-killing cannibal.

"Flo taught me to honor the role of the mother in society," Jane wrote in *Through a Window*, her sequel to *In the Shadow of Man*, "and to appreciate not only the importance to a child of good mothering, but also the joy and contentment which that relationship can bring to the mother."

Over and over Jane emphasizes that human and chimp babies develop similarly. "The human baby has a program built into it," she says. "It wants something, it cries. The human mother is programmed to respond to its needs." But if the mother isn't there with the child, or if she allows the child to scream unattended in its playpen or crib, "these things destroy the trust built into the child."

For this reason, Jane frowns upon "mothers who dump their children at day care centers and go off to pursue their careers." Day care, she says, can seldom provide a child with the comfort and solace it needs. "They are understaffed and the people are underpaid. There is such a turnover of staff that the child's trust is stifled. The biggest issue any government should face is doing something for the children of people who have to work and can't afford an expensive day care center."

Not everyone is eager to accept the chimpanzee as the role model for women in human society. After giving a lecture at Yale University in 1972, Jane was interviewed by a Sunday *New York Times* reporter, a woman. "You're suggesting that for the chimp female it is adaptive to be so submissive?" she asked Jane.

"Well, yes," Jane replied. She smiled. A student, she said, had recently asked her the same question. The young man had told her that he was studying primate behavior and had concluded that females were submissive. His conclusion had made him, he complained, "unpopular" in his group. Jane had told him that if we were looking for "women's lib" in the animal world, the chimp was not the animal to show it.

Some of Jane's comments made her unpopular with feminists, who saw her as reinforcing the stereotypical female role just as they were succeeding in enlarging women's horizons. But Jane best remembers the comments of young mothers who would come up to her after her talks. "Thank you," she remembers one young woman saying, "for giving me the courage to spend time with my children."

After Grub turned three, Jane and Hugo hired two African nannies to watch over him in the mornings so he could play on the beach safely while Jane wrote or spoke with her students, and Hugo worked on photography. Jane's afternoons were reserved for her son. Though he never whimpered when she left him with his nannies, Grub would always greet her at lunch with delighted cries of "Mummy, Mummy!" and jump into her arms to hug her neck.

Grub, an outgoing little boy who learned KiSwahili and KiHa along with English, found many African age-mates to play with. They came from a culture that relied on witchcraft and ritual to keep evil spirits at bay, to bring rain and children, to ensure the harvest of fish and crops.

And Grub knew some magic of his own. He remembers instructing his playmates in a peculiarly Christian magic: just as lion fat and ritual prayer could heal sickness, just as amulets worn around the neck would protect against evil, Grub discovered after a Christmas holiday in England that hanging an old sock at the end of the bed would yield a rich harvest of toys. He couldn't wait to share the news.

"I was onto a good thing here," Grub, now grown, remembers. "I told them, 'It's very simple: if you want lots of presents, here's what you do. Wait till Christmas, write out a list of the things you want, and put it in the fire and wish for it, and then put a sock at the end of your bed. You'll get all the stuff you want.' "

Grub pauses and laughs. "Then of course it came to Christmas and my stocking got filled, and they came complaining theirs were empty. And I always wondered, why not them?"

He was happy growing up at Gombe. He remembers the sound of the lake. "You always remember that. I always liked the rainy season, because you get a lot of tropical storms. I liked the lightning and thunder. Usually the rain is almost warm. You can go out in it. You get a certain smell, and the sound, and — I don't know what it is exactly — you get a kind of spiritual feeling."

At Gombe the only problem was that he didn't like the chimpanzees very much. "I wasn't jealous of the chimps," Grub says. As an adult, he's given that idea some thought. "People have asked me that. But at that age I was frightened of chimps, yes."

Flint was Grub's particular nemesis. When Hugo used to walk though the forest with Grub on his shoulders, young Flint would hide in a tree and then suddenly reach out from a branch and pull the child's hair. Jane saw this a few times, and she remembers being "overcome with quite irrational anger." And it was then that she finally understood what Flo had felt and why she had so viciously attacked Evered when he had been squabbling with Figan.

At this point Jane had begun to consider Flint a bit of a spoiled brat. When Flint was five, his mother gave birth to a pretty little female Jane named Flame. Flint became increasingly demanding. He would ride on Flo's back, "looking like a ridiculous big baby" while Flame clung to Flo's stomach. Flint would throw tantrums, hurling himself on the ground, screaming in frustration, when Flo suckled Flame at her breast. He would hit and bite and kick his old mother. Once he actually pushed her out of a tree, making her fall to the ground. "At times I felt like slapping him," Jane confessed.

Yet Flo seldom punished her son. Her patience seemed infinite. Again and again she would gently push his hands away when she was suckling her daughter, or try to distract him with grooming or play. Sometimes, when Flint threw a particularly violent tantrum, Flo would bite or cuff him, but she always held him close at the same time, as if to reassure him.

When Flame was six months old, Flo became ill with a flulike disease. She left the camp, and Jane didn't see her or Flint for six days. When Jane's students finally found Flo, the old mother was so weak she could hardly move. Flint was with her, but Flame had disappeared and was never seen again.

As Flo recovered, Jane began to supplement Flo's diet with hen's eggs, a favorite treat. Fresh food for the research staff was often hard to come by at Gombe. Fresh vegetables, meat, and eggs had to come from Kigoma, a day's boat trip away. But whenever Jane saw Flo, she would stop what she was doing, go to the kitchen hut, and hand her friend a precious egg. Flo would pop the egg in her mouth and chew it with a wad of leaves.

One of Jane's assistants found Flo's body on an August morning in 1972. She was lying face down in Kakombe Stream as if she had dropped dead in midcrossing. Jane came to the scene right away. She turned the body over and looked into her old friend's face: it was, Jane remembers, "peaceful and relaxed and without sign of fear or pain. Her eyes were still bright and her body supple."

Jane sat vigil over Flo that night; she says she did not want the body violated by marauding bush pigs and did not want Flint to discover his mother's body in shreds. But surely, also, in the bright moonlight, Jane wanted to pay homage to her friend, to honor and mourn her, and to remember the stories they had shared. She had known and loved Flo for eleven years. Even a month after Flo's death, Jane confessed, it was hard for her to believe that her friend was really dead. She wrote an obituary for Flo, which was printed in the *London Sunday Times*.

> Flo has contributed much to science. She and her large family have provided a wealth of information about chimpanzee behaviors — infant development, family relationships, aggression, dominance, sex. . . . But this should not be the final word. It is true that her life was worthwhile because it enriched human understanding. But even if no one had studied the chimpanzees at Gombe, Flo's life, rich and full of vigor and love, would still have had a meaning and a significance in the pattern of things.

Flint spent many hours hunched on the bank of the stream near Flo's body. From time to time he pulled at her hand as if begging her to come back to life. Three days after Flo's death, Jane saw Flint climb slowly into a tall tree near Kakombe Stream. He walked along a branch and then stopped and stared. Jane followed his gaze: Flint was staring down at the empty nest he had shared with Flo a few nights before.

For the next three days Flint became increasingly lethargic, then the researchers lost sight of him for six days. When he was next seen, he had deteriorated markedly. Two weeks later he died.

Flint was eight and a half years old when he died, long past the stage when he depended on his mother for milk. An autopsy on his body revealed signs of gastroenteritis and peritonitis. "It seems likely that psychological and physiological disturbances associated with loss made him more vulnerable to disease," Jane wrote in her scholarly book, *The Chimpanzees of Gombe*. But in her heart Jane knew it was simpler than that: "Flint," she said, "died of grief."

Even Grub, then five, was saddened at the death of his young nemesis. "I was very upset when Flint died, actually," Grub recalls nearly two decades later. "Although I didn't like him, I was quite sad."

Grub, twenty-two, is well spoken, courteous, handsome, and adventurous. From his years on the lakeshore at Gombe, he has become an expert swimmer and fisherman, a keen observer, a fluent African linguist. He is an explorer in his mother's mold. Recently he was invited to serve as ichthyologist on a research expedition to Zaire to search for a dinosaurlike creature reportedly living in a virtually unexplored 55,000-square-mile swamp. A German magazine commissioned him to research an article on chimpanzee poaching in Sierra Leone, Ivory Coast, Liberia, and Guinea. He has also been offered a job exporting tropical fish from Lake Tanganyika. "Every month I get a new opportunity," he says, "a new offer to do something else."

"People thought it was quite peculiar, the way we raised Grub," Jane says. "They were particularly concerned that he would be very clinging, that he would have no independence. I've always said that if you give them an early confidence, a sense of security, that would remain central, and that'll spill over and they'll become confident. Well," she says with pride, "it worked."

Jane is somewhat gaunt but still supple at fifty-five. She wears her graying hair in the same characteristic ponytail. But her girlishness is gone. In place of eagerness, in her brown eyes you now see wisdom and calm. She is no longer a girl guide wandering wide-eyed in an unexplored Eden. She is a wisewoman passing on her knowledge of a world as rich and intense as our own to her initiates: the humans who watch her films, attend her lectures, read her books, who consider with her what it is like to be a chimpanzee.

Jane has survived deep tragedy: the divorce from Hugo when Grub was seven, the death of her second husband from cancer in 1980. Most of the chimps she knew when she first came to Gombe are dead now: Flo, David Graybeard, Goliath, Olly, Mr. McGregor are all gone. Jane personally cleaned their bones to preserve them for study.

But Fifi lives on. When Jane goes back to Gombe these days, she especially enjoys spending time with Fifi and her large family: adult sons Freud and Frodo, and daughters Fanni, an adolescent, and Flossi, still a child. And in 1989 Fifi gave birth to Faustino.

When I first saw him, Faustino was only three weeks old, and still unnamed. Fifi was cradling the infant in her arms, sitting partly in the sun, with Flossi watching from a palm tree nearby. The baby gave a toothless yawn, then formed his lips into an O. Fifi's lower lip hung open, drooping, as she looked down into her baby's pink face.

Freud descended from a nearby tree and began to groom his mother. She hunched protectively over her infant, then stood, raising a right leg, inviting her son to groom the back of her thigh. Frodo descended from another tree with an orange palm nut in hand, walked over to Fifi, and began to groom her head. Flossi came down from her tree, and Fanni emerged from the forest and greeted Frodo by presenting her backside for inspection. Fifi, reclining on her side with her infant at her breast, was surrounded by her entire family, and everyone was grooming. In the dappled sunshine in this parklike setting, it seemed like a family picnic on a Sunday afternoon.

When Fifi's first baby, Freud, was born in 1971, one of Jane's students reported something unusual, something the student had never seen a chimpanzee mother do before: Fifi, on her back, was dangling her son above her, holding him with her foot and tickling him with her hand.

3 Dian Fossey and Digit

EVERY BREATH was a battle to draw the ghost of her life back into her body. At age forty-two it hurt her even to breathe.

Dian Fossey had been asthmatic as a child and a heavy smoker since her teens; X-rays of her lungs taken when she graduated from college, she remembered, looked like "a road map of Los Angeles superimposed over a road map of New York." And now, after eight years of living in the oxygen-poor heights of Central Africa's Virunga Volcanoes, breathing the cold, sodden night air, her lungs were crippled. The hike to her research camp, Karisoke, at 10,000 feet, took her graduate students less than an hour; for Dian it was a gasping two-and-a-half-hour climb. She had suffered several bouts of pneumonia. Now she thought she was coming down with it again.

Earlier in the week she had broken her ankle. She heard the bone snap when she fell into a drainage ditch near her corrugated tin cabin. She had been avoiding a charging buffalo. Two days later she was bitten by a venomous spider on the other leg. Her right knee was swollen huge and red; her left ankle was black. But she would not leave the mountain for medical treatment in the small hospital down in Ruhengeri. She had been in worse shape before. Once, broken ribs punctured a lung; another time she was bitten by a dog thought to be rabid. Only when her temperature reached 105 and her symptoms clearly matched those described in her medical book for rabies had she allowed her African staff to carry her down on a litter.

Dian was loath to leave the camp in charge of her graduate students, two of whom she had been fighting with bitterly. Kelly Stewart and Sandy Harcourt, once her closest camp colleagues and confidantes, had committed the unforgivable error of falling in love with each other. Dian considered this a breach of loyalty. She yelled at them. Kelly cried and Sandy sulked.

But on this May day of 1974 Sandy felt sorry for Dian. As a gesture of conciliation, he offered to help her hobble out to visit Group 4. Splinted and steadied by a walking stick, she quickly accepted.

Group 4 was the first family of mountain gorillas Dian had contacted when she established her camp in Rwanda in September 1967. A political uprising had forced her to flee her earlier research station in Zaire. On the day she founded Karisoke — a name she coined by combining the names of the two volcanoes between which her camp nestled, Karisimbi and Visoke — poachers had led her to the group. The two Batwa tribesmen had been hunting antelope in the park — an illegal practice that had been tolerated for decades — and they offered to show her the gorillas they had encountered.

At that first contact, Dian watched the gorillas through binoculars for forty-five minutes. Across a ravine, ninety feet away, she could pick out three distinctive individuals in the fourteen-member group. There was a majestic old male, his black form silvered from shoulder to hip. This 350-pound silverback was obviously the sultan of the harem of females, the leader of the family. One old female stood out, a glare in her eyes, her lips compressed as if she had swallowed vinegar. And one youngster was "a playful little ball of disorganized black fluff . . . full of mischief and curiosity," as Dian would later describe him in *Gorillas in the Mist*. She guessed then that he was about five years old. He tumbled about in the foliage like an animated black dustball. When the lead silverback spotted Dian behind a tree, the youngster obediently fled at his call, but Dian had the impression that the little male would rather have stayed for a longer look at the stranger. In a later contact she noticed the juvenile's swollen, extended middle finger. After many attempts at naming him, she finally called him Digit.

It was Digit, now twelve, who came over to Dian as she sat crumpled and coughing among the foliage with Sandy. Digit, a gaunt young silverback, served his family as sentry. He left the periphery of his group to knuckle over to her side. She inhaled his smell. A good smell, she noted with relief: for two years a draining wound in his neck had hunched his posture and sapped his spirit. Systemic infection had given his whole body a sour odor, not the normal, clean smell of fresh sweat. During that time Digit had become listless. Little would arouse his interest: not the sex play between the group's lead silverback and receptive females, not even visits from Dian. Digit would sit at the edge of the group for hours, probing the wound with his fingers, his eyes fixed on some distant spot as if dwelling on a sad memory.

But today Digit looked directly into Dian's eyes. He chose to remain beside her throughout the afternoon, like a quiet visitor to a shut-in, old friends with no need to talk. He turned his great domed head to her, looking at her solemnly with a brown, cognizant gaze. Normally a prolonged stare from a gorilla is a threat. But Digit's gaze bore no aggression. He seemed to say: I know. Dian would later write that she believed Digit understood she was sick. And she returned to camp that afternoon, still limping, still sick, still troubled, but whole.

"We all felt we shared something with the gorillas," one of her students would later recall of his months at Karisoke. And it is easy to feel that way after even a brief contact with these huge, solemn beings. "The face of a gorilla," wrote nature writer David Quammen after just looking at a picture of one, "offers a shock of what feels like total recognition." To be in the presence of a mountain gorilla for even one hour simply rips your soul open with awe. They are the largest of the great apes, the most hugely majestic and powerful; but it is the gaze of a gorilla that transfixes, when its eyes meet yours. The naturalist George Schaller, whose year-long study preceded Dian's, wrote that this is a look found in the eye of no other animal except, perhaps, a whale. It is not so much intelligence that strikes you, but understanding. You feel there has been an exchange.

The exchange between Digit and Dian that day was deep and long. By then Digit had known Dian for seven years. She had been a constant in his growing up from a juvenile to a young blackback and now to a silverback sentry. He had known her longer than he had known his own mother, who had died or left his group before he was five; he had known Dian longer than he had known his father, the old silverback who died of natural causes less than a year after she first observed him. When Digit was nine, his three age-mates in Group 4 departed: his half sisters were "kidnaped" by rival silverbacks, as often happens with young females. Digit then adopted Dian as his playmate, and he would often leave the rest of the group to amble to her side, eager to examine her gear, sniff her gloves and jeans, tug gently at her long brown braid.

As for Dian, her relationship with Digit was stronger than her bonds with her mother, father, or stepfather. Though she longed for a husband and babies, she never married or bore children. Her relationship with Digit endured longer than that with any of her lovers and outlasted many of her human friendships.

In her slide lectures in the United States, Dian would refer to him as "my friend, Digit." "Friend," she admitted, was too weak a word, too casual; but she could find no other. Our words are something we share with other humans; but what Dian had with Digit was something she guarded as uniquely hers.

A mountain gorilla group is one of the most cohesive family units found among primates, a fact that impressed George Schaller. Adult orangutans live mostly alone, males and females meeting only to mate. Chimpanzees' social groupings are so loosely organized, changing constantly in number and composition, that Jane Goodall couldn't make sense of them for nearly a decade. But gorillas live in tight-knit, clearly defined families. Typically a group contains a lead silverback, perhaps his adult brother, half brother, or nephew, and several adult females and their offspring.

A gorilla group travels, feeds, plays, and rests together. Seldom is an individual more than a hundred feet away from the others. The lead silverback slows his pace to that of the group's slowest, weakest member. All adults tolerate the babies and youngsters in the group, often with great tenderness. A wide-eyed baby, its fur still curly as black wool, may crawl over the great black bulk of any adult with impunity; a toddler may even step on the flat, leathery nose of a silverback. Usually the powerful male will gently set the baby aside or even dangle it playfully from one of his immense fingers.

When Dian first discovered Group 4, she would watch them through binoculars from a hidden position, for if they saw her they would flee. She loved to observe the group's three infants toddle and tumble together. If one baby found the play too rough, it would make a coughing sound, and its mother would lumber over and cradle it tenderly to her breast. Dian watched Digit and his juvenile sisters play: wrestling, rolling, and chasing games often took them as far as fifty feet from the hulking adults. Sometimes a silverback led the youngsters in a sort of square dance. Loping from one palmlike *Senecio* tree to another, each gorilla would grab a trunk for a twirl, then spin off to embrace another trunk down the slope, until all the gorillas lay in a bouncing pileup of furry black bodies. And then the silverback would lead the youngsters up the slope again for another game.

Within a year, this cheerful silverback eventually took over leadership of the group, after the old leader died. Dian named him Uncle Bert, after her uncle Albert Chapin. With Dian's maternal aunt, Flossie (Dian named a Group 4 female after her as well), Uncle Bert had helped care for Dian after her father left the family when she was three. While Dian was in college Bert and Flossie gave her money to help with costs that her holiday, weekend, and summer jobs wouldn't cover. Naming the silverback after her uncle was the most tender tribute Dian could have offered Bert Chapin: his was the name given to the group's male magnet, its leader, protector—and the centerpiece of a family life whose tenderness and cohesion Dian, as a child, could not have imagined.

Dian was a lonely only child. Her father's drinking caused the divorce that took him out of her life; when her mother, Kitty, remarried when Dian was five, even the mention of George Fossey's name became taboo in the house. Richard Price never adopted Dian. Each night she ate supper in the kitchen with the housekeeper. Her stepfather did not allow her at the dinner table with him and her mother until she was ten. Though Dian's stepfather, a building contractor, seemed wealthy, she largely paid her own way through school. Once she worked as a machine operator in a factory.

Dian seldom spoke of her family to friends, and she carried a loathing for her childhood into her adult life. Long after Dian left the family home in California, she referred to her parents as "the Prices." She would spit on the ground whenever her stepfather's name was mentioned. When her Uncle Bert died, leaving Dian $50,000, Richard Price badgered her with cables to Rwanda, pressing her to contest the will for more money;

after Dian's death he had her will overturned by a California court, claiming all her money for himself and his wife.

Her mother and stepfather tried desperately to thwart Dian's plans to go to Africa. They would not help her finance her lifelong dream to go on safari when she was twenty-eight. She borrowed against three years of her salary as an occupational therapist to go. And when she left the States three years later to begin her study of the mountain gorillas, her mother begged her not to go, and her stepfather threatened to stop her.

She chose to remain in the alpine rain forest, as alone as she had ever been. She chose to remain among the King Kong beasts whom the outside world still considered a symbol of savagery, watching their gentle, peaceful lives unfold.

Once Dian, watching Uncle Bert with his family, saw the gigantic male pluck a handful of white flowers with his huge black hands. As the young Digit ambled toward him, the silverback whisked the bouquet back and forth across the youngster's face. Digit chuckled and tumbled into Uncle Bert's lap, "much like a puppy wanting attention," Dian wrote. Digit rolled against the silverback, clutching himself in ecstasy as the big male tickled him with petals.

By the end of her first three months in Rwanda, Dian was following two gorilla groups regularly and observing another sporadically. She divided most of her time between Group 5's fifteen members, ranging on Visoke's southeastern slopes, and Group 4. Group 8, a family of nine, all adult, shared Visoke's western slopes with Group 4.

Dian still could not approach them. Gorilla families guard carefully against intrusion. Each family has at least one member who serves as sentry, typically posted at the periphery of the group to watch for danger—a rival silverback or a human hunter. Gorilla groups seldom interact with other families, except when females transfer voluntarily out of their natal group to join the families of unrelated silverbacks or when rival silverbacks "raid" a neighboring family for females.

Adult gorillas will fight to the death defending their families. This is why poachers who may be seeking only one infant for the zoo trade must often kill all the adults in the family to capture the baby. Once Dian tracked one such poacher to his village; the man and his wives fled before her, leaving their small child behind.

At first Dian observed the animals from a distance, silently, hidden. Then slowly, over many months, she began to announce her presence. She imitated their contentment vocalizations, most often the *naoom, naoom, naoom,* a sound like belching or deeply clearing the throat. She crunched wild celery stalks. She crouched, eyes averted, scratching herself loud and long, as gorillas do. Eventually she could come close enough to them to smell the scent of their bodies and see the ridges inside the roofs of their mouths when they yawned; at times she came close enough to distinguish, without binoculars, the cuticles of their black, humanlike fingernails.

She visited them daily; she learned to tell by the contour pressed into the leaves which animal had slept in a particular night nest, made from leaves woven into a bathtub shape on the ground. She knew the sound of each individual voice belching contentment when they were feeding. But it was more than two years before she knew the touch of their skin.

Peanuts, a young adult male in Group 8, was the first mountain gorilla to touch his fingers to hers. Dian was lying on her back among the foliage, her right arm outstretched, palm up. Peanuts looked at her hand intently; then he stood, extended his hand, and touched her fingers for an instant. *National Geographic* photographer Bob Campbell snapped the shutter only a moment afterward: that the photo is blurry renders it dreamlike. The 250-pound gorilla's right hand still hangs in midair. Dian's eyes are open but unseeing, her lips parted, her left hand brought to her mouth, as if feeling for the lingering warmth of a kiss.

Peanuts pounded his chest with excitement and ran off to rejoin his group. Dian lingered after he left; she named the spot where they touched Fasi Ya Mkoni, "the Place of the Hands." With his touch, Peanuts opened his family to her; she became a part of the families she had observed so intimately for the past two years. Soon the gorillas would come forward and welcome her into their midst.

Digit was almost always the first member of Group 4 to greet her. "I received the impression that Digit really looked forward to the daily contacts," she wrote in her book. "If I was alone, he often invited play by flopping over on his back, waving stumpy legs in the air, and looking at me smilingly as if to say, 'How can you resist me?' "

At times she would be literally blanketed with gorillas, when a family would pull close around her like a black furry quilt. In one wonderful photo, Puck, a young female of Group 5, is reclining in back of Dian and, with the back of her left hand, touching Dian's cheek—the gesture of a mother caressing the cheek of a child.

Mothers let Dian hold their infants; silverbacks would groom her, parting her long dark hair with fingers thick as bananas, yet deft as a seamstress's touch. "I can't tell you how rewarding it is to be with them," Dian told a New York crowd gathered for a slide lecture in 1982. "Their trust, the cohesiveness, the tranquility . . ." Words failed her, and her hoarse, breathy voice broke. "It is really something."

Other field workers who joined Dian at Karisoke remember similar moments. Photographer Bob Campbell recalls how Digit would try to groom his sleeves and pants and, finding nothing groomable, would pluck at the hairs of his wrist; most of the people who worked there have pictures of themselves with young gorillas on their heads or in their laps.

But with Dian it was different. Ian Redmond, who first came to Karisoke in 1976, remembers one of the first times he accompanied Dian to observe Group 4. It was a reunion: Dian hadn't been out to visit the group for a while. "The animals filed past us, and each one paused and briefly looked into my face, just briefly. And then each one looked into Dian's eyes, at very close quarters, for half a minute or so. It seemed like each one was queuing up to stare into her face and remind themselves of her place with them. It was obvious they had a much deeper and stronger relationship with Dian than with any of the other workers."

In the early days Dian had the gorillas mostly to herself. It was in 1972 that Bob Campbell filmed what is arguably one of the most moving contacts between two species on record: Digit, though still a youngster, is huge. His head is more than twice the size of Dian's, his hands big enough to cover a dinner plate. He comes to her and with those enormous black hands gently takes her notebook, then her pen, and brings them to his flat, leathery nose. He gently puts them aside in the foliage and rolls over to snooze at Dian's side.

Once Dian spotted Group 4 on the opposite side of a steep ravine but knew she was not strong enough to cross it. Uncle Bert, seeing her, led the entire group across the ravine to her. This time Digit was last in line. "Then," wrote Dian, "he finally came right to me and gently touched my hair. . . . I wish I could have given them all something in return."

At times like these, Dian wept with joy. Hers was the triumph of one who has been chosen: wild gorillas would come to her.

The great intimacy of love is only-ness, of being the loved One. It is the kind of love most valued in Western culture; people choose only one "best" friend, one husband, one wife, one God. Even our God is a jealous one, demanding "Thou shalt have no other gods before Me."

This was a love Dian sought over and over again—as the only child of parents who did not place her first, as the paramour of a succession of married lovers. The love she sought most desperately was a jealous love, exclusive—not *agape*, the God-like, spiritual love of all beings, not the uniform, brotherly love, *philia*. The love Dian sought was the love that singles out.

Digit singled Dian out. By the time he was nine he was more strongly attracted to her than were any of the other gorillas she knew. His only age-mates in his family, his half sisters, had left the group or been kidnaped. When Digit heard Dian belch-grunting a greeting, he would leave the company of his group to scamper to greet her. To Digit, Dian was the sibling playmate he lacked. And Dian recognized his longing as clearly as she knew her own image in a mirror.

Dian had had few playmates as a child. She had longed for a pet, but her stepfather wouldn't allow her to keep even a hamster a friend offered, because it was "dirty." He allowed her a single goldfish; she was devastated when it died and was never allowed another.

But Digit was no pet. "Dian's relationship with the gorillas is really the highest form of human-animal relationship," observed Ian Redmond. "With almost any other human-animal relationship, that involves feeding the animals or restraining the animals or putting them in an enclosure, or if you help an injured animal—you do something to the animal. Whereas Dian and the gorillas were on completely equal terms. It was nothing other than the desire to be together. And that's as pure as you can get."

When Digit was young, he and Dian played together like children. He would strut toward her, playfully whacking foliage; she would tickle him; he would chuckle and climb on her head. Digit was fascinated by any object Dian had with her: once she brought a chocolate bar to eat for lunch and accidentally dropped it into the hollow stump of a tree where she was sitting next to Digit. Half in jest, she asked him to get it back for her. "And according to script," she wrote her Louisville friend, Betty Schwartzel, "Digit reached one long, hairy arm into the hole and retrieved the candy bar." But the chocolate didn't appeal to him. "After one sniff he literally threw it back into the hole. The so-called 'wild gorillas' are really very discriminating in their tastes!"

Dian's thermoses, notebooks, gloves, and cameras were all worthy of investigation. Digit would handle these objects gently and with great concentration. Sometimes he handed them back to her. Once Dian brought Digit a hand mirror. He immediately approached it, propped up on his forearms, and sniffed the glass. Digit pursed his lips, cocked his head, and then uttered a long sigh. He reached behind the mirror in search of the body connected to the face. Finding nothing, he stared at his reflection for five minutes before moving away.

Dian took many photos of all the gorillas, but Digit was her favorite subject. When the Rwandan Office of Tourism asked Dian for a gorilla photo for a travel poster, the slide she selected was one of Digit. He is pictured holding a stick of wood he has been chewing, his shining eyes a mixture of innocence and inquiry. He looks directly into the camera, his lips parted and curved as if about to smile. "Come to meet him in Rwanda," exhorts the caption. When this poster began appearing in hotels, banks, and airports, "I could not help feeling that our privacy was on the verge of being invaded," Dian wrote.

Her relationship with Digit was one she did not intend to share. Hers was the loyalty and possessiveness of a silverback: what she felt for the gorillas, and especially Digit, was exclusive, passionate, and dangerous.

No animal, Dian believed, was truly safe in Africa. Africans see most animals as food, skins, money. "Dian had a compulsion to buy every animal she ever saw in Africa," remembers her friend Rosamond Carr, an American expatriate who lives in nearby Gisenyi, "to save it from torture." One day Dian, driving in her Combi van, saw some children on the roadside, swinging a rabbit by the ears. She took it from them, brought it back to camp, and built a spacious hutch for it. Another time it would be a chicken: visiting villagers sometimes brought one to camp, intending, of course, that it be eaten. Dian would keep it as a pet.

Dian felt compelled to protect the vulnerable, the innocent. Her first plan after high school had been to become a veterinarian; after failing chemistry and physics, she chose occupational therapy; with her degree, she worked for a decade with disabled children.

One day Dian came to the hotel in Gisenyi where Rosamond was working as manager. Dian was holding a monkey. She had seen it at a market, packed in a carton. Rosamond remembers, "I look and see this rotten little face, this big ruff of hair, and I say, 'Dian. I'm sorry, you cannot have that monkey in this hotel!' But Dian spent the night with the animal in her room anyway.

"Luckily for me, she left the next day. I have never seen anything like the mess. There were banana peels on the ceiling, sweet potatoes on the floor; it had broken the water bottle, the glasses had been smashed and had gone down the drain of the washbasin. And with that adorable animal she starts up the mountain."

Kima, as Dian named the monkey, proved no less destructive in camp. Full grown when Dian bought her, Kima bit people, urinated on Dian's typewriter, bit the heads off all her matches, and terrorized students on their way to the latrine, leaping off the roof of Dian's cabin and biting them. Yet Dian loved her, built a hatchway allowing Kima free access to her cabin, bought her toys and dolls, and had her camp cook prepare special foods for her. Kima especially liked french fries, though she discarded the crunchy outsides and ate only the soft centers. "Everyone in camp absolutely hated that animal," Rosamond says. "But Dian loved her."

Another of Dian's rescue attempts occurred one day when she was driving down the main street of Gisenyi on a provisioning trip. Spotting a man walking a rack-ribbed dog on a leash, she slammed on the brakes. "I want to buy that dog," she announced. The Rwandan protested that it was not for sale. She got out of her Combi, lifted up the sickly animal, and drove off with it.

Rosamond learned of the incident from a friend named Rita who worked at the American embassy. For it was to Rita's home that the Rwandan man returned that afternoon to explain why the dog, which he had been taking to the vet for worming, had never made it to its destination. "Madame, a crazy woman stopped and stole your dog, and she went off with it in a gray van."

"Rita got her dog back," Rosamond continues. Dian had taken it to the hotel where she was staying overnight; when Rita tracked her down, she was feeding the dog steak in her room. "And that was typical of Dian. She had to save every animal she saw. And they loved her—every animal I ever saw her with simply loved her."

When Dian first came to Karisoke, elephants frequently visited her camp. Rosamond used to camp with Dian in those early days before the cabin was built. The elephants came so close that she remembers hearing their stomachs rumble at night. Once she asked Dian if she undressed at night. "Of course not, are you crazy?" Dian replied. "I go to bed in my blue jeans. I have to get up six times at night to see what's happening outside."

One night an elephant selected Dian's tent pole as a scratching post. Another time a wild elephant accepted a banana from Dian's hand. The tiny antelopes called duiker often wandered through camp; one became so tame it would follow Dian's laying hens around. A family of seven bushbucks adopted Karisoke as home, as did an ancient bull buffalo she named Mzee.

Dian's camp provided refuge from the poacher-infested, cattle-filled forest. For centuries the pygmylike Batwa had used these volcanic slopes as a hunting ground. And as Rwanda's human population exploded, the Virungas were the only source of bush meat left, and poaching pressure increased. Today you will find no elephants in these forests; they have all been killed by poachers seeking ivory.

If you look at the Parc National des Volcans from the air, the five volcanoes, their uppermost slopes puckered like the lips of an old woman, seem to be standing on tiptoe to withdraw from the flood of cultivation and people below. Rwanda is the most densely populated country in Africa, with more than 500 people per square mile. Almost every inch is cultivated, and more than 23,000 new families need new land each year. In rural Rwanda outside of the national parks, if you wander from a path you are more likely to step in human excrement than the scat of a wild animal. The Parc des Volcans is thoroughly ringed with *shambas*, little farm plots growing bananas, peanuts, beans, manioc, and with fields of pyrethrum, daisylike flowers cultivated as a natural insecticide for export. The red earth of the fields seems to bleed from all the human scraping.

The proud, tall Batutsi have few other areas to pasture their cattle, the pride of their existence; everywhere else are shambas. From the start Dian tried to evict the herders from the park, kidnaping their cows and sometimes even shooting them. On the Rwandan side of the mountain, cattle herds were so concentrated, she wrote, that "many areas were reduced to dust-bowls." She felt guilty, but the cattle destroyed habitat for the gorillas and other wild animals the park was supposed to protect. Worse were the snares set by the Batwa. Many nights she stayed awake nursing a duiker or bushbuck whose leg had been mangled in a trap. Dian lived in fear that one of the gorillas would be next.

The Batwa do not eat gorillas; gorillas fall victim to their snares, set for antelope, by accident. But the Batwa have for centuries hunted gorillas, to use the fingers and genitals of silverbacks in magic rituals and potions. And now the hunters found a new reason to kill gorillas: they learned that Westerners would pay high prices for gorilla heads for trophies, gorilla hands for ashtrays, and gorilla youngsters for zoos.

In March 1969, only eighteen months into her study, a friend in Ruhengeri came to camp to tell Dian that a young gorilla had been captured from the southern slopes of Mount Karisimbi. All ten adults in the group had been killed so that the baby could be taken for display in the Cologne Zoo. The capture had been approved by the park conservator, who was paid handsomely for his cooperation. But something had gone wrong: the baby gorilla was dying.

Dian took the baby in, a three- to four-year-old female she named Coco. The gorilla's wrists and feet had been bound with wire to a pole when the hunters carried her away from the corpses of her family; she had spent two or three weeks in a coffinlike crate, fed only corn, bananas, and bread, before Dian came to her rescue. When Dian left the park conservator's office, she was sure the baby would die. She slept with Coco in her bed, awakening amid pools of the baby's watery feces.

A week later came another sick orphan, a four- to five-year-old female also intended for the zoo. Her family had shared Karisimbi's southern slope with Coco's; trying to defend the baby from capture, all eight members of her group had died. Dian named this baby Pucker for the huge sores that gave her face a puckered look.

It took Dian two months to nurse the babies back to health. She transformed half her cabin into a giant gorilla playpen filled with fresh foliage. She began to take them into the forest with her, encouraging them to climb trees and vines. She was making plans to release them into a wild group when the park conservator made the climb to camp. He and his porters descended with

Orphaned gorillas Coco and Pucker cling to Dian
Fossey as she takes them out for their daily romp in
the forest. *Bob Campbell*

both gorillas in a box and shipped them to the zoo in West
Germany. Coco and Pucker died there nine years later, within
a month of one another, at an age when, in the wild, they would
have been mothering youngsters the same age they had been
when they were captured.

Thereafter Dian's antipoaching tactics became more elaborate.
She learned from a friend in Ruhengeri that the trade in gorilla
trophies was flourishing; he had counted twenty-three gorilla
heads for sale in that town in one year. As loyal as a silverback,
as wary as a sentry, Dian and her staff patrolled the forest for
snares and destroyed the gear poachers left behind in their tem-
porary shelters.

Yet each day dawned to the barking of poachers' dogs. A field report she submitted to the National Geographic Society in 1972 gave the results of the most recent gorilla census: though her study groups were still safe, the surrounding areas of the park's five volcanoes were literally under siege. On Mount Muhavura census workers saw convoys of smugglers leaving the park every forty-five minutes. Only thirteen gorillas were left on the slopes of Muhavura. On neighboring Mount Gahinga no gorillas were left. In the two previous years, census workers had found fresh remains of slain silverbacks. And even the slopes of Dian's beloved Karisimbi, she wrote, were covered with poachers' traps and scarred by heavily used cattle trails; "poachers and their dogs were heard throughout the region."

It was that same year, 1972, that a maturing Digit assumed the role of sentry of Group 4. In this role he usually stayed on the periphery of the group to watch for danger; he would be the first to defend his family if they were attacked. Once when Dian was walking behind her Rwandan tracker, the dark form of a gorilla burst from the bush. The male stood upright to his full height of five and a half feet; his jaw gaped open, exposing black gums and three-inch canines as he uttered two long, piercing screams at the terrified tracker. Dian stepped into view, shoving the tracker down behind her, and stared into the animal's face. They recognized each other immediately. Digit dropped to all fours and ran back to his group.

Dian wrote that Digit's new role made him more serious. No longer was he a youngster with the freedom to roll and wrestle with his playmate. But Dian was still special to him. Once when Dian went out to visit the group during a downpour, the young silverback emerged from the gloom and stood erect before his crouching human friend. He pulled up a stalk of wild celery — a favorite gorilla food that Digit had seen Dian munch on many times — peeled it with his great hands, and dropped the stalk at her feet like an offering. Then he turned and left.

As sentry, Digit sustained the wound that sapped his strength for the next two years. Dian did not observe the fight, but she concluded from tracking clues that Digit had warded off a raid by the silverback leader of Group 8, who had previously kidnaped females from Group 4. Dian cringed each time she heard him coughing and retching. Digit sat alone, hunched and indifferent. Dian worried that his growth would be retarded. In her field notes she described his mood as one of deep dejection.

This was a time when Dian was nursing wounds of her own. She had hoped that Bob Campbell, the photographer, would marry her, as Hugo van Lawick had married Jane; but Bob left Karisoke for the last time at the end of May 1972, to return to his wife in Nairobi. Then she had a long affair with a Belgian doctor, who left her to marry the woman he had been living with. Dian's health worsened. Her trips overseas for primatology conferences and lecture tours were usually paired with hospital visits to repair broken bones and heal her fragile lungs. She feared she had tuberculosis. She noted her pain in her diary telegraphically: "Very lung-sick." "Coughing up blood." "Scum in urine."

When she was in her twenties, despite her asthma, Dian seemed as strong as an Amazon. Her large-boned but lanky six-foot frame had a coltish grace; one of her suitors, another man who nearly married her, described her as "one hell of an attractive woman," with masses of long dark hair and "eyes like a Spanish dancer." But now Dian felt old and ugly and weak. She used henna on her hair to try to cover the gray. (Dian told a friend that her mother's only comment about her first appearance on a National Geographic TV special was, "Why did you dye your hair that awful orange color?") In letters to friends Dian began to sign off as "The Fossil." She referred to her house as "the Mausoleum." In a cardboard album she made for friends from construction paper and magazine cutouts, titled "The Saga of Karisoke," she pasted a picture of a mummified corpse sitting upright on a bed. She realized that many of her students disliked her. Under the picture Dian printed a caption: "Despite their protests, she stays on."

By 1976 Dian was spending less and less time in the field. Her lungs and legs had grown too weak for daily contacts; she had hairline fractures on her feet. And she was overwhelmed with paperwork. She became increasingly testy with her staff, and her students feared to knock on her door. Her students wouldn't even see her for weeks at a time, but they would hear her pounding on her battered Olivetti, a task from which she would pause only to take another drag on an Impala *filtrée* or to munch sunflower seeds. Her students were taking the field data on the gorillas by this time: when Dian went out to see the groups, she simply visited with them.

One day, she ventured out along a trail as slippery as fresh buffalo dung to find Group 4. By the time she found them, the rain was driving. They were huddled against the downpour. She saw Digit sitting about thirty feet apart from the group. She wanted to join him but resisted; she now feared that her early contact with him had made him too human-oriented, more vulnerable to poachers. So she settled among the soaking foliage several yards from the main group. She could barely make out the humped black forms in the heavy mist.

On sunny days there is no more beautiful place on earth than the Virungas; the sunlight makes the *Senecio* trees sparkle like fireworks in midexplosion; the gnarled old *Hagenias*, trailing lacy beards of gray-green lichen and epiphytic ferns, look like friendly wizards, and the leaves of palms seem like hands upraised in praise. But rain transforms the forest into a cold, gray hell. You stare out, tunnel-visioned, from the hood of a dripping raincape, at a wet landscape cloaked as if in evil enchantment. Each drop of rain sends a splintering chill into the flesh, and your muscles clench with cold; you can cut yourself badly on the razorlike cutty grass and not even feel it. Even the gorillas, with their thick black fur coats, look miserable and lonely in the rain.

Minutes after she arrived, Dian felt an arm around her shoulders. "I looked up into Digit's warm, gentle brown eyes," she wrote in *Gorillas in the Mist*. He gazed at her thoughtfully and patted her head, then sat by her side. As the rain faded to mist, she laid her head down in Digit's lap.

On January 1, 1978, Dian's head tracker returned to camp late in the day. He had not been able to find Group 4. But he had found blood along their trail.

Ian Redmond found Digit's body the next day. His head and hands had been hacked off. There were five spear wounds in his body.

Ian did not see Dian cry that day. She was almost supercontrolled, he remembers. No amount of keening, no incantation or prayer could release the pain of her loss. But years later she filled a page of her diary with a single word, written over and over: "Digit   Digit   Digit   Digit . . ."

II *Scientists*

4 The Prodigal Faith of Louis Leakey

FOR TWENTY-EIGHT YEARS the son of an Anglican missionary searched for the ancestors of Adam. On hands and knees, as if in prayer, Louis Seymour Bazett Leakey scraped at the crusty soils of Tanzania's Olduvai Gorge with shovel and trowel and dental instruments. With the faith of Jesus at the tomb of Lazarus, he called to the dead to come out.

Few but he believed, when he began that search in 1931, that the fossilized bones of man's ancestors would be found beneath African soil. At a time when the prehistoric map of East Africa was practically a blank, most other paleoanthropologists were certain that man had originated in Asia or Europe. But Louis Leakey was convinced that Africa, his own birthplace, was also the cradle of humanity and that the lineage of apelike ancestors leading to man was far longer and more ancient than anyone else dared believe.

At the center of Louis's convictions was a prodigal faith. He was, above all, a believer: he believed in God's will, which he credited with directing his life; he believed in "wild" theories, which would eventually revolutionize the study of human origins; and he came to believe in three inexperienced young women, who would transform modern views of both man and ape.

Louis Leakey was world famous when he died in 1972. Responsible for some of the most spectacular fossil finds of the century, he had established Africa as the birthplace of mankind and had proved that the ancestral line leading to humanity was indeed very long. At a South African symposium in Leakey's honor a year after his death, the eminent paleoanthropologist Philip Tobias said, "No single person has done more to unravel man's past in Africa than the late Dr. Leakey."

Louis, more explorer than scientist, was a man in constant motion. He scurried rather than walked, theorizing at every turn. (Though some of his theories proved brilliant and elegant, some were just plain strange: he thought that warthog's warts evolved as "pincushions" for thorns, and that women could conceive only when their diet contained the elusive "Vitamin X.") His life was riddled with what many considered paradoxical allegiances. A self-described "White African" (the title of his first autobiography), he attacked white settlers, administrators, and missionaries in his 1935 book, *Kenya: Contrasts and Problems*. A Biblical scholar, he devoted his career to the study of evolution, which his church decried. "There are some people whose faith in their own belief about God is so feeble that they dare not face the facts of science lest they shatter their religion," he once wrote; he saw Genesis and evolutionary biology unified in what he called "the One Truth of Creation." At one time or another he embarrassed almost everyone he knew, from his missionary parents to his Cambridge professors to his scientific colleagues — a feat in which he seemed to take mischievous pride.

His brand of Christianity was prodigal, too. "I don't need to flop down on my knees to pray," he sometimes said. "I pray anywhere—everywhere." Louis did not have his children christened; he believed they should decide for themselves. But on visits to London he nearly always attended a service at St. John's or King's Chapel at Cambridge; and in his final days of illness he asked his American friends Hugh and Tita Caldwell to take communion for him at the Wednesday healing service at their Episcopal church.

It was not until late in his career that Louis envisioned studies of the great apes. He was fifty-seven when he sent Jane Goodall into the field, sixty-three when he secured funding for Dian Fossey. By the time he picked Biruté Galdikas to head up his orangutan study, when he was sixty-six, the trend was clear: he favored female protégées. To account for this preference he offered yet another of his "wild theories": that women are better observers than men.

The idea of long-term, close-range studies of the large primates was new in 1959. "This was something extremely unusual," remembers his friend Barbara Isaac, an archeologist who was working at the time in Kenya with her husband, Glynn. "Everyone said it couldn't be done." When Louis announced the names of the women he'd selected to head the studies, Barbara remembers, "people questioned his mental health."

For the study on wild chimpanzees Louis picked a twenty-six-year-old former waitress and secretary. For a study of mountain gorillas he chose an occupational therapist who had flunked out of veterinary school. The young woman he selected to head up an orangutan study was a graduate student in anthropology, but that didn't matter; he chose her on the basis of how she scored on a playing-card test he had devised.

Louis Leakey always defied convention, and he never allowed the experts to deflect him from his beliefs. When he announced to his professors at Cambridge University his plans to search for traces of early man in Africa, they told him the idea was foolish.

"Without exception, they told me it was a waste of time to return to Kenya," Louis later recalled. "I was just being mad." But Louis's destiny was tied to Africa. When he was born, on August 7, 1903, at Lower Kabete, a small village near Nairobi, the Kikuyu neighbors sneaked into his parents' mud and thatch mission to spit on him. He was the first white baby they had ever seen, and they were eager to bestow on him, with their spittle, the traditional Kikuyu blessing. At age thirteen he was initiated into the Kikuyu tribe.

Even in his old age Louis often thought and dreamed in Kikuyu. He once told an interviewer: "I am African born and bred, with African sensitivities. I happen to be white."

So in 1926, against all advice, he returned to Kenya. At Gamble's Cave, his first dig, he promptly found shards of pottery he dated at 20,000 years B.C., four times earlier than the date at which pottery was then presumed to have been made. As Louis planned to announce the finds at an upcoming anthropology conference, his Cambridge supervisor warned him in a letter, "Do not go in for wild hypotheses. These won't do your work any good and it's foolish to try to make a splash."

Advancing wild hypotheses — drawing dramatic and often premature conclusions from his finds — was the hallmark of Louis Leakey's career. With obvious enjoyment and theatrical flair, he would call press conferences before his findings had been "properly" published; before the assembled reporters he would pull a fossil from a breast pocket and brandish it for dramatic effect. (Once his own PR backfired: after he explained to a journalist that his finds were uncovered with dental instruments, the reporter cabled the newspaper: Mr. Leakey Discovers the First Dentist.) His colleagues did not appreciate his bravado. As biographer Sonia Cole wrote in her book *Leakey's Luck*, throughout his adult life Louis remained "a needle embedded in the armchair of the 'experts.' " What may have needled them most was that Louis's wild claims were often right.

In 1931, on his first expedition to Olduvai Gorge, he bet his colleague Hans Reck ten pounds that he would find stone tools on his first day. Within hours Reck had to pay up: Louis had found several ancient hand axes made from basalt lava.

But it would be nearly three decades before Louis found the evidence he was really seeking at Olduvai. Under the shadeless African sun his hair turned from brown to white. He collapsed several times from heat stroke. He persisted under conditions others would consider nightmarish. At Olduvai a party of ten had to drive an hour and then walk eighteen miles to and from the single water source, a hippo wallow that yielded drinking water flavored with the animals' urine. Fine black dust blew constantly, covering buttered bread before the slice could be brought to the mouth; often rations were so short that the party was reduced to eating rice flavored with marmalade. At another dig, at Kanjera in western Kenya, the field party ate with their trousers tucked into Wellington boots and towels covering their faces to protect them from mosquitoes. Even so, one person killed a hundred mosquitoes on his face during a single meal.

Leakey's persistent digs uncovered a plethora of fossil material. In 1948 his second wife, Mary, found the first nearly intact skull of the extinct manlike ape known as Proconsul. At Olduvai the Leakeys unearthed stone tools and the skeletons of giant prehistoric animals: giraffes twice as tall as modern ones with horns the size of moose antlers, pigs the size of rhinos, and skeletons of *Dinotherium*, a cousin of the modern elephant. But for twenty-eight years Leakey found no trace of the being who used stone tools to hunt these animals.

Everything changed on the morning of July 17, 1959. Louis was in bed in his tent at Olduvai with an attack of flu. Mary Leakey went out to the site known as FLK, named, ironically, after Louis's first wife, Frida. The rains had exposed new bones in the earth. Mary looked closely at one and saw that it was part of an upper jaw. She ran to fetch Louis from bed. "I've got it! I've got it! I've found the man!"

The skull came to be called *Zinjanthropus*, though the popular press called it "Nutcracker Man" because of its huge teeth. Mary and Louis called the skeleton "our dear boy," for it was with this find that Louis achieved world fame. The fossil, he concluded, was twice as ancient as human evolution had previously been estimated to be. "Here at last," said Louis, "was the earliest known man in the world."

A year after *Zinjanthropus* came another startling Leakey discovery: the skull, and then parts of the hands and feet, of a prehistoric child. This fossil, of a species Louis named *Homo habilis* ("Handy Man" as it was called in the press) soon displaced Zinj, in Louis's opinion, as the direct forerunner to man.

Louis was seeking an answer to one of the central questions of human religion and philosophy: What is man? Where did we come from? Once Leakey was asked by a radio interviewer, "What has kept you going all these years?" He replied, "I want to know: Who am I? What was it that made me what I am?"

Louis realized this question could not be answered by bones and stones alone. The skeletons could reveal what early man looked like; how the bones articulated could show how he might have moved; his tools hinted at his early culture. But as Louis liked to say, "Behavior doesn't fossilize." To flesh out the fossilized bones of Adam's ancestors, Louis proposed long-term, close-up studies of humankind's closest living relatives — the chimpanzee, the gorilla, and the orangutan.

With this proposition he alarmed even Mary, who did not think that study of the great apes was relevant to understanding early man. But what truly confounded his colleagues at the time was his selection of the young Jane Goodall to head up this study.

Jane, who had come to Africa without a job, had finagled a position at the Coryndon Museum in Nairobi, which Louis directed, and had worked with the Leakey family at Olduvai. The

Louis Leakey spent most of his career scraping the
soils of Olduvai Gorge for remains of early man.
Ian Berry/Magnum Photos

idea to study chimps wasn't hers; it was Louis's, and he had to
convince even Jane that she could do it.

"There seriously were people who told Louis he was practically insane," Jane later recalled, "and that this wasn't the sort
of thing he should do at all." It was bad enough, in the opinion
of the experts, that Jane had no academic qualifications. But the
real reason Louis's colleagues were horrified, Jane remembers,
was that "I was a defenseless young female going out in the
wild."

In 1966 Louis selected Dian Fossey, then thirty-four, to study
the mountain gorilla. Responding to Louis's plea to help finance
Dian's first expedition, the president of the New York Zoological
Society, Fairfield Osborn, wrote to him in consternation: "What

new breed of human beings is this? These young women go out
to far places, obviously relishing the risks involved. Do you think
they are trying to prove they are better than men? A subconscious
motivation of which they may not be aware?"

By the time he chose twenty-three-year-old Biruté Galdikas as
his "orangutan girl" in 1969, no one was terribly surprised. As
his right-hand people, Louis nearly always chose women.

It was his wife Mary—ten years Louis's junior—who actually
discovered most of the famous Leakey finds: *Proconsul* and *Zinjanthropus*, and later the prehuman footprints embedded in the
ash of Laetoli. When Louis established a center for primate
studies at Tigoni, outside Nairobi, he chose a woman as its
director and staffed it almost entirely with young women. The
last major dig of his life—at Calico Hills in California—was
also headed by a young woman.

For work in fields traditionally dominated by experienced
men, youth and womanhood were not faults Louis managed to
overlook. They were qualities he actively sought. For in these
young women he saw the attributes to which he credited his
own success.

Louis's first archeological finds came about as a result of jumping
to an incorrect conclusion simply because he didn't know any
better.

When he was twelve, an English cousin sent him a book for
Christmas that excited his imagination. *Days Before History*, by
H. N. Hall, told of flint arrowheads and axheads found in Europe. Though Louis did not know what flint looked like, he
decided to look for flint tools in Kenyan soils.

What he found was not flint at all. His parents dismissed his
"prehistoric tools" as "pieces of broken glass." Louis did not
know that two years earlier two American archeologists had
dismissed similar finds with the same conclusion. In search of
prehistoric stone implements, the archeologists had visited Na-

kuru and Naivasha lake basins. When they found only "pieces of broken glass," which they assumed originated from a nearby hotel serving bottled beer, they canceled the detailed study they had envisioned.

Young Louis took his finds to Arthur Loveridge, assistant curator of the natural history museum in Nairobi. Loveridge told him that the pieces were not broken glass—nor were they flint. They were worked obsidian. The Kikuyu call all pieces of obsidian *nyenji cia ngoma*: razors of the spirits. Loveridge confirmed that Leakey had found the knives and weapons of a long-dead race, tools made by Stone Age man.

"Had I known what flint was," Louis concluded in *White African*, "I might never have found any stone implements at all."

With none of the bias of a conventional Western education, Louis learned to think for himself. With the spittle of his Kikuyu neighbors bestowed at birth he was doubly blessed: his unfettered childhood gave him the freedom to explore and the local Kikuyu taught him the skills to see.

Joshua, a teacher of mixed Kikuyu and Ndorobo blood, taught Louis the habits of the neighborhood animals: duiker, dik-dik, mongoose, porcupine, aardvark, jackal, hyena, and genet. Firsthand observation was paramount.

To demonstrate that man needed tools to survive, Louis tried skinning animals with his teeth ("most unsatisfactory," he concluded). To better understand early tool making, he became an expert flint knapper. So, in later life, he did not look for conventional qualifications in the applicants he interviewed for his projects.

Geza Teleki, who later worked with Jane Goodall at Gombe, recalls his first interview with Louis, in the mid-1960s. It took place at a Washington hotel, across from Louis's perennial source of funds, the National Geographic Society:

"The whole room was full of fossils, and you couldn't sit down anyplace, and he was drinking sherry out of a tumbler the size of a basketball, and it was just very odd. He sort of exploded at you with everything. He'd jump up and accost you with a question. There were all these little rocks and stuff, and he'd say: 'What is it?' I didn't know. He'd pick something off a table, stick it in your hands and say: *What is it?* I think he almost couldn't contain himself. He'd run over next to you and ask it right to your nose.

"It was not the kind of interview I expected," Geza continues. "I thought he'd want me to tell him what I was interested in, why I would go and all that stuff. He asked me three questions: was I a Boy Scout, could I fix a car, and could I cook. Then he asked me to prepare a meal for him. He had some pork chops in the refrigerator and a kitchen in his suite. And I made him a meal. He didn't give a rat's ass about where I'd gone to school, what I had studied, or whether I was properly equipped intellectually."

At Biruté Galdikas's first interview with Louis, he did not ask about her academic qualifications. Instead he subjected her, she remembers, to "weird little intelligence tests like you see in magazines." He turned over some cards and asked her to recall which were red and which were black. She immediately mentioned that half of the cards were slightly bent.

Men, Louis said, seldom noticed this detail; women usually did. And this, says Tita Caldwell, a founder of the Leakey Foundation, was the key to the interview: in observing the lives of nonspeaking primates, Louis considered attention to detail — especially details that others might consider of little consequence — of paramount importance. "Louis was looking for a *quality of perception*," Tita said. "He was testing them for their powers of observation. Louis firmly believed that women were more observant than men, so there's a lot less training to do with them. Whenever Louis was interviewing someone for a position, if there were three applicants and he only had time to interview one, he would interview the woman."

Dian recalled that Louis continued to test her powers of observation from time to time. After she had been in the field for some months, she visited him in Nairobi at the Coryndon Museum. In front of the building he suddenly asked her what she saw at a certain spot. "I would look and see a spider web, thinking myself very, very observant," she wrote in an unpublished memorial to Louis after his death. "He would see a spider web, a bee, a dead fly—he would see twenty-odd things when I would see one. So I learned to use my eyes, and that's what he wanted."

"My Kikuyu training taught me this," Louis once wrote in a *National Geographic* article: "if you have reason to believe that something should be in a given spot but you don't find it, you must not conclude it isn't there. Rather, you must conclude that your powers of observation are faulty."

When each of the three women met the famous Dr. Leakey for the first time, they believed he was not particularly impressed with them.

Jane's introduction to Louis was far from warm. Having gathered the courage to telephone the museum to ask for a job, she timidly asked the voice who answered the phone if she could speak with Dr. Leakey. "I'm Dr. Leakey," the voice announced brusquely and then demanded: "What do you want?"

Dian wrote in a Leakey Foundation tribute to Louis after his death, "A less propitious beginning to a deep and prolonged friendship with a man who was to shape my life and destiny could not be imagined." On her first African safari in 1963 she traveled to the Leakey digs at Olduvai. Louis dismissed her as "another bothersome tourist" and charged her fourteen shillings to tour the excavations. (She did prove bothersome: she fell down a ravine, broke a precious fossil with her fall, and then, nauseated by the pain of her sprained ankle, vomited on the specimen.)

Biruté spoke to Louis of her deep wish to study orangutans after hearing his lecture at the University of California at Los Angeles, where she was pursuing a master's degree in anthropology. She recalls, "Dr. Leakey looked at me very coldly and didn't say much. I could have been telling him he had dandruff for all his interest."

It was only when she told him that she had already begun to make arrangements for her study by contacting orangutan researchers in Sarawak that she elicited a glimmer of interest. "I only support people who know what they want to do and are determined to do it," Biruté remembers Louis telling her.

The depth of Dian's determination was foreshadowed from the start. After Mary bandaged her sprained ankle, she insisted upon leaving Olduvai to stagger up a 10,000-foot volcano in search of mountain gorillas. Three years later, after Louis agreed to secure funding for her study, he suggested jokingly that she have her appendix removed as a precaution. Before she received his letter telling her he was only joking, she had already undergone the surgery. (Biruté went one better: at her job interview with Louis she offered up her tonsils as well.)

For the studies Louis had in mind, tenacity was as important as keen observation. Jane, Dian, and Biruté were not the first people to study the great apes. Henry Nissen had ventured to French Guinea in the 1930s to study the chimpanzee; he stayed two and a half months. George Schaller had spent a year among the mountain gorillas of Zaire in the 1950s. And, before Biruté, John MacKinnon had undertaken the longest study of orangutans. After spending a year at Gombe with Goodall, he began an orangutan study that spanned three years. These early male primatologists all went on to study other animals in other places. And this, remarks Biruté, is "the typical way males do things."

The men were fine naturalists, but basically they were "adventurers," Biruté says. "It must be exhilarating—to go to a new place, find the lay of the land . . . and then you move on to a new area. That's the way men are. You conquer, and you move on to the next conquest."

Throughout his career Louis scorned "armchair anthropologists" who were "only prepared to devote a few months to research and then return to more lucrative and comfortable work in the universities." The genius of Louis Leakey's vision was that he insisted upon long-term studies. (When he first told Goodall he expected her to stay at Gombe for ten years, she laughed and thought, "Well, maybe three.")

Louis believed that women were particularly well suited to long-term studies. Both biology and society encourage women to invest their time in long-term projects, he pointed out: raising a child to adulthood, for instance, demands two decades of commitment. Women, he believed, were of necessity tougher and more tenacious than men.

And for Louis's three "ape ladies," as well as for his own work at Olduvai, tenacity was the source of the achievement: it was not that they went, but that they stayed.

Many people raised eyebrows at the idea that Louis took on young female protégées in his "dotage." In *Leakey's Luck*, biographer Cole suggests that Leakey launched his primate studies after the fashion of the older middle-aged man suddenly buying a new sports car, a classic response to "male menopause."

"His sons had flown the nest . . . his wife was ensconced at Olduvai . . . Leakey became disabled physically, unable to do active field research and reluctant to adopt modern techniques," she notes. Perhaps he encouraged the careers of young women in part to "ease his loneliness."

That Mary did not take kindly to many of Louis's female protégées fueled the rumors. Penny Caldwell, an early student of Louis's at his Tigoni primate center, remembers the reception she got from Mary when she first arrived in Nairobi. "She looked me up and down, up and down, up and down, and finally said,

'Well, everyone to his own taste.' " When Glynn Isaac, one of the few male archeologists who worked successfully under Louis, brought his bride-to-be to meet his employer's wife, Mary Leakey made the meeting extremely stressful, Barbara Isaac recalls. Mary immediately subjected her to a spelling test. ("I did very well," Barbara recalls. "I got most of them right, but no more than had Mary's mother.")

Mary, who had married Louis after he left his first wife pregnant with their second child, could not have failed to notice that her aging husband basked in the attention of his entourage of pretty young women.

Although strikingly handsome as a square-jawed young man, by the time Louis was made famous by the *Zinjanthropus* discovery, he looked old. Pained by an arthritic hip, in his fifties he already walked with a cane (later he used crutches), and his neck-forward posture had collapsed to an old man's hunch. A 1966 National Geographic TV special showed him at Olduvai seated on a rock, his legs framing a paunch. A long slip of white hair, wagging in the breeze, flopped sillily over the wrong side of his part. His voice seemed almost effeminate in a professorial way. Yet women swarmed.

"I first met him when he was old and ugly and had practically no teeth left and had a belly hanging over his belt," recalled the anthropologist wife of one Harvard professor, "and still he was one of the most attractive men I had ever met. Women just fell all over themselves for him."

A charismatic speaker, a charming and witty dinner guest, Louis was a male magnet who dominated a room. Biruté found him "extraordinarily inspirational," attributing his charisma to "his total self-confidence."

Yet his female followers may have been equally attracted by his own deeply feminine qualities. Louis was in many ways a traditional nurturer. When Mary and Louis's first child, Jonathan, was born, Mary was too enthralled with prehistory to spend much time with him; a nurse cared for the baby by day, but at night it was Louis who bottle-fed him and changed diapers. His mothering extended also to orphaned animals. His "field pets" included adopted wildebeest calves, a colobus monkey, and an infant baboon named Baby, with whom he often slept. When he gave his and Mary's second son, Richard, a pony as a pet, he allowed it to sleep in their house at Langata while a paddock was being constructed.

He loved to cook. At Olduvai he often baked bread, and he often cooked at get-togethers, whether he was host or not. Jane's mother, Vanne, remembers his "specs, completely opaque with flour and other tit-bits from a sputtering pan . . . perched atop his head" as the smells of a succulent roast—the joint chosen personally by Louis at the butcher shop that morning—wafted through the Goodall kitchen.

Louis himself may not have considered these qualities particularly feminine. But "one of the main things Louis stressed about women," said Tita Caldwell, "was that women are blessed and cursed with sensitivity and intuition that only one in a million men have. It is very rare in men. But Louis had it."

Tita and her husband, Hugh, called this intuition "Louis's weird antennae." Even when mobbed by fans after a successful lecture, he would somehow spot, across a crowded room, the one person who was in distress or needing assurance and would gravitate to that person. Many people have noticed this same ability in Jane and Dian and Biruté. Martta Marshalko, who works at the National Geographic Society, was struck by this quality in Dian. The two would converse briefly each time Dian visited her sponsor in Washington. "In 1984 she came by and I told her, 'Next time you come I won't be on the fifth floor.' She looked at me sharply and said, 'You were very very unhappy here, weren't you?' I had never complained to Dian. But I had been miserable. I said, 'How did you know?' She said, 'It was obvious to me.' "

"People don't realize," said Tita Caldwell, "that to these women, who can interpret the minds of a nonspeaking primate, to sit in a room full of speaking animals and interpret their behavior is duck soup!"

As a consequence of his weird antennae, Louis was constantly adopting people, many of them young women in distress. He would write letters, phone them from Africa, give them jobs. One of the women he encouraged was Joy Adamson, who came to him almost penniless after her divorce from her first husband. He gave her a job at the museum and encouraged her artistic skills and love of nature. She later moved on to study lions and to write the classic *Born Free*.

In his most successful protégées, Jane, Dian, and Biruté, Louis took special pride. Joan Travis, a cofounder of the foundation that bears Leakey's name, recalls that he always carried with him the latest communication from any one of the three; he would often whip out their telexes from a breast pocket to read aloud at his lectures. He called them his "three primates" — a phrase that always prompted his breathless, body-heaving laugh. Louis showed the typical African delight in word play in the expression, a triple play on words: not only were the women primates studying primates, but the highest post in the Anglican church is that of primate — a position only a man could hold.

But though Jane, Dian, and Biruté would always be linked publicly to Louis as a trio, his personal relationships with them were as different as the women were from one another.

To Louis, Jane was a best-loved, golden-haired daughter. His first child, with his first wife Frida, was a daughter, but he divorced Frida when little Priscilla was five. Louis's investment in Jane — and his involvement with her sister and mother — was far stronger than the attachments he maintained with his first family. And in his final years he spent more time with the Goodalls, particularly Jane's mother, than he did with his second wife.

In her 1984 autobiography, *Disclosing the Past*, Mary Leakey wrote ruefully: "I am sure he derived from [Vanne's] kindness and friendship much of the support I myself could no longer provide."

After agreeing to hire Jane as an assistant secretary at the Coryndon Museum, Louis almost immediately adopted her as his "Foster Fairy Daughter," as he called her. This "adoption" quickly extended to the entire Goodall family.

When Vanne, who was divorced, came to visit Jane in Nairobi, Louis squired mother and daughter around on safari. To ease Jane into her new role as "chimp girl," Louis packed her off for training at Dr. John Napier's primate unit at the Royal Free Hospital in London. He then secured funding for both Vanne and Jane to go to Gombe. Two years later he persuaded the English weekly newspaper *Reveille* to pay for Jane's sister, Judy, to go out to Gombe also — ostensibly as a photographer, though Judy had little previous experience with a camera.

Louis continued to orchestrate the careers of his foster family. He decided that Jane needed a doctorate, and arranged for her to work toward one at his alma mater, Cambridge — despite the fact that she did not have a bachelor's degree. He set Judy up in a fossil-casting business — "FD [for Foster Daughter] Castings" — provoking the jealousy of his son Richard, who was trying his hand at paleoanthropology himself. Louis later helped Judy and her husband get a loan to buy their first house.

In a letter in 1962, Louis informed Vanne of yet another prize he had secured for his family: "I've found the perfect husband for Jane," he announced. He had met Hugo van Lawick through friends. Hugo worked briefly with Louis, filming his work at Olduvai for a National Geographic program. Louis arranged for Hugo to film Jane's work at Gombe for another National Geographic documentary, and the couple fell in love and married.

Though Louis never visited Jane at Gombe — at first he deliberately kept out of her way, and later his bad health prevented

a visit — they wrote each other constantly, she signing her letters
with the initials FC for Foster Child. The Goodall flat in London
became a frequent stopover on Louis's flights from Kenya to the
United States. Vanne and he would go to plays and ballet, and
he often went to church with Judy. Vanne, a talented writer,
helped edit Louis's books and articles and coauthored the book
Unveiling Man's Origins with him in 1969.

Louis's fatherly pride in Jane never flagged. One day, Vanne
remembers, Louis predicted to friends gathered at the flat that
someone would raise a statue to Jane. "And somebody said,
'Oh, no — to you first, Dr. Leakey.' And he said, 'No — to
Jane.' "

Louis's relationship with Biruté was less intense. Perhaps because
she was his third "primate," perhaps because she was married,
perhaps because her field work was not in Africa, Biruté was
"very much the third daughter," as she recalls. He invited her
and her first husband, Rod, to join him on an African safari, as
a "vacation" on their way to Indonesia; he encouraged her with
frequent, inspirational letters, like a kindly uncle. Though his
influence upon her was profound, she admits that she didn't get
to know him very well; he died only three years after she met
him.

Dian, however, was no daughter to Louis. With Dian he fell
hopelessly, adolescently, in love.

In October 1969, nearly three years into her study, she went
to Nairobi for medical tests and to Louis for solace. She was
depressed about the poachers at Karisoke and sick with what
she feared was tuberculosis. Louis proposed accompanying her
on a luxurious, weeklong safari in south central Kenya to cheer
her up. At age sixty-six Louis was smitten.

His love letters, which Dian kept with her mementos, read
like a teenager's: "I love you," he wrote her in his almost un-

intelligible, sprawling scrawl, "quite simply, deeply, whether you are miles and miles away or very, very close."

"It was lovely just seeing you," he wrote Dian. "Even briefly and knowing that you do love as I can do deeply love you. . . . I feel we belong and so I was very very happy."

Whether his love for Dian was ever physically consummated is not known; but that they "belonged" was in a sense true. Dian seldom spoke to anyone about her sad childhood, but the moment Louis met her, he told Tita Caldwell, he recognized her past and future, as if he had known her in a previous life: "Her life was a tragedy and will always be a tragedy," Louis predicted. "She is a tragic person, and I want you to promise me you will never desert her." Louis begged others to be tolerant of Dian, "because she has been through so much."

Dian attracted many suitors in her youth, but it may have been her tragedy that touched a chord in Louis. He shared with her a dark side. Most people recall him as constantly ebullient, but Vanne Goodall remembers moods that would "envelop him in a dark fury, or in a martyr's gloom." They came on suddenly, unpredictably, making him "testy and irritable, harshly critical, sometimes rude." The description is almost exactly like what other people said of Dian's mood swings and outbursts.

He also shared with Dian an African sense of humor. They both delighted in lampooning people, particularly the self-important. Exaggeratedly miming the gait, inflection, and facial expression of some official, they'd draw howls of laughter from their respective African staffs. They both enjoyed word play, especially when Dian would produce a scatological or obscene double-entendre.

Louis showered love letters upon his "dearest love" for the next three years. He bought her a ruby ring. From entries in her diaries, it seems that Dian didn't know what to make of his romantic attentions. She never obeyed his urgings to write him at his private post office box in Nairobi, a secret he kept from his wife. But she did care for him. She visited him in the hospital in London after his first heart attack in 1970. A year later Louis was attacked by African bees and stung hundreds of times; when he hit the ground in pain, the fall caused a concussion that left him comatose for a week. During his recovery Dian regaled him with cheerful, humorous letters.

When Louis awoke from his coma, his first thoughts were of Dian. He feared she was short of funds, and immediately dictated a letter to her. Whatever she needed, he'd fix it somehow. He had plans to visit her for the first time at Karisoke in April 1972. She worried endlessly whether his health could withstand the trip. He did eventually cancel the plans because his health was failing.

Louis did not live long enough to visit the study sites of any of his three primates. He felt the first symptoms of his fatal heart attack at Vanne's London flat in the autumn of 1972. There, before starting his planned lecture tour in the States, he was putting the finishing touches on his second autobiography, *By the Evidence.* He was scheduled to fly to New York on October 2.

On September 30 he felt weary; his doctor advised him to postpone the flight. On the morning of October 1 he suffered a coronary. Vanne left the hospital at nine A.M., and he died half an hour later.

Not long before he died, when Jane's sister and some friends were visiting him at the flat, Vanne recalls that the conversation turned to death. Someone asked, "Are you afraid of dying, Dr. Leakey?"

"Dying? Why should I mind dying?" he replied. "My spirit will live on in my family—but I—my soul will go on forever."

5 *"Science with a Capital S"*

SITUATED to the west of the eastern fork of the Rift Valley of Tanzania, Olduvai Gorge is a thirty-mile-long moonscape, flooded with white-hot light. There is little soil here: in places, all the eye can see is a vast expanse of cracked and bouldered white and gray calcrete, a type of limestone. The summer sun sears your skin, burning right through cotton clothing. Grass dries to straw; the tops of the few acacias seem flattened by the brittle heat. It is so dusty that if you blow your nose at the end of the day, mud comes out. Everything your senses tell you is sharp-edged, metallic, stark. It seems as if bones are the only thing this soil will grow.

But as Louis Leakey searched for those bones, in his imagination this land was ripe and lush. When Jane Goodall first came to Olduvai in 1957, accompanying Louis and Mary on a dig, he told Jane of the paradise early man would have found here. The gorge exposes the graveyards of vanished lakes and streams, whose waters would have drawn plentiful game, easy hunting.

Nearby forests would have offered cool shade, shelter, nuts, and fruits. When Jane first came to Olduvai, *Zinjanthropus* and *Homo habilis* were yet to be unearthed, but Louis was sure such finds awaited him. Man's ancestors, he knew, would have flourished by Olduvai's lakeshores.

On that dig Jane remembers holding in her hands the fossilized bone of a prehistoric animal that early man might have hunted by the vanished lake. It was then she realized the full extent of Louis's quest: here was the fossil, but what had this being really looked like? How did it communicate with others of its kind? How was its family organized? How did it move? What was the scent of its skin?

These were the questions Louis pondered about the ancestors of mankind. For clues Louis looked to another lakeshore, several hundred miles to the west. There, roaming a thirty-square-mile park, still lived large-brained, agile-handed primates, animals so like man that early explorers had described them as human. And though others of their kind lived mostly in dense tropical rain forests, here, by the shores of Lake Tanganyika, they shared the environment that primitive man had enjoyed at Olduvai two million years ago. It was at Olduvai that Louis first told Jane about them: they were the chimpanzees of Gombe.

To travel to Gombe from Kigoma, the largest town in the region, you wait for the water taxi to make its wet landing on the shore of Lake Tanganyika. You may have to wait under a hot sun for many hours because the boat doesn't adhere to a schedule; meanwhile dozens of children crowd around, whispering "Muzungu!" (white person) while eyeing and interpreting your every movement with murmurs of KiSwahili or KiHa. The water taxi is a long, low, rough-hewn wooden boat, crowded with perhaps eighty people and their gear: live chickens, baskets of fruit, furniture, logs, neatly tied bundles of clothes. There aren't any seats; people sit on the rim of the boat or on fat burlap sacks stuffed with the odoriferous sardinelike fish called *dagaa*. Mud-and-thatch fisherman's huts dot the shore. On moonless nights the fishermen hoist their red nets, heavy with *dagaa*, by lamplight; at every fishing village you approach along the trip, you'll see *dagaa* on the beach, drying in the sun, glittering like tinsel. As the boat approaches the shore to take on passengers and cargo, the shallows sparkle with the silver-blue, iridescent scales.

The twelve-mile journey takes two or three hours, depending on how frequently the motor cuts out. When it breaks down, passengers discuss the problem animatedly, and finally the men search their pockets for a penknife with which to attempt repairs. Women wrapped in bright-patterned cloth, on their way to visit other villages, pass their babies back and forth among the other passengers, trying to shelter them from the sun with their *kangas*.

As the boat nears the shore of the park, Gombe looks much as Jane Goodall found it when she landed here, in a government-owned aluminum dinghy, with Vanne, a game ranger, and an African cook on July 16, 1960. The beach is narrow, only a dozen yards of brown sand and pastel pebbles. The mountains rise sharply from the beach to tower 2,500 feet above the lake. They are fissured with gorges and streams, their valleys thick with tropical trees. Vanne was secretly horrified at the steepness of the slopes, the density of the forests; but to Jane, Gombe was a storybook dream fulfilled.

The forest looks like a *Tarzan* movie set: palms and ferns on the lower slopes and, higher up, buttressed trees soaring to 100 feet, vines tangling in the canopy. The light is diffused by the tracery of leaves above, dappling the ground like a fawn's back. The tops of the mountains are covered with golden, grassy slopes, inviting one to climb.

Despite the steep slopes, Gombe is a comfortable place. The temperature here by day is seldom hotter than 85 degrees Fahrenheit, seldom cooler than 60. The dry season, which lasts from June to October, is idyllic. On the beach the sun's bright heat is cooled by the breeze off the lake. You can swim in the clear blue water; it harbors none of the snails that infect so many other African lakes with deadly bilharzia. Cold streams bubble through every valley; the water is safe to drink. Biting insects, poisonous snakes, and toxic plants are few. In the glorious dry season, this is a place that invites walking in sandals and shorts.

Once the boat leaves, you hear only the sound of the waves lapping, as peaceful as breathing. A few dozen yards takes you to the edge of the forest, and you can hear the bubbling of Kakombe Stream, the rattling of dry palm fronds ready to fall, the cackling trills and high-pitched chirps of birds, the barks of the beetle-browed baboons. Little lizards trickle down tree trunks like raindrops. Within an hour of your arrival, you may glimpse coppery red-tailed monkeys cascading through the canopy or the chestnut flash of a bushbuck, a goat-sized antelope with spiral horns. Entering this jungle paradise of clear water, cool shade, and bright sun feels like a homecoming, familiar as a half-remembered dream.

When Jane embarked on her great adventure, she thought it might occupy at most two years of her life. She and her mother unpacked their gear: tents and tins and bedding, old binoculars borrowed from Louis, and tableware consisting of two tin plates, a cup without a handle, and a thermos top. Jane remembers feeling a curious sense of awed detachment that first day. "What had I, the girl standing on the government launch in her jeans, to do with the girl who in a few days would be searching those very mountains for wild chimpanzees?" she recalls in her book *In the Shadow of Man.* "Yet by the time I went to sleep that night the transformation had already taken place." That night she pulled her cot from the tent to sleep out under the open sky.

Studying primates as a route to understanding man is an idea whose roots go back to the 1920s. Robert Yerkes, the American psychologist who founded and ran the Yale Laboratory of Primate Biology from 1924 to 1943, considered chimpanzees "psychobiological gold mines." The chimp, in his view, was to be "a servant of science." To accomplish this goal, men were to "shape it intelligently to specification, instead of trying to preserve its natural characteristics." Using chimps as surrogate humans, scientists could, it was hoped, experiment in the laboratory to pioneer new ways to remodel humans psychologically, to make people happier and more productive.

The purpose of investigating the natural lives of primates was primarily to learn the "substrate" upon which man's "artificial" culture and language was imposed. Yet even in these so-called naturalistic studies, man's controlling hand often willfully manipulated the "natural" lives he had come to observe. Clarence Ray Carpenter's studies of "free-ranging" monkeys on Cayo Santiago in the late 1930s are considered one of the more important naturalistic studies of the era. But the 450 rhesus monkeys in his study colony had been captured in India and transported to Cayo Santiago in 1938. Attempting to investigate issues of sex and dominance in the group, he experimentally manipulated the social structure. In one experiment he removed the leader, then the emerging new leader, and so on down the line. "Naturalistic" studies included experimentally implanting electrodes in the brains of free-ranging monkeys and castrating and releasing males.

But Jane Goodall, sleeping out under the open sky, envisioned no experiments, no manipulation. Her vision was one of approach, of trust: she asked only that the chimpanzees admit her silent presence into their lives.

"We soon realized it would be impossible to habituate them to our presence," wrote the primatologist Vernon Reynolds in 1960 after a nine-month study of wild chimpanzees in Uganda. He and his wife, Frances, had hoped the chimps would become used to their presence; they never did. The chimps fled as soon as they saw the two researchers.

This had also happened to Henry Nissen. In his forty-nine

days of observation in French Guinea, he was unable to study
them at close range. He was forced to hide from the chimps in
order to see them, and the foliage that hid him from view often
obscured his view of the animals.

Before leaving for Gombe, Jane had spoken with wildlife researchers in both Nairobi and London, and they all said she
should not get her hopes up. The chimps would never get used
to human observers.

When Jane began her study, her two Tanzanian scouts located
chimps for her daily. Crawling through the clotted undergrowth
of the lower valley forests, crisscrossing streams, hiking up the
mountain slopes, they would follow the chimpanzees' hooting
calls. But once the animals were located, Jane could watch them
only from far away. Through her binoculars she saw mostly
groups of chimpanzees climbing up tree trunks and then, many
hours later, climbing back down. The chimpanzees' movements
were obscured by the leaves of the *msulula* trees in which they
were feeding. Jane and her scouts tried to approach closer for
a better view, but even at 500 yards the chimps would flee from
the three approaching humans.

From the beginning Jane had wanted to pursue her study
alone. Her mother had come with her because the local government officials—Tanzania was then Tanganyika, under British
rule—would not hear of a young English girl working in the
jungle without a proper British chaperone. The two scouts accompanying her daily were there by order of the game warden,
for Jane's safety. There were buffalo in the forests, and Jane
remembered the gashes left on a tree by a bull that had charged
in fury at a fisherman, who climbed the tree to escape. She
occasionally saw leopards at close range; one left a neat pile of
dung at a spot where she often sat. And the chimpanzees themselves could be dangerous. Waha tribesmen told her that once
a man had climbed a palm to pick the fruits and failed to notice
an adult male chimp was there. The animal charged down the
tree, swiped at the man, and knocked out his eye.

Yet Jane longed to be alone in the forest. She reasoned that it would be easier for the chimps to accept a single human. The first few months of study were frustrating, and she felt pressured. Louis had secured only enough funds to cover six months; no more money would be forthcoming if she could report only a few glimpses of black hairy arms reaching down from the foliage to pull fruits out of sight. At one point Jane wrote her "Fairy Foster Father": "Life is depressing—wet, chimpless, and it seems impecunious. Fruit not fruiting. Chimps vanishing. Me being ill. Oh, just ——— everything." She signed off, "A despondent and sad FC."

By the third month both Jane and Vanne were ill with malaria. The doctor in Kigoma had assured them, for reasons Jane still cannot fathom, that there was no malaria in Gombe, so they had brought no malaria pills. Vanne's fever soared to 105 each night. When Jane's fever finally broke, nearly two weeks later, she stole out of the tent at dawn. She headed, alone, for the mountain that rose directly above her two-tent camp.

A twenty-minute climb brought her to an open overlook about a thousand feet above the lake. A large flat rock offered a seat for an excellent view of the forested valleys below. It is not a hidden vantage point; any animal with reasonable eyesight can see a person up here from a quarter of a mile away. Heart hammering from the climb, Jane sat quietly, her legs folded beneath her.

She had been there scarcely fifteen minutes when three chimps appeared in a ravine below, only eighty yards away. They stood and stared at her boldly, considering, then calmly moved on. At that point Jane knew: the peak was the altar on which she could offer them her presence, like a promise: I am here. I am harmless. I wait.

Jane now says that day marked the turning point in her study. Later that morning she watched a group of chimps, screaming and hooting, careen down the opposite mountain slope and begin feeding on figs in the valley below. Another group appeared about twenty minutes later in the bare ravine where she had earlier seen the three. They stopped also to stare at her and then moved on without alarm.

Thereafter, nearly every day she would make the predawn pilgrimage to the Peak (when Jane writes about the Peak it is sanctified with a capital letter). No longer did the scouts need to accompany her; they knew Jane was safe up there. They knew where to reach her. Carrying her clothing and a thermos, she would often climb the mountain naked in the glimmering dawn. Though she carried her clothes so they would not become wet and cold in the dew, she came to enjoy the feel of the wet grass against her legs, the cool darkness wrapping her body. It was like a purification ritual before going to a sacred place. Though the spot is still used today by Gombe research workers, it is considered to belong in some way to her alone; they call it Jane's Peak.

At the Peak Jane always donned the same dull-colored clothing, and once seated, she remained utterly still. Clearly visible, with her presence Jane reiterated her promise to the chimps, an incantation, an offering: I am here. I am harmless. I wait. To you, said her silent form, I give the choice: to flee or approach or ignore.

The chimps passed by her nearly every day to get to the figs fruiting in the valley. She came to recognize the individuals. And like Adam in the Garden of Eden, one of her first acts was to name the animals. Mr. McGregor was an old, balding male who reminded her of the gardener in *The Tale of Peter Rabbit*. She named Olly after her own aunt. Goliath was a powerful male in his prime; his gentle, handsome friend she called David Graybeard. Often, she noticed, when Goliath's body would grow huge with excitement, his hair erect, David would wrap an arm around his friend or gently touch his groin. Goliath's hair would go flat and smooth again.

Earlier naturalists and explorers had portrayed chimps as violent brutes. Their journals emphasized the chimps' "maniacal screams," their "murderous rages," their sudden, powerful movements.

"They goe many together, and kill many negroe that travaile in the woods," claimed the African traveler Andrew Battel in the 1623 volume *His Pilgrims*. He claimed that chimpanzees were strong and vicious enough to kill elephants, "which come to feed where they be, and so beat them with their clubbed fists and pieces of wood that they will runne roaring away from them."

"These monkeys have an ugly face," quotes another seventeenth-century text. "They are very wicked and bold . . . so bold that they attack man."

But watching these animals that men had seen as violent, maniacal, and murderous, Jane was most impressed by the chimps' gestures of gentle affection, their quest for comfort. The difference in perception recalls the results of a study conducted by psychologists Susan Pollak and Carol Gilligan. They showed men and women a picture of acrobats performing on a trapeze and asked the respondents to write stories about the image. The men wrote stories of violence and betrayal. One imagined a scene in which one of the acrobats purposely drops another, who then plunges to her death. The women wrote stories about the two acrobats working together carefully and gently. Many women included in their stories a safety net that was not shown in the picture.

From her perch on the Peak, Jane watched the chimps greet each other with embraces and open-mouthed kisses. Sometimes a chimp would offer a hand to be kissed in greeting, like a Victorian lady. She often saw them hold hands with each other, as people do walking down the street. She watched them build their sumptuous leafy nests at dusk, high in the trees. When she could reach them, Jane would climb into the nests after the chimps had left for the day. She could feel the springy softness of the carefully woven branches and leaves. Often, she found, the chimps would construct pillows for their heads. Each individual slept in its treetop nest alone, except for infants, who slept in their mother's nest, curled in her arms.

Jane learned that the chimps' "maniacal screams" were often hoots of pleasure, heralding the discovery of a tree laden with fruit. Sometimes in their excitement they would hug one another, as if in joyful congratulation. Before picking a fruit, a chimp would often test it for ripeness, squeezing it gently with thumb and fingers, like a canny old lady at the grocery store.

Jane would taste the fruits the chimps ate: often they were bitingly acidic. She even tried eating termites, which she found rather tasteless. She began to share the chimps' sensory world, their perceptions: she will speak of a tree "laden with luscious fruit," even though to human tastes the fruits are too tart. She could almost feel the calm spreading through the bodies of the chimpanzees as they sat grooming one another, lavishing intense concentration on bringing pleasure to another.

Jane would watch and write down what she saw in her notebook. At night she would return to camp to exchange news with her mother over a dinner prepared by Dominic, the cook: he baked bread in a pit oven and made stews from tinned meat and fresh vegetables bought in Kigoma. A houseman washed her clothes, laying them out to dry on the dagaa-scented beach, and then pressed them with a hand iron filled with hot coals.

While Jane observed the chimps, her mother began a sort of clinic at the base camp, dispensing aspirin and bandages to the local fishermen. After dinner Jane would transcribe her notes into narrative, typing by the light of the kerosene lamp. Sometimes she would spend the night at the Peak to be nearer the chimps.

When Vanne left after five months at Gombe, Jane was lonely at first, but within a few weeks she came to cherish her solitude, especially her nights at the Peak. She had her scouts carry a trunk up there, with some tinned beans, a mug and some coffee, a blanket, and a sweater; these were her luxuries. "There's a special fascination about the sudden nightfall in the forest, when the sounds of the day give place to the more mysterious sounds of the night," she later said of her nights at the Peak. "I felt part of the mountain world around me, completely alone, completely at peace."

In the fifth month of her study, Jane made two discoveries that caused worldwide excitement. "For both of them," she wrote, "I had David Graybeard to thank."

One day Jane saw David sitting in the branches of a tree with a female and a youngster, who were reaching toward his mouth with outstretched hands, as if begging. In David's mouth was a pink object. Jane realized that it was meat.

David, after chewing the meat with bits of leaves, often spat out the wad into the hands of the female. Once he dropped a piece of flesh, and when it fell to the ground the youngster followed it. An adult bushpig ran from the undergrowth, charging at the young chimp. Jane saw three striped piglets with the adult and realized that the chimps were eating a piglet.

Until that time scientists had thought that chimps were vegetarians. Though it was believed they might supplement their diet with insects and perhaps small rodents, no one had imagined that chimps might hunt, kill, and eat mammals this large.

Within two weeks of that discovery, when Jane was on her way up to the Peak, she saw David Graybeard again in the grass sixty yards away. Focusing her binoculars, she saw that he was sitting by the red, drip-sand castle of a termite mound, pushing a long grass stem inside. After a few minutes he withdrew the stem and plucked something from the end with his lips.

For more than a week Jane watched and waited near the termite mound. David reappeared on the eighth day, along with Goliath. She saw them bite off the ends of their fishing stems

With dexterous fingers, this chimp is gently grooming
his partner, an activity that not only removes burrs
and parasites but also cements social bonds. It is
obvious from the expressions on their faces
that this feels wonderful. *Michael K. Nichols/
Magnum Photos*

when they became bent. She saw them carefully select new
stems, twigs, and vines, often collecting "spares" from far away.
She saw them carefully peel the leaves from twigs to fashion the
tool.

She cabled Louis with her discoveries: like man, chimps hunt
and eat large mammals and share the meat. Like man, chimps
both use and make tools.

Ironically, the agency that had funded her first months of
study, the Wilkie Brothers Foundation, was begun by Leighton
and Robert Wilkie, inventors of cutting tools, machines, and
processes. The brothers firmly believed that making and using
tools was what had made man human; it was Louis's finds of
primitive tools that had drawn their attention to him and his
projects. "Man is a tool-using animal. . . . Without tools he is

nothing, with tools he is all," read the brochure for their foundation. Indeed, tool use was part of the definition of man at the time. After receiving Jane's cable, Louis wrote to her: "I feel that scientists holding to this definition are faced with three choices: they must accept chimpanzees as man, by definition; they must redefine man; or they must redefine tools."

Louis wrote to the National Geographic Society about his protégée's findings. In her first eighteen months of research she had made "completely outstanding discoveries . . . of the very highest scientific importance." Louis's perennial funder soon offered £500, the equivalent at that time of $1,500, to continue the study.

Louis decided that Jane would need proper credentials in order for her findings to be taken seriously; she had only a diploma from a secretarial school in London. Louis negotiated an unprecedented agreement with Cambridge University: Jane would bypass the usual bachelor's degree and, after several semesters of courses at Cambridge, would submit the writeup of her study as a thesis for her Ph.D. in ethology, the study of animal behavior.

To Jane this was a huge nuisance. "I didn't want a Ph.D.," she recalls. "I spent as little time there [Cambridge] as possible." From the beginning of 1962 until her thesis was accepted in 1965, her observations at Gombe were broken up each year by a dreary Cambridge semester. She remembers cold gray days, frozen water pipes, and longing to be with the chimps. And she remembers being told politely, again and again, that she was doing it all wrong.

In her first eighteen months of study, Jane had taken few measurements; she described in words, not numbers. She did not begin with a theory; instead she wrote down what she saw and what she felt, receptive to the dramas unfolding. Her focus was on the individual, not the archetype. Her subjects were not numbered but named. Her approach was intuitive, personal, receptive, and narrative at a time when ethology was becoming increasingly theoretical, impersonal, experimental, and statistical.

Hers was the approach that women typically take in configuring the world: emphasizing relationships rather than rules, individuals rather than generalities, receptivity rather than control. Jane's approach was maverick for the very reason it was rejected: she was applying a feminine approach to a field that was dominated and defined by male views and values.

Women had seldom worked in field primatology; when they did, it was usually in the company of a Ph.D. husband. Her name would appear in the acknowledgments of scientific papers that came out of the field work or, less frequently, she would be listed as coauthor. An extensive search of the scientific literature by biologist Donna Harraway, author of *Primate Visions*, revealed not a single book written by a woman Ph.D. primatologist before 1960.

Jane's Cambridge adviser, Robert Hinde, was dismayed with her methods. He pushed measurement and numerical analysis. Jane remembers, "He would suggest things like, 'When you get back to Gombe,' — and this was after I had spent only eighteen months there — 'you should measure the distances between where the chimps are feeding and the level they are in the canopy.' " Numbers, not narrative, would tell the scientific truth, he insisted; statistics, not intuitions, would reveal empirical reality.

A highly respected English ethologist, Hinde stood at the forefront of a field whose practitioners were at that time struggling to transform themselves from naturalists to scientists. Naturalists, typified by the self-taught nineteenth- and early twentieth-century explorers, merely scribbled descriptions in their notebooks. In the 1960s scientists, those bright young men in white coats, were supposed to be the saviors of the world. Guided by logic, propelled by measurement and experiment, scientists promised the breakthroughs leading to the Great Big Beautiful Tomorrow lauded at every World's Fair, when, thanks to man's increasing control over the universe, life would be easier, more comfortable, more productive, more affluent.

Robert Hinde was one of the young Turks taking ethology in a direction new and different from that envisioned by Konrad Lorenz, its founder. Lorenz, a Bavarian naturalist, is best known for his discovery of the phenomenon known as imprinting; newly hatched ducklings and goslings will follow the first moving object they see and respond to it as to a mother. In a front-page photo in the *New York Times* tagged to his February 1989 obituary, Lorenz is pictured as he is best remembered: a white-bearded old man followed by a parade of greylag goslings that have imprinted on him.

Lorenz discovered and named many of the basic principles of animal behavior, especially many of the stereotyped inborn behaviors of birds. But he firmly believed that animals had thoughts, feelings, and motives. He made most of his discoveries without performing a single experiment. He did not intend to interfere with the behavior of any animal in the wild; a keen observer, he relied on his senses, intuition, and many thousands of hours of observation to reveal the *gestalt* of an animal's natural behavior.

But by the late 1950s Lorenz's influence was waning. The new ethology was largely an experimental science, as characterized by the work of Niko Tinbergen, Lorenz's friend and colleague, best known for his work on wasps and other insects. No longer was it enough to present narratives of field notes, as the naturalist-explorers had. The new ethology was problem-oriented, quantitative, experimental. The old naturalists were now dismissed as mere "butterfly collectors." "In science, butterfly collecting isn't good enough anymore," said Nancy De Vore who, with her husband, Irven De Vore, was studying baboons in Kenya at the time. "If you don't have a theory informing what you're doing, and the numbers to back it up, it doesn't do to just write down everything you see."

The 850 pages of meticulously typed, carefully observed notes Jane had amassed over her first eighteen months at Gombe amounted to little more than a huge and immensely colorful butterfly collection. Hers was a collection of portraits of individual animals: Flo playing with her youngsters; David soothing the irritable Goliath with a touch of his hand; timid Olly, crouching and uttering soft grunts in front of more dominant individuals.

From the start Jane focused on the differences between individuals. And this, too, Carol Gilligan tells us, is a feminine characteristic: women tend to "insist on the particular . . . resisting a categorical formation." Men see things clearly ordered by theories, laws, and rules; but when a woman makes a decision, it is "a contextual judgment, bound to the particulars of time and place," Gilligan explains in her book on psychological theory and women's development, *In a Different Voice*.

But exploring individual differences was precisely the opposite of the goal ethology set for itself in the 1960s. "Today you wouldn't dream of not recognizing individuality," says primatologist Alison Jolly, well known for her research on lemurs. But when Jolly was a graduate student, about the same time Jane was studying at Cambridge, she remembers that "there was constant pressure for scientists to talk about *the* adult male, *the* adult female—archetypes." Ethology was mainly concerned with discovering the "mechanisms" underlying universal behaviors, not individual motives sculpting differing responses.

Because animals were considered "models" rather than thinking, feeling individuals, animals under study were typically numbered, not named. Jane was not the first to name her study animals—Irven De Vore had named his baboon subjects in 1958—but she was still frowned upon for doing so. The first journal to which she submitted a scientific paper, *Annals of the*

New York Academy of Science, sent it back, insisting she number the chimps instead of naming them. The editors crossed out Jane's references to chimps as "he" or "she" and replaced each one with "it"; they changed each "who" to "which." Jane refused to make the changes, and the paper was published anyway.

Regardless of her methods, Jane's discoveries at Gombe were too spectacular to ignore. As her renown grew, thanks to articles in *National Geographic*, her fame bruised academic egos. What right had this young female amateur to steal the spotlight from those to whom it rightfully belonged, those who had devoted years of study and meticulously calculated methodology to their theories? Whispered attacks on Jane swelled, focusing on the aspects that set her apart from the male Ph.D.s whose turf she had invaded: many scientists dismissed her as a "blond bimbo" recalls Mary Smith, Jane's editor at *National Geographic*. "It was easy to make jokes about 'Me Jane, you Tarzan and the apes,' " she said.

Biruté Galdikas remembers that when she was an undergraduate at UCLA, one of her female professors offered this assessment of Jane's career: "The only reason she's so famous is because of her great legs in those short shorts in the films." Many years later Biruté told Jane about that comment. "I don't let that sort of thing bother me," Jane told her. "I just don't listen to it anymore."

Nor did Jane heed all her adviser's suggestions. She continued to record her observations mostly as a narrator, writing in her notebook, later speaking into a tape recorder. She continued to focus on individual differences. She continued to name her study subjects. Jane doesn't like to talk about her early disagreements with her Cambridge colleagues; neither does Robert Hinde. "He's totally different now, anyway," she says, dismissing the past; Hinde is now a close friend and an adviser to the institute that bears Jane's name.

In spite of their early disagreements, Jane's thesis was accepted and her degree awarded in 1965. Not awarding it would have caused much embarrassment at Cambridge; by that time her work had been heavily publicized in *National Geographic*, and in both 1963 and 1964 she had been awarded the society's Franklin Burr Award for Contribution to Science. But her thesis was not widely respected by her colleagues. When Dian Fossey was sent off to Cambridge to get her Ph.D., she wrote to her friends the Schwartzels that Jane's thesis "is now considered in the University School the perfect example of what not to do."

When you mention these criticisms today, Jane replies in a voice a shade sharper and louder than her normal speaking voice: "I didn't give two hoots for what they thought. They were wrong, and I was right. That's why I was lucky that I never was going into any of these things for science. And as I didn't care about the Ph.D., it didn't matter. I would listen, I just wouldn't do what they said. Then I would go back to what I was doing at Gombe."

During the rainy season of Jane's first year at Gombe, after Christmas, the chimpanzees became bold in her presence. Sometimes she would find herself surrounded by screaming, thrashing chimpanzees: black shapes, yellow teeth, hurling at her an angry wall of sound. With hair erect, they would shake branches, scream threats, and then vanish, their voices hanging in the air. Once as Jane was lying flat on the wet ground, sheltered under a plastic sheet from the rain, a large male hit her hard on the head with his hand. When she sat up, he moved away. And Jane felt a sense of triumph along with relief: this was contact of a sort.

After she returned from her first semester at Cambridge, she found the chimps more accustomed to her. Now she could follow them through the forest. David Graybeard was particularly patient and tolerant of her follows; sometimes he even seemed to welcome her company. He would wait for her to catch up to him, pausing to look back in her direction as she stumbled over vines or belly-crawled along overgrown pig trails, just as he would wait for his friends Goliath and William.

Jane spent many hours alone with David Graybeard. One day as she sat with him near a stream, she saw a red palm nut on the ground nearby; she picked it up and offered it to him on her open palm. At first he turned his head away. But when she moved her hand closer, she recalls in *Shadow*, "he looked at it, and then at me, and then he took the fruit, and at the same time held my hand firmly and gently with his own. As I sat motionless he released my hand, looked down at the nut, and dropped it to the ground."

David had not accepted her gift, but he had given her one far more profound:

> At that moment there was no need of any scientific knowledge to understand his communication of reassurance. The soft pressure of his fingers spoke to me not through my intellect but through a more primitive emotional channel: the barrier of untold centuries which has grown up during the separate evolution of man and chimpanzee was, for those few seconds, broken down.

On another evening Jane returned to camp to find Dominic very excited: a large male chimpanzee had walked into her camp and spent an hour feeding in the fruiting palm tree near her tent.

The next day Jane stayed in camp. About ten in the morning David Graybeard walked past her tent to climb the palm tree. He returned daily, as long as the tree continued to fruit. And although "there was a limit to the amount of information one could gain from watching a lone male guzzling palm nuts," she wrote in *Shadow*, she would sometimes stay in camp and wait for him, "just for the intense pleasure of seeing him so close and so unafraid."

A few weeks later Jane suffered another bout of malaria. A different palm in camp was fruiting, and David resumed his visits. One day when she left a banana on a table, David, hair suddenly erect with boldness, snatched it. Thereafter Jane told Dominic to leave bananas out when he saw David around. The chimp began to visit regularly and occasionally would bring his high-ranking friend Goliath and, later, timid William.

At about this time Hugo van Lawick came to Gombe. The bananas proved to be a filmmaker's bonanza. Judy Goodall's efforts to photograph the chimps at Gombe had been ruined by constant rain and fleeing subjects. Hugo's skill and luck were greater. Drawn to the pile of bananas, the chimpanzees came to camp regularly. Before Hugo's whirring camera they shared and squabbled over the fruits, occasionally arguing with baboons over the provisions. They also discovered the salty taste of sweaty garments left out to dry, and chewed and sucked on them. Hugo filmed David accepting a banana from Jane's hand: first he swaggered from side to side, hair erect, and then very gently grasped the offering.

Jane's provisioning the chimps with bananas was later strongly criticized, even by Louis, who vehemently objected. "I feel it is creating a most dangerous and impossible situation," Louis wrote her in 1964, "which might lead to these chimpanzees being shot." Provisioning could make the chimpanzees dangerously bold and greedy, he warned; having lost their fear of humans, they might begin to raid villagers' houses, and if this happened, the Africans would probably retaliate: "It is not right and I cannot be a party to it."

But in 1962 the bananas provided a bridge to a new level of intimacy. It was while David Graybeard was eating a banana that Jane first ventured to touch him. Squatting close beside him, Jane slowly moved her hand toward his shoulder and parted his fur with her fingers. David brushed her hand away as casually as if it were a fly. When she reached for him again, he let her groom him for a full minute. It was Christmas Day.

*

The photos and films that Hugo took of Jane among the chimps deeply moved Western audiences. Jane, girlish in her ponytail, shorts, and sandals, rounds a bend, stepping from the bushes into a clearing, as a young chimp raises a hand to her as in greeting. Jane reaches out, her pale arm balletic, to touch the outreached hand of Flo's infant son Flint—the image of the reaching hands of God and Adam in the Sistine chapel.

Never had National Geographic found such a treasure trove for its films and magazine. Jane's first article on her work, "My Life among Wild Chimpanzees," which appeared in 1963, was so popular that the issue sold out and the society had to reprint it. Between 1962 and 1989 National Geographic made five films about her, more footage than they have devoted to any other investigator, including Louis Leakey.

Edwin Snider, the society's vice president, had been skeptical when he first met Jane. Shy and slim, so proper and English that even her smile seemed restrained, her lips covering her teeth, she didn't seem tough enough to do the job. "She looked like some-one who would seem more at home at an English garden party than in the jungle," he recalls. But it was Jane's fragility, her vulnerability before the chimpanzees' great strength, that made her story so compelling: the beauty among the beasts, at once myth, fable, and adventure story.

Introducing Jane to an audience gathered at National Geo-graphic's Washington headquarters in 1964, Melvin Payne in-voked Edgar Rice Burroughs's tales of Tarzan and his English bride, Jane: "Truth is stranger than fiction, and fiction can be transformed into prophecy," he said. "Here we have a per-fect example of that evolution, for this lovely English lady called Jane has likewise traded her comfortable home in England for the primitive life of the African wilderness among the great apes."

Jane's work and life had a storybook quality, echoing the themes of the childhood books she had cherished growing up.

In her *National Geographic* articles and her books, Jane's own story was entwined with that of the chimps, and it read even more like a fairy tale: in 1964 the brave young adventuress's bylines include the title "Baroness." In 1967 she gave birth to a golden-haired son, and *Grub the Bush Baby*, as she titled a 1971 book, gave occasion for more films and articles. Many of Jane's early lectures were given titles befitting children's books: "Family Life in Chimpland"; "My Life among the Wild Chimpanzees." In an English-accented voice as low and steady as a lullaby, Jane was constantly pointing out the ways in which chimps were "just like people": "Every chimpanzee, just like every human being, has his own character and personality," begins her narration to Hugo's 1963 film shown at National Geographic, which introduces David Graybeard and Goliath, Flo and Fifi, Olly and her daughter Gilka. Often her words seem to have been borrowed from Doctor Dolittle, who talked with the animals. Chimps call as they wake in the morning in their treetop nests: "Here David is telling Goliath it is time to get up." A family of chimps forms a grooming chain: "Here you see a sort of forest beauty parlor." At a time when scientists regarded animals as "stimulus-response machines" with no conscious purpose, Jane freely spoke of the chimps' emotions, moods, and motives. As Olly's one-and-a-half-year-old daughter clutches herself with crossed arms, Jane narrates: "Gilka still feels far more confident if she can hang onto something, even if it's only herself."

As Louis had wooed audiences with his showmanship and bravura, Jane enchanted her listeners with her storytelling. Her slight shyness before the microphone — she still sometimes looks at a mike as if she's never seen such an object before — only set off her poise, a large jewel in a slender setting. Her story is the drama of contact, of touch, of equality between species. "This is not the story of man's stewardship," writes Donna Harraway in *Primate Visions*, "but of his homecoming, not just in peace, but in equality . . . a narrative not of civil rights, but of natural rights."

But this is not the story that Science was constructing for man. The year National Geographic published Jane's first book, *My Friends the Wild Chimpanzees*, 1967, an American named Harry Harlow received the National Science Medal for his work with rhesus monkeys. He did not work in a jungle; he did not need binoculars to make his observations. He did not wait, as Jane did, for the dramas of his subjects' lives to unfold. Harlow created the dramas he was to witness; in his laboratory at the University of Wisconsin in Madison, he exercised absolute control over both the actors and the stage.

Harlow used monkeys as psychological stand-ins for man. He is best known for his invention of the "surrogate mother": this was a model to which baby monkeys, raised in isolation, would pitifully cling when confronted with a frightening stimulus. The baby monkeys would rush to the surrogate mother, frantic for comfort and solace, even if the model was equipped with a catapult to toss the infant away, even if it blasted compressed air into the infant's face. He powerfully demonstrated the psychological need for contact, a need deeper even than that of relief from physical pain.

While Jane was quietly, patiently watching and waiting, it was Harlow's genius that was honored in Western science: the genius of manipulation, of experiment. "The taproot of science is the aim to control," Donna Harraway comments in *Primate Visions*; the laboratory, not the wild, yields the kind of knowledge that enhances control.

Harlow's experiments brought control of primate minds and emotions to undreamed-of levels of sophistication. His laboratory inventions read like a Christmas shopping list for the Marquis de Sade: the "well of despair" was an isolation chamber designed to produce, for study, profound depression in baby monkeys. He created the "iron maiden," a surrogate mother covered with hidden brass spikes that would emerge at a touch of the experimenter's button. This device, like the other "evil mothers" he created, was supposed to demonstrate the infant's deep need for maternal comfort, even when the mother was inherently punishing and evil. He developed the "rape rack," a device to immobilize the female monkey while artificially inseminating her. Using artificial means, Harlow produced far more baby monkeys with which to stock other labs than healthy wild animals could produce.

Honored with some of the most prestigious awards in his field, founder of two major research laboratories, Harry Harlow epitomized the role of the scientist as male manipulator, inventor, experimenter. Godlike in his power over his research subjects, the scientist was equally Godlike in promising a future in which man's increasing control over the universe would exalt his power.

In universities, Jane says, these messages still persist: "First of all, it's wonderful to be a scientist. Secondly, if you become a scientist, you become one of the elite, you wear a white coat, you're ranked with God, and what you say will be believed. Thirdly, if you're going to be a scientist you've got to be very objective; you mustn't get emotionally involved about those things.

"So what the message is that's coming out, you must be a scientist first and human being second. And I think that's what's gone wrong. I mean it's appalling to me to see science with a big capital S: it's turning people into machines."

Jane's science is lowercase, a woman crouching humbly in the grass, receptive, allowing approach. When Geza Teleki arrived at Gombe in 1968—never having worked in Africa, never having worked with primates—he asked Jane to explain her approach to him, how she expected him to work with the chimps. "And she couldn't do it," he remembers. "She got really exasperated. She ended up saying to me, 'Look, I can't explain it to you, you'll find out when you get there. There's only one thing to keep in mind: if you're going down the trail, and you see a chimp coming the other way, you are the one to get off the trail, not the chimp. You don't belong here. The chimp belongs here.'

"And that, to me, summarizes Jane Goodall," Geza continues. "Everything else is less important. Career is less important. Science is less important. Fame is less important than doing the right thing when you're dealing with the natural environment. I didn't understand it at the time. I thought she was a little weird. It's not the kind of thing you want to deal with when your only interest is starting a career as a professional. But that message has directed my life for the past twenty years."

"Doing the right thing when you're dealing with the natural environment." At no time was this credo thrown into sharper, more revealing relief than during the Gombe polio epidemic of 1966. "Nothing that happened at Gombe before or since that has been as horrible—nothing," Jane says. "They were among the darkest days of my life—a living nightmare."

In the dry season of that year, Olly's four-week-old baby became ill. At first it seemed that the infant was having trouble gripping its mother's belly as they traveled; the next day his four limbs hung limply. The following day Olly appeared in camp, with Gilka, her adolescent daughter. The infant's corpse was slung over Olly's shoulder.

At the time Jane and Hugo did not know that Olly's infant was the first victim of an epidemic of polio that would eventually claim the lives of six of the Gombe chimps. Jane was then pregnant with Grub; neither she nor Hugo had had the full course of polio vaccine. But when the couple linked the chimps' paralyzing disease to an outbreak of polio among Africans in a nearby village, they panicked.

Reaching Louis by radio telephone, they engineered an arrangement with Pfizer Laboratories in Nairobi. The firm would donate oral polio vaccine and fly it in to Gombe for Jane, Hugo, their staff, and the chimps. The vaccine would be administered to the chimps hidden in bananas. But for some of the chimps, help came too late. The nightmarish agony of Mr. McGregor haunts Jane to this day.

In November 1966, Hugo saw Flo and Fifi and Flint staring into a low bush and giving soft, *hoo* calls; he could not see what they were looking at. At dusk, when Jane and Hugo went to investigate, they first saw swarms of flies. "We were expecting to see some dead animal as we cautiously moved closer," Jane wrote in an article for *National Geographic*. But instead they found Mr. McGregor. Sitting on the ground, the old chimp was reaching for some purple berries on a bush over his head. "It was not until he wanted to reach another cluster of the fruit that we realized the horror of what had happened, for to move he had to seize hold of a low branch, both his legs trailing uselessly behind him," she wrote. They realized later he must have traveled a long way in this manner; even the tough callosities on his buttocks were raw and bleeding from dragging along the ground. Polio had robbed him of control of the sphincter muscles; his feces, urine, and blood had drawn the flies.

That night they watched in amazement as McGregor, using only his arms, pulled himself into a low-branched tree and built himself a nest. The next morning they followed his trail and were staggered at the distance he had dragged himself: more than 150 yards. "For the next ten days — and it seemed ten years — we followed, hoping in vain we might see some flicker of life return [to his legs]," Jane wrote.

"We did all that we could to help," she wrote. At first, nervous when they approached him too closely, he threatened them by raising an arm and barking. But after two days "he seemed to sense that we were only trying to help," Jane wrote. He would lie still while she squeezed water from a sponge into his open mouth. Hugo and Jane prepared a basket of bananas, palm nuts, leaves, and berries and with a long stick pushed it up to him in his nest. To kill the flies that were torturing him, they sprayed him with insecticide.

One evening when they went out with his supper, they found McGregor on the ground. From the angle of his shoulder, they saw he had dislocated an arm. "We knew that in the morning we would have to shoot our old friend," Jane wrote. She spent much of that last night with him. As dusk fell he looked up frequently into the tree above him; Jane realized he wanted to make a nest. She cut some vegetation and took it to him in a large pile; without hesitation, he took the leafy twigs and branches and with his good hand and his chin tucked them beneath himself to make a comfortable pillow. She returned to see him later that night. "It says very much for the extent to which we had won his trust and confidence, that, having heard my voice, he closed his eyes and went back to sleep, three feet away, and with his back to me and my bright pressure lamp."

The next morning, while he was grunting with pleasure over two eggs they had brought him — his favorite food — Hugo and Jane shot their old friend.

Decades later Jane is still defending the choices she made during the polio epidemic: to act instead of watch, choosing empathy over objectivity. Anthropologists, working with groups of "primitive" peoples, are often faced with similar dilemmas. When sickness or famine strikes a village, the anthropologist must choose either to act — providing Western medicines, nursing care and food, interfering in the lives she has come to observe — or to merely watch and chronicle, leaving the group "unpolluted" by Western "interference."

There were other times in her study when Jane chose to "interfere." When chimps were sick, she provisioned them with antibiotic-laden bananas. When Gilka developed a fungal growth on her face, Jane had the growth biopsied and later gave Gilka medication to control the disease. When old Flo was dying, Jane fed her eggs to make her last days more pleasant.

"There are some scientists who frown upon such practices, believing that nature should run its course," Jane wrote in an early chapter of *The Chimpanzees of Gombe*, a scholarly compilation of her first twenty-six years of work. "It seems to me, however, that humans have already interfered to such a major extent, usually in a very *negative* way . . . with so many animals in so many places that a certain amount of *positive* interference is desirable."

At many of her lectures, when the polio epidemic is mentioned, a member of the audience asks: "Why did you interfere?" Usually the question comes from a man. For men, observes psychologist Carol Gilligan, "the moral imperative appears rather as an injunction to respect the rights of others and thus to *protect from interference* the rights to life and self-fulfillment" (italics mine). But for women, "The moral imperative that emerges repeatedly in interviews . . . is an injunction to care, a responsibility to discern and *alleviate* the 'real and recognizable trouble' of this world" (italics mine).

More recently Jane spoke about the polio epidemic to a group of physical therapists, most of whom were women. Their question, at first mention of the disease, was different: "Did you try to help?"

By the second decade of Jane's research, her tiny campsite had been transformed into the Gombe Stream Research Centre, an international collaborative research community. Her first three students arrived in 1966; by 1972 more than a hundred people —African staff and their families, American and British undergraduate and graduate students—were supporting a study of fifty-four chimpanzees and the troops of baboons who shared their land.

By this time most of the chimps were regularly visiting Jane's banana feeding station, which by now had a building of its own and was equipped with underground bins that the researchers could open or close as the situation demanded. They monitored attendance rates at the station daily and maintained charts on group structure and activities, vocalizations, and gestures. Increasing emphasis was placed on following individual chimps and groups in the forest. "There was so much to be found out, one person couldn't begin to answer all the millions of questions springing to mind," Jane remembers. "I needed the help badly."

After Grub's birth in 1967, Jane spent less time with the chimps. She and Grub often accompanied Hugo to his camp in the Serengeti while he worked on a documentary and a book on wild African dogs. Students took over the day-to-day collection of data from 1967 to 1969, when the Serengeti project ended. From 1971 to 1975 Jane spent a semester each year as a visiting professor at Stanford University in California.

Many of Jane's students were recruited from this institution and from Cambridge. By this time conditions at camp were more comfortable, though still Spartan. The students lived in prefab metal cabins, the windows covered with wire mesh to prevent the chimps from climbing in, the tin roofs covered with thatch (Jane hated the appearance of gleaming metal). In 1972 a brick dining hall was built near the beach, and the students dined there at night with Jane and Hugo when they were in residence. Emelie Bergman (who later married Gombe researcher David Riss) recalls dinners as decorous and pleasant, a "familylike atmosphere." After a bath in the lake, the students would dress neatly for dinner—a nod to Jane's proper English upbringing. They'd wait politely for everyone to arrive before eating the meal of rice, cabbage, and fish, or sometimes fresh meat and fruit from the market in Kigoma. After the meal a student would often give an informal talk about her work, or, if the generator was working, they might all listen to music on a cassette player.

But of course the chimps dominate students' memories of Gombe. "Everyone who worked at Gombe had chimps that they especially identified with," remembers Geza Teleki. Typically, male chimps got on best with male workers, and females with females. Geza had a special relationship with Leakey. Easily recognized because of a scar under one eyelid, which revealed a white patch around that iris, Leakey had, of course, been named in honor of Jane's mentor. He was also the first male chimp Jane knew who would try to take away two females to mate with at the same time. By the time Geza met him, Leakey was old and, as he puts it, "semi-retired." The wonder of that relationship stays with him now, two decades later.

"I never gave Leakey anything, never coerced him with anything, never rewarded him, never willingly touched him," Geza remembers. The relationship "was not based on interaction, favors, or any of the usual things whereby we forge links with animals around us. Yet there was a sort of mutual attraction, for reasons I can't explain. There were times I would sit down some distance from him, and like as not he'd come and sit next to me, and then lie down and put his head on my tennis shoe. I did a lot of follows of Leakey simply because he seemed to like to have me around. If I got left behind or lost, he'd come back and find me."

Geza had not dreamed that such a relationship was possible between himself and a wild animal. He had read, of course, of Jane's relationships with David Graybeard, Flo, Mr. McGregor, and the others; he knew that she had bridged the gap between human and animal. But until he experienced this himself, he did not realize that Jane had built a bridge strong enough for others to cross.

That the chimps were far from harmless only augmented the human observers' awe at their normally gentle behavior. When the chimpanzees did become aggressive, they usually directed their actions toward male observers. Richard Wrangham was once used as a "display tool" by a seventeen-year-old male named Charlie. Hair erect, Charlie rushed down a bank at the student, grabbed his ankle, and dragged him several dozen yards through the foliage in an attempt to impress some other chimps watching nearby. "While I squawked and thrashed, I added a lot to his display," Richard recalls thoughtfully. "I was much better than if he had used relatively silent and immobile branches."

Although there were several other such incidents, during the first decade of research no chimpanzee ever seriously injured a human observer at Gombe; this seemed a powerful testament to the animals' inherent gentleness. It bore out the portrait Jane had been painting of them: excitable at times, but intrinsically peaceful beings, an attractive ancestor of the potentially peaceful human species.

But with other eyes watching them, during the second decade of Gombe research, "My Friends the Wild Chimpanzees" turned out to be cannibals, infant killers, and warmongers.

"The picture painted of these animals today is very different from what Jane initially saw alone," says John Mitani, a primatologist who has studied all three species of great apes. "Goodall, like Fossey, went into the field thinking these were cute, cuddly creatures. They were prone not to see things happening." John's suggestion recalls the stories women wrote about the pictures of trapeze artists in Pollak and Gilligan's psychological study: they imagined safety nets when none were present in the picture. "The single most important reason they didn't see these things [cannibalism and warfare]" John quickly adds, "is the fact that they're tough animals to study, and these are rare events; but these women also had ingrained biases. And this isn't a criticism," he emphasizes. "It points to the need for perseverance."

At first, said Jane, "I couldn't believe it." Jane had heard reports, from the Japanese researchers working south of Gombe in the Mahale Mountains, of cannibalism and warfare among chimps. "We were all scornful," she remembers. "We all said, 'They must have made a mistake.' " But soon the evidence was too obvious to ignore.

In 1972 the researchers recognized the existence of a new group at Gombe. The Kahama community, as it was called, comprised six mature males, including the powerful Goliath, and three females. They had broken off from the study community, known as the Kasakela group, and had set up new territory to the south. Males from the Kasakela community set out on regular raids with one objective in mind: to murder the members of the Kahama group.

Emelie Bergman recorded one such raid in February 1975:

Faben, Flo's eldest son, led the Kasakela party of five adult males and one adolescent. They traveled slowly, cautiously south until they reached a tree, which they climbed. For forty-five minutes they stared toward the Kahama group's range.

It was then that the group spotted Goliath, who was now quite old. His head and back were partially bald; his teeth were worn to the gums. Faben gave pant-hoots and raced toward the old male, pushing him to the ground. Then all the chimps attacked. For twenty minutes they savaged Goliath, twisting his limbs, dragging him along the ground, pounding his shoulder blades, biting his thigh. At first Goliath tried to protect his head with his arms, but then he gave up and lay still. Roaring pant-hoots, drumming on trees with feet and hands, the war party dispersed to the forest, victorious.

When they had gone, Emelie saw Goliath try to sit up; he couldn't. She left him shivering and bleeding; she wanted to help but, without any medical supplies, she was unable to do so. The students and staff searched intensively for Goliath for many days thereafter; but like all the other victims of these systematic brutal attacks, Goliath was never seen again.

That time, says Jane, was the most brutal in Gombe's history.

Soon the humans, too, would be held hostage to a wave of brutality. It was as if evil had seized the community, both chimps and humans, in a fist of rage. It was during the early part of the chimpanzees' era of warfare, on May 19, 1975, that violence struck the humans of Gombe Wildlife Research Institute and changed its history forever.

That evening Jane retired early; she had a sore eye, and the brightness of her kerosene lamp further pained her, so she turned it out earlier than normal. Had it not been for that sore eye, surely, she says today, she would have been kidnaped.

A few minutes later Jane heard the motor of an approaching boat; she assumed it was the water taxi stopping at Gombe to see if they had petrol.

She did not realize until hours later, when Grub's tutor came running along the beach to her house, that Gombe was facing an emergency. At first she learned only that Emelie Bergman's typewriter had been found lying upside down on a path and Emelie's house was empty.

Forty armed guerrillas, members of the Marxist Popular Revolutionary Party, had crossed the lake from Zaire. They had kidnaped Emelie, along with three Americans: Stanford graduate student Barbara Smuts, twenty-four, and undergraduates Kenneth Smith, twenty-two, and Jane Hunter, twenty-one. The terrorists had beaten a member of Jane's Tanzanian staff, but the man refused to reveal where the other American students were sleeping.

The student hostages later made a pact that they would never talk about the kidnaping. "There are so many terrorists, they might get ideas," Emelie explains today. She will only say that she and the others were held in a jungle hut forty miles across the lake in Zaire, and that the terrorists never knew their hostages were participants in the most famous field study in Western history. "All they knew about us was that we were white," Emelie said. That was bait enough. Emelie was released to carry the captors' demands to the Tanzanian government: $460,000 in cash, the release of party leaders from Tanzanian jails, and dozens of rifles. Otherwise the remaining three hostages would be killed.

Gombe was evacuated when negotiations began. "Tanzania will not be blackmailed," pledged President Julius Nyerere. Nonetheless a deal was negotiated with the help of the parents of the kidnaped students and Stanford University. The students were released safely and returned home to their parents. But from that time on, whites at Gombe were considered terrorist bait. Her African staff returned to the research station to take data on their own, but Jane was marooned at Dar es Salaam, where her new husband, Derek Bryceson, lived. Derek and Jane had married a year after her divorce from Hugo, when Grub was seven years old.

In August Jane's staff reached her in Dar by radio with fresh horror: Passion, with the aid of her adolescent daughter, Pom, had seized Olly's three-week-old granddaughter. The mother-daughter team had then spent five hours eating the body of the infant.

To Jane the news was a stunning blow. "This was the hardest thing to understand and accept that's ever happened at Gombe," she says today. Though the news of the Kasakela warriors shocked her, essentially their actions made sense: brutal, warring males staging a takeover of territory closely mirrored the be-havior of modern man; here, in the chimps, lurked the "dawn warrior"; the roots of our violence ran deep. The terrorist raid on Gombe horrified and angered Jane: but it was part of an understandable pattern of human violence—a pattern to which her Gombe chimps had provided such an Edenic and peaceful alternative. But females preying on babies—that was different. The mother-daughter bond had been contorted into a grotesque cannibalistic partnership.

Jane still does not understand what drove Passion and Pom

to their attacks. But she vividly remembers that Passion, when Pom was born in 1965, had proved "extraordinarily inefficient and indifferent" as a mother. Unlike solicitous Flo, who responded with comfort to her offspring's every whimper, when Pom would cry with hunger, Passion would not guide the infant's mouth to her nipple; Pom had to find it for herself. As Pom became older, Passion did not always gather her baby in her arms and tuck her under her belly before moving off; instead she would simply walk away, and Pom would run, whimpering, to catch up.

Jane had known Passion since her early days at Gombe; she appears along with David Graybeard in many of Hugo's early photographs. When Jane named this chimp, she was not thinking of passion in the sense of suffering.

Over the next two years Jane's African staff saw Passion and Pom kill and eat three infants of the Kasakela community. Between 1974 and 1977 two other infants vanished during their first month of life, and three mothers, known or thought to be pregnant, miscarried. During the period of Passion and Pom's cannibalistic attacks, only one Kasakela mother — Flo's daughter, Fifi — successfully raised an infant.

Jane herself observed none of the incidents of cannibalism. After the hostage crisis she was prohibited from returning to Gombe for a time; when she finally was allowed to go back, it was only for a few days a month. She did, however, witness Passion's unsuccessful solo attack on a female with her baby, which occurred in the top of a tree. Jane realized that without Pom's help Passion was unable to kill other mothers' babies.

In November 1976, two African staff members recorded an attack by Passion and Pom on the three-week-old daughter of the gentle female named Melissa. Melissa's other daughter, six-year-old Gremlin, ran to the field assistants, stood upright and looked into their eyes, then at the scene before her, as if she were begging for help. The two assistants threw rocks at Passion and Pom, and some of the rocks hit them, but the pair didn't seem to notice. Passion held Melissa to the ground as Pom bit the baby's head. Using one foot, Passion pushed at Melissa's chest while Pom pulled at her hands; finally Pom ran off with the infant, who was already dead.

Fifteen minutes later Melissa approached Passion. The two mothers stared at each other, then Passion reached out and touched Melissa's bleeding hand and embraced her. As Jane interprets it, "It was as if to say, 'I have no quarrel with you, I only want your baby.' "

Jane and her staff debated what to do to stop the killing. At one point they discussed tranquilizing Passion and disabling a nerve in her arm. The operation would have to be extraordinarily delicate, for Jane could not in conscience permanently cripple any chimp, no matter how much she personally disliked the animal. The disability would have to be reversible. But in 1977 Passion bore another baby, and motherhood was the functional equivalent of a disabled arm, said Jane: for the first few months one arm was always holding the baby. The killings and cannibalism stopped. Jane named the baby Pax—peace.

Jane doesn't relish talking about that violent era. In 1980 she reluctantly delivered a lecture titled "Cannibalism and Warfare in Chimp Society" at an L. S. B. Leakey Foundation fundraiser.

"The title of the lecture was chosen for me," she told the audience, as if in apology. "This isn't a subject that I prefer to emphasize above other aspects of chimpanzee behavior."

Yet for all its horror, the violence at Gombe proved beyond doubt the centerpiece of Jane's thesis: that the animals' individual temperaments, family backgrounds, and decisions were the basis of their history. "An individual chimp can have as much influence on the history of his or her community as an individual human can have on his or her tribe or country," Jane said. Passion and Pom's cannibalism affected a whole generation of chimpanzees: for three years they prevented all but one of the Kasakela mothers from raising an infant. And that the chimpanzees' era of warfare, cannibalism, and infanticide occurred against the backdrop of the terrorist raid on Gombe underscored Jane's point: "Chimpanzees are far more like humans than even we ever thought."

For Jane this era of violence was followed by a time of unparalleled fame and unparalleled sorrow. Between 1974 and 1984 she was honored with five internationally respected awards, including the J. Paul Getty Wildlife Conservation Prize of $50,000. Journalists seized upon the lurid behavior of the chimpanzees to produce a flood of publicity; National Geographic filmed another TV special.

What these stories and the film didn't mention was that Jane was by now spending very little time at Gombe. After the kidnaping, the Tanzanian government forbade her to have white students stay there for any long-term study, and her own visits to Gombe were short, secretive, and restricted to a few weeks at a time.

When she was not lecturing abroad to wildly enthusiastic audiences, Jane spent much of her time with her new husband. Friends describe Derek as "the love of her life" and their marriage as "blissful." Jane had loved Hugo, remembers Emelie Bergman-Riss, but their relationship, like the chain-smoking baron himself, was always "high-pressure." The couple had once had to make a rule that they would take one evening off a week, forcing themselves to simply enjoy each other's company. Their separation and divorce in 1974 occurred after Hugo had complained to friends that he was "tired of being Mr. Goodall." He was no longer willing to set aside his photography to be administrator of his wife's camp.

But with the easygoing "Mr. B.," as Jane's students called Derek, life became more relaxed. In the days before the kidnaping he visited Jane at Gombe often, and when they were apart they talked daily on the radio-telephone. Often they took vacations together, flying in the plane he piloted or boating and fishing with Grub near Derek's home in Dar es Salaam. An RAF pilot during World War II, Derek was a close friend and next-door neighbor of Tanzania's first president, Julius Nyerere. Derek had served as the only white member of parliament after Tanzania won independence in 1961. His political power allowed him to protect his new wife's project; his clout as director of Tanzania's national parks was crucial to resolving the kidnaping dilemma; and during his years in that position he took over many administrative chores. He also embargoed tourism at Gombe.

But after only five years of blissful marriage, Derek became ill with cancer. By the time it was diagnosed, the doctors said it was too late to intervene. In desperation he sought treatment at an alternative medical clinic in Hannover, West Germany. Jane stayed in a pensione while Derek was receiving treatments; she often picked wildflowers for her husband on her walk across the field that separated her flat from the hospital. Jane was devastated when Derek died in October 1980. She still wears his gold wedding band.

The prohibition on tourists to Gombe was lifted after Derek's death. Today the students' dining hall has been transformed, with flimsy particle-board partitions, into guest rooms for tourists. Tanzanian park officials have moved into the tin-roofed quarters Jane had built for her African research staff and their families; her thirty workers have had to double up under the new arrangement to accommodate the park officials and rangers. Though a dozen or so tour operators now bring white visitors to Gombe, white researchers are still prohibited from working at the site except under special conditions. Jane now gets out to Gombe only a few times a year for only a few weeks at a time.

Today, a recent poll reveals, Jane Goodall is the most easily recognizable living scientist in the Western world. Her studies at Gombe "will rank forever as one of the great achievements of scientific dedication combined with stunning results," wrote the eminent Harvard biologist and historian of science Stephen Jay Gould in a 1989 column in the magazine *Natural History*.

"Her work is almost comparable with Einstein's," says Roger Fouts, whose work with the sign-language-using chimpanzee Washoe has challenged man's claim to uniqueness as a language user, just as did Jane's findings of hunting, warfare, and the use of tools by chimps.

Jane's approach, once ridiculed as amateurish, is now often held up as a standard to which other field ethologists should aspire. Now some respected scientists are beginning to argue that it is the lens of theory and methodology that clouds vision, not the focus of empathy. "Most scientists come supplied with theories and force the animals to fit the theory," continues Roger Fouts. "Jane's is a humble science. She asks the animals to tell her about themselves."

Says John Mitani: "One of the maladies of the field today is the studies are too methodologically rigorous. People don't watch the animals anymore. You have an idea and go out to test your idea—and you have blinders on."

He echoes the lament of Konrad Lorenz; in his 1981 book, *The Foundations of Ethology*, Lorenz wrote that many modern researchers "do not accept perception as a source of knowledge. . . . I regret that a very large proportion of the younger researchers who consider themselves ethologists show a deplorable lack of knowledge of animals." Lorenz called for a resurgence of "amateurism," of long-term endeavors sustained by the observer's sheer love of his subject: this, he wrote, "can only be accomplished by those men whose gaze, through a wholly irrational delight in the beauty of the object, stays riveted to it."

Jane's work has ushered in the glimmerings of a new way of doing science, a scientific outlook that draws upon the feminine emphasis upon individuality, relationships, and empathy. Stephen Jay Gould wrote in the introduction to the 1988 revised edition of Jane's *In the Shadow of Man*: "We think of science as manipulation, experiment, and quantification. . . . The laboratory technique of stripping away uniqueness and finding quantifiable least common denominators cannot capture the richness of real history."

Jane's strength is that she relinquished control. Today this strength is honored, not as a passive act, as the men before her might have seen it, but as an achievement—one that allowed her to see and inspired her to stay. In *The Chimpanzees of Gombe* Jane wrote: "I readily admit to a high level of emotional involvement with individual chimpanzees—without which, I suspect, the research would have come to an end many years ago."

Many women ethologists have followed Jane's path, bringing an emotional and empathetic involvement to their long-term relationships with the animals they study. Many of them, like Jane, are storytellers, whose tales are of approach, of equality, of homecoming. Alison Jolly has written numerous popular books about the troops of lemurs in Madagascar that she has studied for more than twenty years; one of her books is titled *A World Like Our Own*. Barbara Smuts, once a student of Jane's, is well known for her long-term studies of baboon troops; and primatologist Shirley Strum concentrates on the role of friendship in baboon society in her recent book *Almost Human*. Cynthia Moss, who entered the field with no scientific training, describes her fourteen years among elephant herds at Amboseli National Park in Kenya in her emotional book *Elephant Memories*.

The most famous and most direct descendants of Jane's approach are Dian Fossey and Biruté Galdikas, who completed Louis Leakey's trio of "primates" and built directly upon Jane's pioneering work. In many ways the paths they took were even rougher than Jane's.

6 The Sacrifice of Nyiramachabelli

S HE BECAME KNOWN in Rwanda as Nyiramachabelli. She told people, with pride and regret, what it meant: the old woman who lives alone in the mountains without a man. Dian Fossey was seldom completely alone in the Virunga mountains. From the start of her study she was accompanied by a Rwandan tracker and a cook; later her staff expanded, and Western students came to study with her. But alone and without a man named the sacrifice she made for her work with the gorillas: alone was how she felt in her struggle against poachers and in her battle with the community of Western scientists who, she felt, did not understand. Alone she struggled against poverty, against a staggeringly tough terrain, and against the conflicts of her raging desires.

The Virunga Volcanoes are corrugated, muddy, cold, dark. Sixty-seven inches of rain fall each year. It rains an average of two hours a day: a claustral curtain of cold gray water that shuts out even the memory of the sun. Every few weeks hail pounds with such ferocity that the eaves of the tin-roofed cabins are bent and twisted as if struck by hammers. This is the weather that precipitated attacks of what Dian called "astronaut blues": uncontrollable crying, shaking, fever, sweating, claustrophobia. Several of her students, she said, suffered these symptoms and had to leave; one left camp after only four days.

Even on sunny days the slopes are difficult—slippery, wet, and tangled. Dian repeatedly broke bones in her falls. Wild celery and nettles grow over six feet tall; it is almost impossible to walk anywhere without cutting a trail with a machete, and every step is a side-heaving struggle up 45-degree slopes. Fields of nettles deliver a punishing sting that feels like electric needles even through two layers of clothing. Once a buffalo dragged Dian through a whole meadow of nettles when she mistook the surprised animal's leg for a handhold as she wriggled through the undergrowth. On the lower slopes there are *siafu*, safari ants with mandibles so tenacious that when you try to pull them off, their heads stay in your flesh; they will bite through two layers of wool socks. And there are traps: wire nooses hidden among leaves or pit traps with sharpened stakes at the bottom or drop traps, piles of logs poised to fall at the touch of a trigger wire. Dian lived in the shadow of these traps, in constant fear for the animals she loved. Worse were the unseen bullets and arrows, which left no trace unless they found their mark.

Every scrap of food in Dian's camp had to be carried up the mountain on someone's head from the village of Kinigi or Ruhengeri. Food would keep two weeks at best; there was seldom any fresh meat or fresh vegetables or bread. She craved fat, sugar, salt; instead she had greasy tinned meat, frankfurters, beans, occasionally cheese—at very high cost—eggs laid by her pet chickens, and potatoes. At the end of the month potatoes were nearly all that was left to eat.

For most of the first two years of her study, Dian's only human companions were her African employees, speaking a language she didn't understand, born of a culture she did not share. Although Dian spoke some KiSwahili, she never mastered Kinyarwanda, the national language of Rwanda. On her first day at Karisoke she thought her cook was announcing plans to kill her; he had only asked if she wanted hot water. She was never fluent in French, a second language for many Rwandans; each word clanged dizzily in her skull, searching for its English equivalent. But the gap between her and her Rwandan trackers was wider than even language could fill. None of these people could remember with her the taste of a well-aged steak; none of them could recall the feel of crisp white bed sheets.

"I can tell you this," Dian wrote to Ian Redmond, then a prospective student, in 1976, "the solitude, the lack of good food, the bloody weather etc. (paperwork, fatigue) has defeated fifteen out of eighteen students. The three that made it loved it because of the gift of being with the gorillas. . . . As far as I am concerned, the gorillas are the reward and one should never ask for more than their trust and confidence after each working day."

When she returned to her cabin at the end of each day, Dian surrounded herself with images of the black furry faces of her friends, her reward: black-and-white photos of Digit, Macho, Kweli, Uncle Bert, Lee, and the others covered an entire wall.

Dian was a woman with large appetites, expensive tastes: Hermès dresses, fine restaurants, gold jewelry, the attentions of handsome men. On her first safari in Africa she brought along a mink stole to impress the other guests at her first stop, a fine Nairobi hotel. She wanted to be noticed, she wanted to be first. She loved being the center of attention at dinner with friends, keeping her listeners spellbound with stories and jokes. She loved dancing and cooking good meals for guests and dressing up.

In Louisville, where she worked as an occupational therapist for ten years, Dian had many boyfriends; she was informally engaged to Alexie Forrester when she left for her gorilla study. Once he came to her mountain cabin to "rescue" her. "If you stay here, you'll be hacked to pieces," he told her. "The Africans don't want you here." She sent him home.

In Kentucky Dian had loved the home she had made for herself in a rented farm cottage; in the fall she would run to the window on waking and be "blinded by the beauty." She had loved the children she worked with at Korsair Children's Hospital, and they had loved her. She was able to communicate with disabled children as could few others; she painted a Wizard of Oz mural on the wall of a drab examination room to cheer her patients, and she lured squirrels from the woods to delight them. Leaving behind the children, her home, her three dogs, and her friends, she wrote in her diary, "was the hardest thing I have ever done."

She chose instead a life soaked with sweat and cold rain, a mountain world cloaked in mists, tangled with looming trees, slippery with mud. Her scientific career was forever overshadowed by famous predecessors; her love life became a string of impermanent affairs. Although she longed for wealth, a family, and children, she spent her nights alone in the little cabin in the Virungas.

By 1977, when students Amy Vedder and Bill Weber first met her in Chicago, Dian had been living in the mountains for ten years; she was forty-five. As they sat in a booth in the hotel restaurant, waiting for their dinner order to arrive, Dian began licking pats of butter off the cardboard backings and sucking sugar out of the paper packets.

On the Louisville stop of his speaking tour in 1966, Louis Leakey remembered Dian from their meeting at Olduvai. He had last seen her three years before, and her image had stayed with him: the tall, handsome, dark-haired woman leaving his camp with a bandaged ankle, prepared to stagger up the slopes of the Virunga Volcanoes to search for mountain gorillas. After his lecture she showed him the articles she had written for the *Louisville*

Courier-Journal about her gorilla safari, and the photos she had taken of the huge, shy primates.

Louis offered to meet with her the following morning. He spent much of the hour praising Jane Goodall, then in her sixth year of study at Gombe. He spoke of Jane with the pride of a father; and now, Dian realized, he was welcoming her into his family of female protégées. She was to be his Number-Two Ape Girl — a position she first assumed with jealousy but later jealously guarded.

Before she embarked on her study, Louis arranged for Dian to retrace Jane Goodall's footsteps almost literally: first a three-day stopover in England to visit with Vanne and Judy Goodall at their London flat, then a visit to Gombe to meet Jane and Hugo.

Once Dian arrived in Nairobi, Louis took her under his expansive wing. He helped her shop for a second-hand Land-Rover, which they named Lily. He ordered two tents for her, and when they arrived at the Coryndon Museum, he insisted on showing her just how a tent should be erected, putting up the larger one, on the museum lawn, in under four minutes, Dian recalled. Dian shopped for provisions, and Louis arranged for photographer Alan Root, whom Dian had met three years earlier on her African safari, to accompany her to the Congo to set up camp.

Root stayed with Dian at Kabara meadow for two days. He left on January 15, 1967, the day before her thirty-fifth birthday. In *Gorillas in the Mist* Dian wrote, "I clung on to my tent pole simply to avoid running after him."

The vacuum of isolation stayed with her for several weeks. She could not bring herself to listen to the shortwave radio that Louis had insisted she bring, nor did she read any of the popular science books she had brought or even use her typewriter. "All of these connections with the outside world simply made me feel lonelier than ever," she wrote. Hers was a purification by longing and loneliness, as she emptied herself into the abyss of the black African night. Once emptied by solitude, she would become a vessel, clean and spacious, and fill herself with the lives of the animals she had come to study.

George Schaller, a young Berlin-born zoologist, camped at 10,200 feet in the saddle between Mount Mikeno and Mount Karisimbi, in the area called Kabara, about twenty-five square miles of mainly *Hagenia* woodland, from August 1959 to September 1960.

Schaller began his study by trying to view the gorillas from the cover of a tree trunk, but the gorillas, whose eyesight he judged comparable to his own, usually detected him and fled. The other method was to approach within 150 feet of a group, in full view. Schaller found that after ten to fifteen prolonged contacts, some groups would allow him to approach within fifteen feet without being disturbed. In his more than three hundred encounters with gorillas — 466 hours of observation — he identified 191 individuals. The members of six groups became completely habituated to his presence. Once a gorilla climbed into the tree in which he was sitting and stared at him with obvious curiosity.

In his scientific papers and his popular 1962 book, *The Year of the Gorilla*, Schaller challenged the image of gorillas as "King Kong monsters" and instead portrayed the huge, powerful apes as "amiable vegetarians" living in close-knit, cohesive family groups. He catalogued their facial expressions, vocalizations, and gestures; mapped their movements; and analyzed their diet. He recorded the care with which mothers groomed and carried their babies and the ferocity of the silverbacks performing their chest-beating displays; he noted each silverback's idiosyncrasies, which colored the group's character as well as determined its movements. His study was touted for its excellence and thoroughness.

In the same meadow where Schaller had worked, Dian established her camp. She hired the tracker, Sanwekwe, who had worked for Schaller seven years before. In six and a half months at Kabara she encountered three of the ten groups he had studied.

Her first attempts at observation were, by her own admission, amateurish and clumsy. While Alan Root was still with her, she began to follow a trail of knuckle prints in the moist black earth. After five minutes she realized that Alan was not behind her. She returned to the place where she had discovered the trail. He told her politely, "Dian, if you are ever going to contact gorillas, you must follow their tracks to where they are going rather than backtrack trails to where they've been."

Although Dian began by approaching the gorillas silently and watching them from a hidden position, she later decided to announce her presence to the gorillas, hoping to calm them by imitating their sounds. As well as scratching, chewing, and making belchlike contentment vocalizations, she often greeted groups by pounding her chest—which Schaller had clearly described as a signal of aggression and challenge.

By July 1967 Dian felt she was on the verge of habituating the gorillas; after six and a half months of tracking and knuckle-walking toward each group, munching wild celery stalks to allay their fears and keeping her eyes averted, she was able to approach members of three groups, totaling fifty animals, within thirty feet.

But on the ninth day of that month her time at Kabara ended abruptly. European mercenaries serving the rebel leader Moise Tshombe had taken the regions of Kisangani and Bukavu; the entire eastern region of the Congo was under siege, and the border with Uganda had been sealed off. Soldiers streamed though village streets. Mail and telephone service were suspended, and all commercial air traffic was stopped. The park director sent soldiers up the mountain to order Dian to leave her research site.

Dian would later embroider the story of her escape from the besieged Congo with tales of incarceration, death threats, and rape. In *Gorillas in the Mist* she wrote that she was held captive, "earmarked" as sexual diversion for a soon-to-arrive Congolese general. She told Bob Campbell that she had been raped by Congolese soldiers. But affidavits she herself signed show that her one run-in with the Congolese military was a hassle over the expired registration for her Land-Rover. She was not raped, no guns were aimed at her, and she was never held captive; but her situation was terrifying, and her escape from the Congo — crossing closed borders in an unregistered car, made possible by quick-witted bribes — was a courageous achievement. That she invented other stories only shows that Dian did not consider her true ordeal harrowing enough.

Once she managed to reach Nairobi, she and Louis Leakey discussed plans for her future: he offered her a study of the lowland gorilla or beginning work on a long-term project on orangutans. But Dian was adamant: she wanted to continue studying the mountain gorillas. Within two weeks she was preparing to set up a new study site less than five miles from the Congolese border in the Rwandan portion of the Virunga Volcanoes.

Later Louis would write her that Nairobi was abuzz with criticism of him for having allowed her to resume the study — news he shared with unbridled conspiratorial pride. "If people like you and me and Jane and others, whose work takes them into strange places, put our personal safety first," he wrote Dian, "we would never get any work done at all. . . . From my point of view, provided one took reasonable precautions, and did not deliberately run undue risks, *work must go on*."

"I don't think many people understand how long it took Dian to habituate the gorillas," says her friend Rosamond Carr. Rosamond was fifty-five when she met Dian. She and Alyette

DeMunck, a Belgian neighbor ten years younger, helped Dian set up her new camp in the saddle between Mount Karisimbi and Mount Visoke. Sometimes they would accompany Dian up the mountain and follow the gorillas' trails with her. Often they heard the gorillas pokking their chests in defiance or hooting to distant groups but, remembers Rosamond, "we never saw gorillas at all."

In her first months at Karisoke Dian, even alone, saw little of the gorillas; an hour here, then weeks without a glimpse. Unlike the gorillas of Kabara, who had known George Schaller, the mountain gorillas of Rwanda knew man only as poacher, commander of vicious dogs, and shooter of arrows and bullets. So it was with great restraint and humility that Dian tried to ease gently into the shy animals' lives.

She did not want to surprise them; at first she tried to stay hidden. Then she began to approach gingerly, gently, on hands and knees, slapping and belching a greeting as soon as she was within earshot of a crunching, belch-mumbling group. Occasionally she would climb a tree, not only to see them, but to honor the etiquette of the relationship she was nurturing: "It was important," she wrote in her thesis, "that the group, especially the silverback, knew the location of the observer." As Jane had done on the Peak at Gombe, Dian offered her promise: I am here. I am harmless. I wait.

She would knuckle-walk to within a hundred feet of them, then eighty feet, then fifty, then thirty. Scratching herself and crunching the bitter wild celery, she would settle down in the foliage, kneeling, sitting, or reclining, harmless and calm. *I am here* she announced with a belch vocalization. *I am harmless* she promised with her posture. But further, crunching celery and scratching herself, she told them *I am one of you.*

For two years she refused to follow the animals past the contact point, "to prevent them from feeling subject to pursuit," as she later wrote in her thesis. Like Jane Goodall, Dian began by offering her presence to the study animals, not imposing it. But Dian was determined that her study, unlike Jane's, would remain "pure." She was well aware of the criticism leveled at Jane for setting up a feeding station for the chimpanzees; it was said that she was altering their natural behavior.

Dian knew she could not have lured the gorillas with food even if she had wanted to: their world is covered with food, so abundant that they sleep on it, walk on it. The danger was that she would disturb them with pursuit or too-close contact. She did not want her intrusion to shatter the tranquility of the family groups, so calm, so perfect.

So when *National Geographic* photographer Bob Campbell arrived at Karisoke in August 1968, nearly a year after she had founded the camp, he found little to film. "The gorillas were very wild and unhabituated at that stage. I had a big problem for eighteen months," he remembers. "She tied me down to her standard methods of observation. She wouldn't have me harassing the animals or doing things to make them react; just go out, find them, sit in a good observation spot and then watch what they do. I wasn't to follow them around.

"Sitting thirty to fifty feet away, it's impossible to even see the whole group. It was obvious I wouldn't get what I wanted, sitting back and waiting for them to expose themselves."

It was equally obvious to Bob that at first Dian didn't want him there. The thought of his frightening the gorillas horrified her. But she was also afraid of his judgment: Dian, at six feet, looked powerful and imposing, but she was struggling up the steep slopes; her asthma made her stop frequently, gasping for breath, and she often slipped and fell. Bob often had to stop and wait for her.

"She was unhappy that a strange person could see how much difficulty she had operating on those mountains," he remembers. "She wasn't prepared to have someone unknown to her witness just how difficult things were with her."

For Bob the work was frustrating. After a year and a half of work, as he remembers it, he had only two scenes of Dian near enough to the gorillas — within ten feet — to be taken in by the movie camera lens. National Geographic by then had film of Jane handing chimpanzees bananas, grooming their fur, playing with their babies. They wanted more from Dian.

At one point, attempting to film Dian with the gorillas, Bob sent her in pursuit of Group 8, which was feeding up beyond a ridge. He suggested Dian approach them from below, giving him a clear view without foliage in the way. She was within forty feet of them when suddenly the silverback of the group — an animal she had named Rafiki, the KiSwahili word for "friend" — charged at her.

"That caused a mob situation," Bob recalls. "The whole lot came down — five gorillas screaming at short distance, pouring out of the foliage down the steep side of the ravine, screaming." The charges and screams continued for half an hour. Dian sat with her back to them, crouching, pretending to feed. She couldn't tell where they were. "The screams were so deafening I could not locate the source of the noise," she later wrote in an article for *Omni* magazine. Again and again they charged and screamed, hair on end, canines flashing, releasing a gagging fear odor. Suddenly these were the gorillas described by the nineteenth-century explorer Paul Belloni Du Chaillu: as "monstrous as a nightmare dream. . . . So impossible a piece of hideousness, . . . no description can exceed the horror of its appearance, the ferocity of its attack, or the impish malignancy of its nature: savage, enormous, hirsute, aggressive, cunning, a predatory beast of violent passions."

When at last the gorillas moved away, Bob ran to Dian, horrified by her ordeal. She wasn't shivering or crying, and she wasn't injured. She was angry at him: it had been *his* idea for her to sneak up on them from below. And she was deeply hurt. "She was emotionally hurt," he said, "that this formerly friendly group could suddenly charge like that, that they could suddenly switch and become these frightening creatures." She felt that somehow she had failed them; their trust in her had been shattered like a pane of glass.

Bob returned to Karisoke for more film footage on and off for the following two years. He gradually won Dian's trust. He would help her cut Batwa poachers' traps and herd away wandering Batutsi cattle. He thoroughly documented the last days of Dian's caring for Coco and Pucker, the two pathetically ill juvenile gorillas captured by poachers for the Cologne Zoo. He helped Dian conduct her census work, often camping with her and Alyette in small tents, carrying all their food and water on their backs. He helped her train her Rwandan staff in tracking skills, fixed broken lanterns and stoves, constructed new cabins from tin sheeting she would then paint green.

But his time was running out. So, he says, it was his photography needs that finally induced Dian to move in among the gorillas.

At his garden-bordered home on the outskirts of Nairobi, Bob Campbell sits in an easy chair, the tea service beside him, as he tells his story. He is still a handsome man, slender, elegant, soft-voiced; he now wears glasses to correct the imbalance in his eye muscles caused by years of looking through a camera lens with one eye and at the object being filmed with the other. "We came to an agreement. I would try my methods, and she would stick to hers. So I started crawling around. I was getting in among them. I got to the state they would come and touch me. As soon as that started to happen, I wanted to get Dian in there so they would do it before my camera.

"It took her a while to break down her resistance to pushing the gorillas. She didn't want to intrude too much," he remembers. Shy as a new bride, Dian would keep her eyes averted, her body low, her voice soft. And then she would lie down before them, vulnerable, still. It was while she was lying prone in the foliage that Peanuts, of Group 8, first came forward to touch his fingers to hers.

"She was at first a little uncertain," Bob remembers. "At first she was trying too hard to be just an observer. And then she had the animals touch her." Bob pauses. "It was almost overwhelming for her."

In January 1970 Dian found herself again following in Jane's footsteps, as the second of Louis's amateur protégées to enter Cambridge in pursuit of academic credentials.

Like Jane, Dian did not have a master's degree to begin with, although she did have a degree in occupational therapy from San Jose State College. Louis had arranged for her, too, to bypass the degree that students were ordinarily required to have before beginning a doctoral dissertation. And, like Jane before her, Dian hated Cambridge. "I hate it here because it isn't Africa," she wrote to Louis during her first semester there. "I feel like a mole." But she realized the necessity for a Ph.D.—her "union card," as she called it, for getting further grants.

Dian did not enter Cambridge with the same flourish as Jane had, for her initial discoveries were not nearly as stunning. When the termites had first begun to swarm at Karisoke, Dian had hoped that she would see, as Jane had, the apes using grass stems and twigs to get at the juicy insects inside; she was disappointed to find no evidence that gorillas use tools. Neither had she any evidence that they hunted; they ate mainly leaves, stems, bark, fungus, earth, snails, and grubs that they dug from rotting bark with their great hands.

Yet Robert Hinde, who had supervised Jane, told Dian he was impressed with her data—hundreds of pages of longhand descriptions of her days, trail signs, vocalizations and, when the gorillas were visible, the actions of every member of the group, the time they spent eating and resting, maps of their range. She

Peanuts has just touched Dian for the first time. She
lies as if entranced. *Bob Campbell* © *National Geographic*

had developed a novel way of recognizing individuals: each animal's nose had a different configuration of ridges, as individual
as a fingerprint.

Like Jane, Dian named her study subjects; but this was 1970,
and even the venerable Schaller named the gorillas he studied.
The idea was less outrageous by then, if still not totally accept-
able. (As late as 1981 the anthropologist Colin Turnbull refused
to reward the galleys of *Gorillas in the Mist* with a favorable
blurb; the reason he gave was that he didn't like the fact that
the animals were named.)

In this second of Louis Leakey's protégées, Robert Hinde may
have hoped for a more malleable convert to the "new ethology"
of statistics, measurement, and maps. He got on well with Dian
and often visited her at her flat. She called him Robert and
listened carefully to what he said. At one point, she wrote her

friends the Schwartzels that she had learned to enjoy searching through her data and writing up scientifically. With jealous pride she added, obviously echoing the words of her adviser: "This is something that Jane Goodall never learned to do."

But Dian failed to learn the most important rule of male-dominated empirical science: the rule of separation, of distance from her study subjects, of the wall thrown up between observer and observed.

"If she ever planned to be solely a detached, dispassionate academic observer," National Geographic's William Grosvenor said of Dian, "that plan was soon abandoned."

Digit from Group 4 would come forward to play with her hair, hang on her head, and playfully whack her with foliage. Puck, a youngster in Group 5 who especially enjoyed playing with Dian's camera gear, would come over "to sit down and 'chat.'" Dian wrote the Schwartzels:

> He comes right up to my side, plops down and, looking me directly in the eyes, begins very seriously a long tirade of relating past events, (?), injustices by his family, (?) how the weather has been treating them (?), and on it goes. All done in soft drones and hums, sometimes with mouth opening and closing as though he were trying to imitate human conversation.

Once an adult female in Group 4, Macho—KiSwahili for "eyes"—split off from her group, which had moved away to feed, to return to Dian and gaze into her eyes. "On perceiving the softness, tranquility and trust conveyed by Macho's eyes," Dian wrote, "I was overwhelmed by the extraordinary depth of our rapport. The poignancy of her gift will never diminish."

Dian wrote to her mentor, "It really is something, Louis, after all these years, and I just about burst open with happiness every-time I get within 1 or 2 feet of them."

At Cambridge, as at other academic institutions, ethology students have a term that encapsulates their most dreaded enemy:

the "dirty data stealer." These are people, other students, *competitors*, who steal your data and use it in their own thesis or paper without giving credit. For this reason many academic researchers keep their file cabinets locked. The fear of theft fosters a paranoia, a possessiveness, unlike that found in almost any other setting.

The ivory towers of academia are rife with petty rivalries, snubs, jealousies, and gossip. Jane Goodall, even after she earned her Ph.D., was still a subject of constant comment at Cambridge: one student who had attended a symposium at which Jane was scheduled to speak wrote that the participants positively dripped with sympathy and concern when they learned that Jane's appearance was canceled by an attack of malaria, "but later privately wondered why she always conveniently suffered these malaria attacks before important speaking engagements abroad." Dian's friend and Cambridge colleague, Richard Wrangham, once wrote her in dismay that no one was speaking to him because his new ideas about social organization in monkeys were unpopular.

For Dian the world "outside," away from her gorilla families, loomed monstrous with inflated egos. At the Leakey Foundation, which along with National Geographic was supporting her work, organizers worried endlessly over the seating arrangements for their functions—for as cofounder Tita Caldwell explained, "people would get really ugly about where they would be seated. They would actually say to me, if I don't get to sit next to Jane Goodall, I'm not going to give you any more money." Often people who gave money to foundations like these were fickle, fawning, false, petty, and power-hungry: many of the trustees used the foundation as a social ladder. "I'd never encountered such tremendous jealousy and resentment," Tita remembers.

When Dian went to the gorillas of Karisoke, she would sometimes sing to them. Not in the human sense of singing; she would sing a gorilla song.

Dian discovers that gorillas love to be tickled. *Harry Van Rompaey*

Ian Redmond has heard gorillas singing among themselves. It sounds, he says, "like a cross between a dog whining and someone singing in the bath." The animals will do this when they are exceptionally happy, usually on sunny days when they are feeding on something particularly delicious like juicy bamboo shoots or rotting wood. Ian tasted the wood the gorillas eat; it tasted "like old wood." But to the gorillas, old wood seemed to have the effect that chocolate does on some human beings. It was a food of good feelings. Feeding in a family group, basking in the sunshine, enjoying a feast of this favorite food, "they are so filled with good feeling that they just have to communicate this," Ian said. Sometimes they throw their arms around each other while they are singing and chomping: a celebration of eating, of the rare warm sun on black fur, of belonging. And sitting among them, Dian would be engulfed by their happiness, and she, too, would begin to sing—a choir of voices, the gorilla song of good feeling, of togetherness, of inclusion.

When Dian was with the gorillas, she was as one of them. But when she returned to her cabin alone at night, she was once again Nyiramachabelli: the old woman who lives alone in the forest without a man.

Dian refused to use check sheets, a standard tool in ethology, to record the behavior of the gorilla groups. A typical check sheet will have column headings for behaviors—grooming, feeding, playing, traveling, resting, for instance—that can be ticked off when observed, as a manager would check off merchandise in a warehouse.

Nor did Dian take her notes on a "sampling schedule," which is usually used in conjunction with check sheets. With a sampling schedule behavior is recorded only at precise intervals—once a minute, clocked by the stopwatch, for example—to assure that the researcher is getting a true "sample" of what the animals are doing.

These methods are useful for organizing percentages—for instance, you can infer from these data that an animal spends, say, 40 percent of its time feeding. But Dian felt that the character and depth of the gorillas' lives could not be accurately portrayed with such mechanistic methods. She did not want to merely "sample" their lives; she wanted to experience them, with all of the associations, feelings, sounds, and images that entails. The normal group life of a gorilla family, except for raids from rival silverbacks or voluntary transfers of females to new groups, is a seamless continuum of attachments; Dian refused to separate them into columns on a check sheet or seconds on a stopwatch. She would portray their lives like a story, whole.

Bob Campbell remembers the conflict that arose between Dian and her thesis adviser: "She told me Hinde was a bit hard on her. He wanted her to take her data in a rigid and scientific manner, and she wanted it to be free-flowing. He wanted numbers. She wanted words."

Dian knew this was not the sort of information revered by science. "Ah, [Sandy] Harcourt—now there's a good scientist. He knows how to do thus-and-so," Amy Vedder remembers Dian saying to her, "not like me."

Amy, an American student who went to Karisoke to work with Dian in 1978, had been schooled in sampling and recording technique while earning her B.A. in biology with honors at Swarthmore College. She remembers that working with Dian was frustrating: Dian did not play by the scientific rules. "We were supposed to record behavior of all individuals—but you can't write down or see all of what happens to all animals all the time. It's simply impossible. We were supposed to note vocalization, but she never edited tapes to use as learning tools to standardize the names of the vocalizations. We were supposed to note nursing, but not the number of seconds, or right or left breast. What she was looking for was not clear."

It was an assessment with which Robert Hinde apparently agreed. Dian's relationship with her supervisor deteriorated so far that in December 1975 she threatened, in two angry cables, to resign from her thesis. And in 1976 she described to Richard Wrangham, whose office in Cambridge was next to hers, how her furious supervisor had harangued her for hours the night before her oral examination:

> In comes the professor screaming his head off about my lack of gratitude. . . . He talked and raved for about 3 hours. . . . On and on it went until I asked him to leave. I couldn't count the number of times he said "after all I've done for you . . ." and that I was exactly like Jane and would fail just like he knew she would. . . . It was as though he had had all of this stored up in him against Jane and was using me for an outlet since he would never dare rant and rave in such a manner to her.

*

Dian felt she was forever living in Jane's shadow. When she began to write her popular book, she joked with friends that she would title it "In the Shadow of *In the Shadow of Man.*"

She was jealous of Jane from the start. When she first met her at Gombe, she wrote to friends in the States about the visit. She chose to highlight an incident in which she had predicted chimpanzee behavior that Jane had not foreseen. Dian worried that the chimps would be frightened by a leopard-print travel bag she had brought. Jane told her the chimps would not notice it. But, true to Dian's prediction, a canny female chimp spotted the bag, screamed, and fled.

Jane, it seemed to Dian, had it all: marriage, a child, fame, and funding. Although Louis had arranged for the same institutions to fund Dian's work that had supported Jane—the Wilkie Brothers Foundation, the National Geographic Society, the Leakey Foundation, and others—the money never seemed to stretch far enough for Dian. At one point she was financing boots and raingear for her staff by charging them on a K-Mart credit card borrowed from a friend. Dian was able to pay for much of her medical and dental care only by going to friends, or friends of friends, who would charge her less.

Neither Dian nor her gorillas seemed able to compete successfully with Jane and her chimps for the limelight. Dian made important discoveries about gorilla life: how females transfer, either voluntarily or via raids from rival silverbacks, out of their natal groups; how raiding silverbacks will sometimes kill the infants of a mother he is kidnaping to bring her into heat so he can mate with her; how gorillas will sometimes eat their own dung to recycle nutrients. But these discoveries were outshone by Jane's findings about chimpanzee hunting and tool use, cannibalism and warfare—behavioral aspects that made the chimps seem more like man.

On at least one occasion Jane and Dian were nominated for the same conservation prize; Jane won it. Once Dian complained to an editor at *National Geographic*, Mary Smith, "If I

had blond hair"—("meaning Jane of course," Smith adds)—
"things would be a lot easier for me."

Years later, though, Dian accepted her place in the hierarchy
of Louis Leakey's "three primates." After Biruté Galdikas became the third "ape woman," completing the trio, Dian vigor-
ously defended her place as second.

The three were scheduled to speak at a symposium at UCLA.
Joan Travis, one of the founders of the sponsoring Leakey Foundation, gave a party and made the mistake of asking Biruté
to introduce Jane at the next day's symposium. When Dian
discovered that Biruté—number three—had been given that
honor, "Dian went into a tantrum," remembers Tita Caldwell,
who watched the scene in dismay. "It was a nightmare, like a
bad movie, like a high school drama. [Biruté and Dian] were
shouting in each other's faces, a real gutter fight.

"Dian stalked out and came back with a phone book in her
hand. People were drifting into the living room, unaware of what
was going on, and people asked, 'Dian, what are you doing?'
From her great height—she was six feet tall and she was standing about three steps up the stairs—she announced: 'I'm looking
for a taxi. I won't stay in this house another minute.' "

Biruté remembers: "People had been telling me all kinds of
things about Dian, but I didn't see them—she'd always been so
kind to me. And then one day she just became hysterical. She
just went insane. I'd never seen a human being like that—she
just blew up? And poor Jane was caught in the middle, and Jane
tried to sort of intercede. It was like sibling rivalry or something—it made absolutely no sense.

"Dian took it most seriously of all—she was number two so
she deferred to Jane, and she expected that kind of deferment
from me. I didn't understand the depth to which she expected
this. [She was] hurt by the lack of deferment on even the smallest
issue."

For the solitary orangutans Biruté was studying, hierarchy has little meaning. For the large community of chimpanzees of Gombe, who travel in constantly changing smaller groups, social rank is of limited importance. But for a close-knit family of gorillas, one's place in the group is all-important. And so it was for Dian. "I didn't realize at that time," said Biruté, "that Dian was a gorilla."

Dian's thesis, "The Behavior of the Mountain Gorilla," is a very technical, dry document, full of maps and charts and graphs. But it is clear that to Dian the gorillas are not numbers to be calculated, their lives not data to be manipulated; they are thinking, feeling individuals, deserving consideration in man's as well as God's moral realm. She begins her thesis with an admonition for the scientists to whom the thesis is addressed: "Love the animals," Dian quotes from Dostoevsky. "God has given them the rudiments of thought and joy untroubled. Don't trouble it, don't harass them, don't deprive them of their happiness, don't work against God's intent."

The thesis was accepted, and her Ph.D. awarded in 1976. But for Dian it was a somewhat hollow victory. Her careful mapping of vegetation zones and gorilla ranges, her catalogues of food plants and dung parasites, her careful analysis of age classes and maternal behavior and female transfer—all this did nothing to protect the gorillas. She began to dismiss such data with a sniff as "theoretical conservation." Science, she was convinced, would not save the mountain gorilla. The animals were disappearing, not for lack of data but because they were being murdered. Increasingly, she forsook data collection for what she called "active conservation."

In the spring of 1977 the poaching situation at Karisoke reached a crisis point. In March Ian Redmond and a tracker, Nemeye, found the naked footprints of Batwa poachers on the trail of Group 5; the area was infested with recently set traps. In one day they found and destroyed twenty-one snares and three poachers' shelters. A month later they searched the remote northwestern portion of the study area, where Group 5 was then roaming: the men found and destroyed thirty-five traps in two days.

Dian feared for the gorillas' lives as never before. "We can't find all the traps," she wrote in her diary. "Sooner or later one of them is going to get caught."

So she made a decision that sickened her: the gorillas of Group 5, animals she had spent years shyly approaching, animals she had dared not even follow until she had known them for two years, would have to be forced to leave the trap-laden portion of the study area. They would have to be herded to a new area, like cattle.

Dian directed her men to do the job. She knew she couldn't bear it: the gorillas' terror before the din of her staff ringing poachers' dog bells, the air rank with the stench of their fear, their trail covered with watery dung. "I stay in and make sure I won't hear anything," she wrote in her diary. "It is HORRID but it must be done."

But only days after this drastic effort, six poachers set their dogs on a different group of gorillas — a fringe group known to Dian from previous censuses. Enraged, Dian and her camp staff set out the following morning to try to capture the poachers. In the hail and bitter cold, Dian's lungs and legs could not keep pace with her fury; her heart pounded; she fell repeatedly. She turned back. The men, continuing on, found only a handful of traps.

Word went out to the park guards: Dian would reward them for any poachers they captured. One bright morning five park guards appeared at her camp with Munyarukiko, the leading Batwa poacher in the Virungas. They paraded him in front of her. He stood, eyes downcast, as she glared at him. Ian remembers: "It was not a pretty sight. I can honestly say that the look in Dian's eyes was hatred, and I hadn't seen hatred like that before."

Dian opened bottles of Primus beer for all the men to celebrate. She gently dressed a graze on a guard's shin. Joyfully she paid the guards the equivalent of $120. They assured her that they would turn Munyarukiko in to the park conservator in Ruhengeri.

Minutes later her woodman asked her why she let them leave. Didn't she know that the guards had met the poacher by prearrangement at a village bar? Didn't she know they were now splitting her reward money with him?

The next day she drove to the Batwa village where Munyarukiko lived to capture him herself. He had fled, leaving his five wives and children behind. In a rage she searched his hut, trying to find his gun. It was gone. She tore down the matting from the walls inside the hut, dragged it outside, and set it afire. She demanded that the wives give her the gun and grabbed one of his children, a four-year-old boy, threatening to hurt him if they didn't obey. The women fled, leaving the boy with Dian.

"I know the details of this because I was the boy's baby sitter for a couple of days," said Ian. "The kid was living happily in my cabin, eating and playing with toys he was given, becoming completely at home."

The boy cried when he learned he had to leave the next day. Munyarukiko had obtained a legal judgment against Dian. While her men's boots rotted from the wet, while her camp lanterns sputtered and died, while her patrols lacked raingear and meat, while she subsisted mainly on potatoes, Dian was assessed a fine of $600.

"Dian," remembers Bill Weber, "was an incredible, incurable romantic. What we saw was what was left of this person who had believed, 'This is great, this person is incredible, this is true love'—and had been disappointed every time."

Dian approached almost every new human friendship with great enthusiasm. Bob Campbell remembers how at first she trusted her African staff so completely that once, when she has just cashed a grant check, she proudly showed the men a huge handful of franc notes and exclaimed, "Look at all this money!" Within a week the money had been stolen. Dian would write enthusiastically to friends about many of the new students who arrived in camp: "This is a person of integrity," she would write confidently and would shower her new helper with extravagant evidence of her affection; Craig Scholley, an American, remembers that while he was a student at Karisoke, Dian threw a birthday party for him in her cabin, a beautiful meal laid out on an ornate African cloth. "I said, 'That's a beautiful tablecloth. Where did you get that?" And she immediately took it off the table and handed it to me and said, 'This is yours.' "

But one by one each student slipped from her favor. Dian trusted too much, expected too much: like the women asked to write stories about trapeze artists in psychologists Pollock and Gilligan's study, she imagined a safety net that wasn't there.

Dian's love affairs always ended sadly. Bob Campbell went back to his wife in 1973. Her subsequent love affairs—almost always with other women's husbands or men otherwise attached —always left her lonely. She subsisted for months on great crates of pornography she had friends ship to her, and she kept a vibrator to satisfy her large appetite for sex. Dian was like a silverback who raided other families for mates. But she could not hold on to them; these affairs, born of deception of another woman, always ended when the men began to lie to Dian instead.

"Dian had been shat upon by a lot of people," Ian Redmond says. "Therefore she was very wary about entering into a relationship. She had been hurt.

"But the gorillas were straight. They were honest in their feelings toward her. If they were angry, you could see they were angry; if they liked you, they showed it. It was very up front. Dian appreciated the honesty of the relationship you have with gorillas, and you don't owe them anything and they don't owe you anything, other than trust. With the gorillas she didn't have to hide her feelings from them. She had a very honest relationship with them."

On the last day of 1977, Digit was killed. Serving as the sentry of Group 4, he sustained five spear wounds, held off six poachers and their dogs, and even managed to kill one of the poachers' dogs before dying. Ian found his handless, decapitated body on January 2.

"I cannot allow myself to think of his anguish, his pain, and the total comprehension he suffered of knowing what humans were doing to him," Dian wrote in "His Name Was Digit," a tribute to her friend.

She photographed the body and had a doctor from Ruhengeri come up to perform an autopsy. On the day of the autopsy her woodman, working only fifty feet from her cabin, began to yell, "Poacher!"

"When they brought him out of the forest onto the meadow, I could see he was one of the Twa from what is basically a poacher village near the park boundary," Dian wrote. "I saw something else as well which froze my blood and nearly caused me to lose all sense of reason. Both the front and the back of his tattered yellow shirt were sprayed with fountains of dried blood, far more than could result from an antelope killing."

"I can't tell you," she wrote in many letters, to friends, colleagues, and lawyers, "how difficult it was for me not to kill him."

The captive admitted to having been one of Digit's killers. He also provided the names of the other five, one of whom was Munyarukiko. It was his dog that Digit had killed.

Dian debated whether to publicize Digit's death. She knew that a public outcry could bring large sums of conservation money to Rwanda, but she feared the money would only line officials' pockets. Finally, however, keeping Digit's death quiet seemed too horrible: "I did not want Digit to have died in vain," she said. A few days later Walter Cronkite reported Digit's death on the CBS Evening News.

Later Dian resumed her contacts with Group 4. But, she wrote in her book, "for countless weeks unable to accept the finality of Digit's death, I found myself looking toward the periphery of the group for the courageous young silverback. The gorillas allowed me to share their proximity as before. This was a privilege that I felt I no longer deserved."

In many ways Karisoke Research Center belied its name. By the time Dian began to host students regularly, as her study neared its second decade, research was clearly secondary on her agenda. She did not accept the notion that humans were by rights more important than gorillas; she did not obey the hierarchy of rules that placed science above love. "She was prepared to put all the [research] money into antipoaching and forget about her research work, as long as the gorillas survived," remembers Bob Campbell.

Students were allowed to gather data, but if they were to work with her, at her home, they would also have to take on antipoaching patrols. These were being paid for by the Digit Fund, which Dian had incorporated in June 1978. Peace Corps volunteers assigned to her camp were asked to carry guns — a request that many refused. They were asked to track down poachers and bring them back to Dian as captives. Karisoke Research Center had become an armed camp.

Unlike Jane's research center at Gombe, with its spacious communal dining hall where students gathered for dinner each night, Karisoke students remember no feeling of community. There was no central gathering place at this center. Dian provided no dining hall, lecture area, or library; there was no place where researchers, students, and Peace Corps volunteers could regularly congregate, not even a common campfire.

The students and volunteers who worked at the camp — at most half a dozen at a time — ate separately, cooking their own meals in the little tin cabins. Dian communicated with them mainly on slips of typewritten scrap paper, delivered cabin to cabin by her African staff. To save typewriter ribbon, Dian would use both the red and the black portions. Among some students the idea arose that her "red notes" were the angry ones, but it turned out that her tone was not predictable from the color.

Dian organized her camp in this manner purposely. When, nearly two years into her study, in 1968, she had resigned herself to the need for student help on a census of the gorilla population, she had written to Louis Leakey asking that the volunteers he chose be willing to pitch their tents a ten-minute walk from her camp; she did not want to spend her evenings talking with people or cooking for them.

She had always been ambivalent about sharing Karisoke and the gorillas with other researchers. Though she was ravenous for human company, she demanded a silverback's control. To work with animals she loved like family, to protect them from unwanted intrusion, to defend them against poachers, Dian expected from her students absolute loyalty, absolute respect, absolute integrity. No human could fulfill all her requirements.

Dian's unpredictable temper was legendary. "If things were generally going badly, anyone could get in the line of fire and be the brunt of her outbursts," said Ian Redmond. Although Ian was one of the few students Dian lauded in her book, she threatened on numerous occasions to throw him out of camp, primarily for sleeping late and for turning in his weekly reports late. "She could be talking to you and then turn and just glare, and then put on this great display, and then turn back to you and talk normally. And I think," Ian muses, "that this was something she developed, possibly, from the gorillas putting on a bluff display, not unlike a silverback."

Dian, by the time students began to arrive, was in nearly constant pain: she suffered from emphysema, sciatica, a bad hip, calcium deficiency, and insomnia. She drank often. Though she directed the antipoaching patrols, she seldom accompanied them. She spent most of her time in her cabin and seemed to resent the intrusion of a student knocking at her door. After Digit's death, students remember that if they knocked, Dian would fling open the door and demand, "Who's dead now?"

Students constantly heard the clatter of her typewriter. She was writing letters. She wrote long, loving letters to the Schwartzels, brimming with concern for and interest in every aspect of the family's life; she answered, personally and promptly, every letter ever written to her by a schoolchild; she kept in touch with Ian Redmond's mother, a widow whose isolation she thought mirrored her own. Even though holed up in her cabin, cutting herself off from her students and staff, Dian was desperately seeking connection.

Few of the volunteers and students who came to Karisoke lasted more than a few months; several left after only days. Before they left the States to work at Karisoke, Amy Vedder and Bill Weber talked to former students who had worked with Dian: "We were warned twice. They said, she drives away everyone who works with her," the couple remembers. And in spite of herself Dian knew she did this. Ann Pierce, an American primatology student who had worked at Gombe, did some work at Karisoke while Dian was overseas. Ann remembers Dian saying to her, "I'd love it if you could come and work with me at Karisoke. But you'd end up hating me."

"Oh God," Dian would write in her diary, on nights when her camp was full of people, "I feel so alone, it hurts like physical pain."

On July 24, 1978, student David Watts encountered wet dung (a nervous reaction) on the trail left by Group 4. Minutes later he found the still-warm body, decapitated, of Uncle Bert, the silverback leader of the group, whom Dian had named for her uncle. A bullet had pierced his heart, and a panga wound stretched fifteen inches along the left side of his chest.

Two days later Bill Weber found Macho's body, face down. A single bullet had pierced the left side of her chest. Her three-year-old son, Kweli, was wounded in the right upper arm. He died that October of gangrenous infection. Soon the growing graveyard of poachers' victims would also receive the body of another baby. Lee, a four-year-old female of Nunkie's Group, which Dian had first met in 1972, had broken free from a poacher's trap, but the snare remained around her left foot. For three months the wire worked deeper and deeper into her flesh. She, too, died a lingering death from gangrene.

On Christmas Day, 1978, Amy Vedder knocked on Dian's cabin door. Amy knew Dian was suffering, and she knew how physically difficult it was for her to hike out to see the gorillas she loved. But Amy had just spent the morning with Group 5, and they were unusually near camp. The weather was sparkling clear and fine. "Group 5 has a Christmas present for you," Amy told her. Dian looked at the student quizzically. "They're only ten minutes away," Amy said.

But Dian's heart had slammed shut. "No," she told Amy. "No." And she closed her cabin door.

News of open warfare at Karisoke began to reach the American and European conservation community. Dian, it was said, was running a police state, not a research camp. Her antipoaching patrols were invading Batwa villages and taking captives. Ian was speared in the wrist, a nerve permanently severed. One of Dian's trackers, Semitoa, suffered a broken nose and brain concussion when he leaped a chasm to escape from an ambush by poachers.

Conservation money earmarked for gorilla protection was

now pouring in from various agencies, but the money did not go to Dian. The bylaws of organizations such as the British Fauna Preservation Society and the African Wildlife Leadership Foundation dictated that funds must be channeled through the governments of the countries involved. Much of the money generated by the publicity about gorilla deaths ended up financing new park vehicles, new roads, and a new gorilla tourism program. Dian called these funds "Digit's blood money."

Stories and rumors flew: Dian shooting at tourists, Dian torturing poachers, Dian wandering about drunk with a gun. Dian, it was said, was clinically insane.

Beryl Kendall, a primatologist studying pottos in the remote rain forest of Uganda, remembers that the rumors reached her even there. "They were unbelievable, incredibly vicious rumors," she said. "The international research community totally cut Dian off."

With Louis Leakey dead, the foundation bearing his name now cut itself off from his second protégée's project. Dian was too great a threat to public relations: even while giving a lecture she was often rude to the audience, cutting off questions by telling people to shut up and sit down.

And in February 1979 Dian received this cable from her most important funding source, National Geographic: RECEIVED SERIOUSLY DISTURBING REPORTS CONCERNING EVENTS YOUR CAMP STOP SUCH ENCOUNTERS CREATE CONCERN AND EMBARRASSMENT NATIONAL GEOGRAPHIC.

Days later, U.S. Secretary of State Cyrus Vance telexed the ambassador to Rwanda, Frank Creigler: NG RESEARCH COMMITTEE BELIEVE IT NECESSARY THAT DR FOSSEY LEAVE RWANDA FOR A WHILE. THIS WOULD HELP DEFUSE LOCAL TENSIONS.

Dian conceded defeat. She wrote, "Have finally realized I can no longer live here. The beauty of the late sun at 5 going down behind the trees that Uncle Bert, Macho, Kweli should be enjoying—what they loved so much. No longer does it hold any beauty for me. It holds only hurt."

On March 4, 1980, Dian arrived in Ithaca, New York, to begin a teaching stint at Cornell and to finish *Gorillas in the Mist*. She would attend to her health, including having a major operation on her back. She would give lectures with Jane Goodall and Biruté Galdikas. She would gather her strength: through her book and through her lectures, she vowed, she would appeal to the American public to care about the gorillas, to help.

During this time Dian's heart began to heal. She wrote warm letters to Kelly Stewart, once a favorite student, from whom she had become estranged. She became good friends with Jane Goodall, and the two exchanged letters. To Tita Caldwell, Dian wrote of Jane's admirable patience, dignity and graciousness. Dian patched up her argument with Biruté Galdikas, who still keeps the last letter Dian wrote to her, in pencil on looseleaf, dated April 1981:

> I remain tremendously proud of you; . . . you are deeply appreciated, respected and even loved. The depth of your integrity, sincerity and feeling not only [for] your animals but humans as well, is manifest in all your interactions with others.

Dian returned to Karisoke in the summer of 1983 after a three-year absence. She went out to contact Group 5. "The females —Effie, Puck, Tuck, Poppy and all their young followed by Pantsy and Muraha—just came to cuddle next to me and all their young followed," she wrote to a friend in Ithaca. "Stacey, they really did KNOW me immediately after staring into my face, belch vocalizing, coming 12 feet upon initial contact, then to rest all on top of me and around me, building their day nests in the sun while allowing their kids to swarm, chew, smell, whack, pull hair. . . . I could have died right then and wished for nothing more on earth simply because they *remembered*."

Dian was ebullient. After a promotional book tour arranged

by her publisher, she returned again to Karisoke, now her permanent home.

All of the time Dian worked in Rwanda, she was forced to renew her tourist visa every two months. She had to hike painfully down the mountain, drive in a waiting van to Ruhengeri, and then ride for two or three hours in the "taxi"—actually an alarmingly overcrowded minibus, similar to the *mattatus* of Nairobi—to the capital, Kigali. Then she would wait for days in the office of the tourism and parks director, who always insisted he was too busy to see her and provide the letter she needed to secure the new visa.

In December 1985, while in Kigali on one such trip, she complained of her problems to a dinner companion. He suggested she see the secretary-general in charge of immigration. She did, and within ten minutes her passport was stamped with a visa good for two years. He told her the next one would be good for ten years if she wanted it.

"She was so ecstatic," remembers Rosamond Carr. "She went running around Kigali, hugging everyone she saw and telling them, 'Now I can go up on the mountain in absolute peace, I don't have to go down, again, I've got a visa for 2 years.' She was literally over the moon."

Two weeks later Dian was killed in her cabin by a swipe of a panga that split her skull diagonally from her forehead to the opposite corner of her mouth. It was the day after Christmas.

When I visited her camp in 1989, a plastic Santa Claus was still hanging on the wall of her living room; her breath was still in the flaccid balloons she had strung along the ceiling. Her blood was still on the carpet.

Dian's murder attracted a storm of press attention. Special memorial tributes were held in Washington, New York, and California. Dian's mother, Kitty, attended the California tribute.

To pay her respects to her daughter, who had subsisted largely on potatoes for nearly two decades, who had given her life to the survival of animals, Kitty Price wore a full-length mink coat.

In her will Dian directed that the proceeds from her book and from the movie rights to it should go to the Digit Fund. Her parents wanted the money for themselves. They contested the will and won on the grounds that the document was only a draft.

Dian was buried in the gorilla graveyard in back of her cabin. The name she had asked to have on her wooden marker was Nyiramachabelli.

Rosamond Carr had always wondered about the name. Nyira, she knew, meant woman or girl in Kinyarwanda, but she had never thought Dian's explanation of the name was quite right. When Rosamond asked her housemen about the name, they told her they didn't know. An educated Rwandan friend said the name meant "Dian Fossey."

Finally Rosamond asked a Rwandan physicist working in Gisenyi: "He said it's hard to describe, but I insisted. He said, 'Well, in Rwanda, when there's a family and in the family there is one little girl who is smaller than the others, and does everything quick, quick, quick, we call her Nyiramachabelli.' But why would anyone call Dian, who was six feet tall, Nyiramachabelli? He said he didn't know."

One of Rosamond's housemen, Sembagare, finally admitted that Nyiramachabelli was what people had called Alyette DeMunck, the small, quick, birdlike woman who used to climb the mountain with Dian; when Alyette stopped coming, they applied the name to Dian. Rosamond talked to Alyette about it. She smiled and said, "Yes, I know. But Dian was very proud to be called Nyiramachabelli. She loved it. I'm very happy Dian never knew."

7 A Study in Patience

I<small>T IS PREDAWN DARK</small> in the rain forest of southern Borneo. The dark is thick and dense with sound. Insects and frogs trill and keen to their kind. Cicadas buzz and whirr, loud as chainsaws. The hot, wet air is heavy with the scents of bloom and decay. There is no breeze; the breath of the forest is its voices, heaving and sighing.

Before first light the gibbons whoop their alien, elastic duets. Tiny, sharp-hoofed deer bark like dogs; birds whistle like trains; you see nothing, hear everything. And then, at daybreak, silence.

Life piles thick upon itself. Vines fat as pythons writhe over buttressed trees. Epiphytic ferns and orchids hang from branches. Barbed rattan, thin as cobwebs, claws at your clothing. Life feeds openly, obscenely on death: a column of ants carries away a dying caterpillar. A butterfly, with curled tongue, sucks salt from the open eye of a dead shrew. The strangler fig, born of a seed lodged securely in the arms of a nursery tree, drops its roots around the trunk of its foster mother. Finally she is suffocated by her fosterling's clasping loins and entombed.

This is at once a hell and an Eden, seething with life and death, growth and decay. Here your senses overwhelm you. But you cannot trust them. Far from the forests of Europe and North America—sturdy, orderly, dry, cool—here the meanings you glean from vision, scent, taste are distorted like a funhouse mirror. Nothing is as it seems.

Walking, you look at drops of water falling on your shoes and think it is raining; but it is only the sweat falling from your face in the ninety-degree heat. A fallen tree bridging a swamp crumbles under your boots, plunging you into thigh-deep muck. Great trees tower 150 feet high; their buttressed roots sink only six inches deep. The knees of mangroves, roots pointed like stalagmites, rise upward from the swamp like hands from a grave in a horror movie.

Here bark can burn you with caustic sap, or river water caress you like satin. Fire ants may pour from a handhold, or butterflies light on your skin. Falling fruit can kill you. One of the main trees here is the durian. Its coconut-sized fruit, which in season falls hourly, is macelike, covered with sharp spines; hit by a falling durian, you could die from the wounds. When opened, the durian fruit smells like rotting onions, but its satiny white flesh tastes like a rich, buttery custard flavored with almonds; "such an excellent taste," commented one traveler, Jan Huygen van Linschoten in 1599, "that it surpasses in flavour all the other fruits of the world."

If you stand still in the forest, inch-long black leeches come toward you from every direction like heat-seeking missiles; they loop forward like inchworms, standing upright and waving their mouths in the air, sensing your warmth. Like a dozen other creatures in this forest, they feed on blood. They inject an anticoagulant as they feed, so the site will gush blood for an hour. Their bite is painless.

The ground is alive with leeches, ants, spiders, sweat bees. The soil, fetid and fecund, digests death so ravenously that within six months, 90 percent of its organic matter will be recycled back into the life of the forest—a process that in dry forest takes three years. The speed of decay is one reason for the great diversity of life forms, compared to those of temperate forests. Great Britain, for example, has 34 species of native trees; here there are 600, as well as 200 species of mammals and 550 species of birds. Life dazzles in profusion and form. Bamboo, a grass that grows out of scale, towers over your head; pitcher plants gape carnivorous and green. Here live the pink-faced proboscis monkey with the gigantic nose; the colugo, or flying lemur, which is not a lemur at all but a glider, the single member of its order; the flying fox, a fruit bat with a wingspan of six feet; the pangolin, a scale-covered anteater; the secretive cloud leopard; and the only Asian great ape, the only red ape: the orangutan.

This is the place Biruté Galdikas has chosen as home.

When Biruté met Louis Leakey, she was working on her M.A. in anthropology at UCLA. She planned to earn money as an archeologist and, with her savings, one day launch a study of wild orangutans in Indonesia. She says she was always fascinated by this most arboreal ape, the one great ape that never left the Garden of Eden, the ape with human eyes. She hoped the orangutan, rather than the chimpanzee or gorilla, would prove to be man's closest relative.

Her meeting with Louis after his lecture to her class was like a promise fulfilled. "I knew, even before I went up to him. As soon as I heard him talk about primates and great ape studies, and sending Jane and Dian into the field, I knew this was it. I knew I'd be going."

Yet destiny is not fate; destiny can be failed or refused. Biruté's confidence wavered when she found herself, on a late summer's day in 1970, knocking on the door of the Goodalls' flat on Earl's Court Road in London. That night Louis orchestrated and hosted the first meeting of his "three primates," Jane and Biruté and Dian. Jane had been working in Tanzania for ten years by then; Dian, in Zaire and Rwanda, for three. Biruté was in awe of them both. "All of a sudden, it hit me," Biruté recalls. "I really was going to the rain forest of Indonesia."

At one point during the evening she turned to Jane and asked, "What am I going to DO?"

"You're going to do exactly as I did," Jane replied. "You're going to go out and find them."

After Biruté's first meeting with Louis, two and a half years passed before he secured funding for the orangutan study. It took so long that at one point, Leakey suggested she study pygmy chimpanzees in Zaire instead. But just as Dian had held out for mountain gorillas when her study was interrupted, Biruté held out for orangutans.

By 1971 Louis had amassed only $9,000 from various sources: the Wilkie Brothers Foundation, the Jane and Justin Dart Foundation, the Leakey Foundation, National Geographic. When Biruté and her husband, Rod Brindamour, left for Indonesia that September, they brought only what would fit in two large backpacks: four sets of clothing, two compasses, some notebooks, two raincapes, cooking and scientific gear, a single flashlight. It was all they could afford.

Only a handful of scientists had studied wild orangutans before. One two-month study had ended without a single orangutan being sighted. During a fifty-two-day survey in North Borneo, a Japanese primatologist, T. Okano, saw only one. Two other researchers, including primatologist George Schaller, had conducted longer studies. Much of their data came from counting the orangutans' empty treetop night nests.

David Horr and John MacKinnon were the first Westerners to conduct long-term studies of the species. They had worked independently of each other in the Malaysian province of Sabah in northern Borneo. Horr's research extended over two years; MacKinnon put in 1,200 hours of observation there, and later another 200 hours watching wild orangutans in Sumatra. They learned that the orangutan was largely solitary, that its favored fruit was the durian, and that it spent most of its time in the trees, building a new nest to sleep in each night.

No one had ever seen an orangutan give birth. No one had observed male orangutans fighting. Little was known about how far an individual might travel, how they selected their mates, how mothers cared for their young, how subadults matured into adults. So little was known about orangutan reproduction that one researcher was convinced that males stopped mating when they became adult.

Biruté and Rod planned to carry out the longest continuous study of wild orangutans ever attempted. They planned to work at Mount Looser Reserve in Sumatra, where orangutans had been studied before.

They never got there.

First there was a stopover in Kenya, to visit with the Leakeys on safari, then a visit to Gombe, observing chimpanzees with Jane Goodall. Then an unplanned-for week in India—both Biruté and Rod were waylaid with intestinal infections and diarrhea. They bought some scientific supplies in Singapore, where they could be purchased cheaply. Their first weeks in Indonesia were spent contacting officials and negotiating for their scientific study permits.

The head of Indonesian parks and nature reserves listened politely to their plans to go to the well-mapped park in Sumatra. Then he told them: "You look like the kind of people who want to be first. You don't want to follow in other people's footsteps." He decided they should go to Tanjung Puting, a roughly 250,000-hectare reserve on a peninsula on the south coast of Borneo. Its boundaries had never been mapped, its interior never explored. But some months earlier, three people from the city of Bogor had visited the reserve and seen orangutans there.

So in the company of an Indonesian forestry official and a

camp cook they had hired in the town of Kumai, Biruté and Rod made the ten-hour boat journey down the weed-choked Sekoyner-Cannon River to the reserve. Their camp, which they named in honor of their mentor, was an abandoned *nipa*-thatched hut that had been built for forest rangers. As the first rain poured through the roof of Camp Leakey, they discovered that the name was doubly apt.

For the first year the short, slim, golden-skinned Melayu people—Moslem farmers and rubber tappers originally from Kumai—were the only humans they saw. At the end of 1972 the first white face they encountered, Biruté wrote, "came as a shock." It would be three years before Biruté left Indonesia, even briefly, for a primatology conference in Europe, and four before Rod would visit the West.

The couple lived in poverty. They ate mainly rice, supplemented with tinned sardines, canned, greasy pigs' feet, and bananas. They cooked over an open fire fueled by fallen branches collected in the forest. Their shoes and clothes rotted. At one point Rod held what remained of his boots together by binding the soles to his feet with rattan.

Biruté would take along only a thermos filled with cold coffee as she searched the forests each day; Rod took their only flashlight as he went to cut trails. They waded through swamps up to their armpits; the skin on their feet shriveled from constant immersion. They hacked their way through vines with machetes. Biruté searched the trees for what one might think would be obvious: a two-hundred-pound primate covered with bright red fur. But all she saw, she remembers, was "a miscellaneous mass of green." The couple would often return after dark, Biruté stumbling over vines and roots.

They found the forest booby-trapped with hidden jaws. Poisonous caterpillars dropped from trees. Long-snouted crocodiles—false garivals—lurked submerged in the tea-colored rivers. Streams of fire ants, whose black bodies had a red sheen, were a constant annoyance. Biruté saw animals caught in traps set by the Dayaks fall victim to these ants; the trapper would find only a skeleton after the ants ate away the flesh.

Snakes were everywhere, coiling arrogantly in patient, perfect camouflage. One night Biruté felt something soft and smooth brush her leg; she walked a few meters and then looked back, shining her flashlight. A cobra reared erect, looking her in the eye.

There were fevers and tick bites, and every scratch seemed to go septic. As Biruté and Rod took off their wet clothes at night, "fat black leeches, bloated with our blood, dropped out of our socks and off our necks and fell out of our underwear," she wrote in a National Geographic article. But all of this did not bother Biruté; though aware of its dangers, she found the forest peaceful, beautiful. What frightened her, depressed her, ate at her, was the fact that she was encountering no orangutans.

"I couldn't find them, I couldn't see them, I couldn't make contact with them—of course I felt pressured," Biruté recalls. It was ten days before she even glimpsed an orangutan—sixty to eighty feet up in the trees, mostly obscured by leaves—and it quickly moved away while Biruté tried to extricate her boots from the sucking ooze of the swamp.

Because the couple had arrived at Tanjung Puting during the rainy season, it was impossible to follow an orangutan in the swollen swamps. On dry ground walking was easier, but, once sighted, the animals were usually irritated by the attention; they would hurl branches, shriek, and, with admirable accuracy, urinate and defecate on their heads. Rod was once hit in the eye with an orangutan turd that exploded all over his face on impact. Orangutans also use dead trees, or snags, to discourage observers. Several times Biruté has watched helplessly as a snag, pushed by a male orangutan, toppled toward her in horror-movie-like slow motion. She would think: This is what it is like to die. Each time the trunk has either broken on its way down or been deflected by vines; but trees have crashed inches from her feet.

It was two months before Biruté was able to follow an orang-utan for more than part of one day. She encountered a female and her offspring one morning at seven and succeeded in following her until dark, when the animal constructed a nest of leaves and went to sleep for the night. Both Biruté and Rod returned to the nest before dawn the next morning and waited beneath the tree in the steaming dark. Long after dawn the nest began shaking, and the female, whom they named Beth, and her infant emerged.

They followed as the two moved and fed, fed and rested. It rained every day. Biruté and Rod tried to dry their clothes each night over the fire; one night the clothes caught fire and burned off one leg of their four pairs of jeans. One afternoon, as the orangutan rested, Biruté sat briefly on a fallen *rangas* log. That night she discovered that her buttocks had been burned black by toxic sap. She could not sit down or sleep on her back for a week afterward.

They followed the mother and infant for five days, encountering no other orangutans the whole time and observing no behavior more revealing than traveling, resting, and feeding. And then they lost the pair. Biruté was not able to establish this long a follow for another three months.

Most primates, including chimpanzees, gorillas, and baboons, travel in groups. If you want to study baboons, for example, you find a troop, pick a different "target" animal to observe each day, and in the course of a month you have data on thirty different individuals. At the same time you are habituating all thirty animals to human presence.

"The orangutan," Jane Goodall agrees, "is the hardest of the three great apes to study." Because they are solitary and arboreal, "it takes Biruté a year to gather information and to see behaviors I might see in one lucky day."

This solitary species must be habituated to human presence one animal at a time. It took Biruté and Rod six months to partially habituate a single animal, a prime male she called Throat Pouch. The beachball-like air sac under his chin was perpetually inflated; most males balloon their normally flaccid pouches only to produce the territorial long call. Biruté was terrified that Throat Pouch had cancer; if he died or left the area, she would have to start all over again. She began to realize just how monumental was the task she had chosen.

Orangutans' lives progress, like most of their movements, with a dignified and serene leisure. Biruté has compared watching them to watching sloths; chimps are positively frenetic in comparison. "The most common complaint of the primatologist intrepid enough to study orangutans," wrote Sarah Blaffer Hrdy, a sociobiologist and primatologist, "is that in hours and hours of observation the adults almost never do anything, almost never meet anyone; rather, they munch endlessly and rest."

Orangutans reveal themselves only slowly. It was eight years before Biruté saw an orangutan use a tool—a thirty-five-second incident in which a male used a stick to scratch his behind. It was more than fifteen years before the female orangutans she first met as infants began bearing their first babies. And this, from the start, was her goal: "I wanted to follow them from the time they were born until the time they died."

In the first four years she and Rod logged 6,804 hours of observation on fifty-eight named wild individuals—four times the observation hours accumulated by her predecessor, John MacKinnon. She followed them even while she was wracked with fever and bleeding from wounds. After she took on the job of rehabilitating former captives, she followed them with orphaned baby orangutans clinging to her body. She followed them on swollen legs, nine months pregnant with her first child. She began to gather their individual life stories.

She watched males battle for females and territory. Sometimes the battles lasted for hours. She watched Throat Pouch grappling with another male in a tree. They grabbed each other like sumo

In the early days, Biruté often pursued the wild orangutans she was studying with an orphaned orangutan clinging to her. *Rod Brindamour,* © *National Geographic*

wrestlers. They bit each other. Often they fell from the tree and chased each other back up to resume fighting, their backs glistening with beads of sweat. Sometimes, she said, they parted and just glared at each other. Finally they separated and sat in adjacent trees. Throat Pouch shoved a dead tree over and then uttered the long call: a series of grumbles, followed by intense roaring and bellowing, subsiding into grumbles and sighs. The other male vanished. The smell of their sweat lingered heavy in the air for hours.

She watched males and females together in courtship and consummation. Most matings occur in the context of consortship: an adult male and female travel together for at least three days, feeding, nuzzling, mating. They make love as humans do, most often belly to belly, and frequently the female reclines against a branch. Usually female orangutans, during the receptive point in their thirty-day cycle, seek the company of an adult male, often moving toward the sound of his long call. Normally shy females may turn brazen: once Biruté saw Beth accost a prime adult male, shake a vine in his face, slap his stomach, and tweak his penis. When all this failed to arouse his attentions, she urinated on his head. Eventually the two moved off together.

But also there is rape. Occasionally males — often subadults — will copulate forcibly with adult females. These instances are not the mild tussles typical of courtship in many other species; the female struggles fiercely and tries to bite the male whenever she can. She emits a peculiar, distressed grunt — Biruté calls it the "rape grunt" — never heard in any other context.

When Biruté first came to Tanjung Puting, the rubber tappers told her that male orangutans will also rape human women. In fact a Dayak legend explains the male orangutan's long call in this light: he is calling for his human lover, a woman he stole from a riverboat but who escaped from the night nest to which he brought her. Biruté knew that many mammals, from dogs to cougars, become excited by the scent of menstruating human females, but she dismissed the legends about orangutans. She would walk through the forest with blood soaking through her jeans each month, for Kotex and tampons were not available in the nearby towns.

Years later a wild adult male orangutan came into her camp and raped a female Indonesian cook. Fortunately the woman was uninjured and she was not socially ostracized for her ordeal. Today Biruté warns women visitors that if they are menstruating they should carry a stick with them and never walk alone among the male ex-captives.

Biruté was one of the first observers to document prolonged social interaction among wild orangutans. Like human teenagers, adolescent and subadult orangutans (from age seven to adulthood) are the most social group, particularly the females. Two or more adolescent females may travel together for days, part, then reunite, sometimes gently grooming or touching one another.

One of the most moving relationships she observed was an odd one, between a subadult male and an adolescent female. Theirs was such a long-lasting friendship that Biruté and Rod thought of them as a pair and called them Mute and Noisy. For years the two orangutans would travel together for more than ten days at a time. This was not a consortship; Mute often raped other females but never attacked Noisy. Once when Mute was forcibly copulating with a female, Noisy attacked Mute's victim. And when Noisy first became receptive, she sought the company of a large cheek-padded male named Nick. Nick and Noisy consorted, mating several times, but Biruté saw Mute several times lurking in the background nearby, sneaking looks at his friend and her lover from behind the trunks of trees.

Unlike Jane and Dian, who initially described what they saw in narrative field notes, Biruté recorded the behaviors she witnessed on a check sheet, minute by minute. She focused on only one orangutan at a time, even when a female was traveling with offspring, or when the animal met up with others—a technique known as focal animal sampling. She carefully catalogued the hundreds of plants and insects the orangutans ate, sometimes tasting them herself. She inventoried every plant in three different plots in the study area, identifying more than 400 species, and meticulously recorded the trees' fruiting and growth.

Biruté's 333-page Ph.D. dissertation was submitted to UCLA in 1978. It was dedicated to the memory of Louis Leakey, who had died in 1972. The thesis was enthusiastically received: independent reviewers called her work "monumental." Jane Goodall, in a letter to the Leakey Foundation, praised Biruté's work lavishly. "Her data are excellent as are her field methods," she wrote. The Washington University primatologist Robert Sussman, echoing many other opinions, called Biruté's work "the best of the three" Leakey protégées.

Unlike Jane and Dian, Biruté was trained in modern data-collecting techniques and statistical analysis. Her thesis presents ninety-one tables of numerical data. She statistically correlates orangutan groupings by sex, age, number of animals present; catalogues long calls by time of day and duration; plots the frequency of consort and nonconsort copulations. The focal animal sampling technique she used from the start had by 1974 been recognized as the most accurate and revealing method available for recording behavioral information.

Biruté was as concerned with theory as with findings. She had hoped her study animal would prove to be man's closest relative, but DNA analysis later gave the chimpanzee that honor. However, her observations yielded the best portrait to date of how man's ancestors may have lived before they left the trees.

A theory she advanced in a 1981 paper, coauthored by Gombe primatologist Geza Teleki, generated much excitement and debate among researchers. The paper argues persuasively that male and female orangutans and chimpanzees use different food resources and that in this "ecological separation" could well lie the origins of human labor division: hunting males and foraging females. Thirteen respected primatologists and anthropologists commented on the paper in the journal *Current Anthropology*. But after an initial flurry of excitement, Western scientists' enthusiasm for Biruté's work began to fade. For after the first decade of her research, Biruté's scientific career, as well as her personal life, diverged dramatically from the Western norm.

Rod Brindamour left his wife in the middle of 1979. He had, he felt, paid his dues to his wife's career. He had surveyed and staked transects and cut more than fifty miles of trails through the swamp and forest. He had meticulously photographed his wife's work. He had helped her develop friendships with Indonesian officials, made recordings of orangutan calls, and managed the camp.

Years of festering tropical ulcers had eaten purple holes in his legs. He was tired of sleeping with ex-captive orangutan orphans in his bed. He had put off his own career plans for seven and a half years. Now Rod wanted to go home. Biruté thought she had made it clear from the start that she wanted to study orangutans for the rest of her life. But Rod had not understood. "He thought it would be more like what most primatologists do, in other words, have a life that's based in North America, and go back and forth to visit," Biruté recalls.

Two years later Biruté married Pak Bohap bin Jalan, a Dayak. It took four months for them to secure official permission to wed; they were even asked to get written approval from the governor of the province. They were the first Indonesian-Western couple ever to marry in the province of Kalimantan Tengah.

It is an unusual partnership. Pak Bohap is seven years Biruté's junior, and at five foot two and 125 pounds, he is significantly shorter and lighter than his wife. He speaks no English; he has never met Biruté's parents and never accompanied her on her yearly visits to North America, not even in 1985 when she left

Biruté presides over dinners and lectures in the dining
room at Camp Leakey, which now attracts hundreds
of volunteers. Orangutans frequently peer in, clinging
to the welded mesh covering every window.
Harold Walker

in the final months before the birth of their daughter, Jane. She
is a member of Bat Conservation International; he hunts bats
for food with the traditional Dayak blowpipe and poisoned
darts. And unlike the Melayu, orthodox Moslems who consider
it a sin to eat pigs or monkeys, the Dayaks, former headhunters
and animists, have no proscriptions against eating orangutans.
But now it is Pak Bohap's work to protect orangutans. After
their marriage, Pak Bohap became the codirector of Biruté's
Orangutan Project and a principal collaborator in her work.

Pak Bohap's forest skills are unparalleled. He can run barefoot
through the swamps. In seconds, while holding a lit cigarette in
one hand, he can climb a tree and triangulate precisely the best
spot from which to view an orangutan from the ground. He can

tell you, from looking at bent twigs, which animal passed by here and how long ago, how quickly it was going, and sometimes what brought it here in the first place. He can pinpoint the source of any forest sound, from bird song to an orangutan long call, with uncanny accuracy.

Unlike the farming Melayu, the Dayaks, Borneo's aboriginal inhabitants, have lived in these forests for centuries. All of Biruté's orangutan trackers are Dayaks, and many of them are relatives of Pak Bohap.

"I've been in the rain forest for seventeen years, and I've come to the conclusion that even though I've been here a long time, nonetheless, I think to me it's a foreign language," Biruté says. "Even though as a child I spent a lot of time in temperate woods, this was a different type of nature. For the people who live here, the Dayaks, the forest is their first language, and they speak it with the native accent."

With skilled Dayak trackers the project can now carry on seven different orangutan follows at once. Two Dayaks go together on a follow, which lasts from before dawn until the orangutan builds its night nest, sometimes after dark. One person makes notations on the data sheet; the other collects food samples and notes the orangutan's direction of travel, using tree markers Rod put in place when creating the transects. If possible, each team will follow an individual orangutan for ten days.

As Biruté's staff has grown, so has the camp's budget. The Orangutan Project has been funded by some of the most prestigious granting organizations in Western science, including the National Geographic Society for more than six years. The organization's long-term support of Louis Leakey's work and that of his "three primates" is unusual; normally it sponsors only single expeditions or short-term projects. Biruté's project also found funding from the World Wildlife Fund, the New York Zoological Society, the Chicago Zoological Society, and the John Simon Guggenheim Memorial Foundation. But the money has never stretched far enough.

From the beginning Biruté worked with only the most rudimentary equipment. The project had a boat but not a car. In April 1972 Biruté cut herself badly with a machete and needed a doctor's attention. She traveled all night on the sputtering wooden boat, the only way to reach the tiny Melayu town of Kumai; once there, she had to wait all the next day to flag down a passing car to take her to the hospital in Pangkalanbuun.

Arlene Masters, whose sixteen-year-old daughter visited Camp Leakey in 1979, wrote to the Leakey Foundation in alarm that the Orangutan Project was "in imminent danger of extinction for lack of funds." That year grants and donations totaling only $8,000 supported a staff of fifteen people. Biruté, who was never salaried, then had no speedboat, no two-way radio. One of her colleagues, Gary Shapiro, had to sell his car and other possessions to fund his passage to work with her at Tanjung Puting.

Biruté remembers that at one point in 1979, only $49 was left in the bank account, and the camp was $5,000 in debt. That year an anonymous donor replenished the account. "We lived from miracle to miracle," Biruté says. National Geographic terminated its support in 1982. "While it has been rewarding scientifically, the committee is reluctant to continue with support for long-term projects," the letter read. Her project was without a sustaining benefactor.

In 1984 Biruté found one in Earthwatch, which pairs volunteer laymen with scientific field projects around the world. The organization, based in Watertown, Massachusetts, offers its members a tax-deductible adventure; to scientists it offers workers who are willing to pay for the privilege of assisting them. Since its first grant to her of $60,000, Earthwatch has provided most of the funds for her work. To work at Camp Leakey with Biruté for two weeks, each volunteer pays Earthwatch about $1,800, not including airfare. Between June and November, about six teams of eight to sixteen volunteers arrive in Pangkalanbuun.

Volunteers nurse orphaned ex-captives and follow Dayak

trackers to observe wild orangutans. They record the interactions of ex-captive mothers and their offspring, using a data sheet modified from one designed by Jane Goodall; they type Biruté's correspondence; occasionally they catalogue botanical plots, work in the herbarium, or go on river patrols to chase illegal fishermen or wild-rubber tappers out of the park.

With so diverse a crowd, problems sometimes arise. Several volunteers have fled Biruté's camp early. One said he left because he found a scorpion under his bed. One Earthwatcher was attacked by a Malayan sun bear, though he escaped without being bitten. One large problem was that the volunteers, usually women, sometimes had affairs with the Dayak staff members; when the women left, the men were heartbroken. This was such a persistent problem that Biruté now delivers a lecture on the subject to Earthwatch teams when they arrive. Since she began delivering the lecture, she says the affairs have stopped.

Volunteers sometimes lack the physical strength needed to follow wild orangutans in the forest. Some of the first English words Dayak trackers learned from Earthwatchers were "God-damnit, slow down!" Biruté found that in the first year of Earthwatch support the orangutan follows got shorter, but the Dayaks' success in finding orangutans in the forest increased by 30 percent. Westerners are considered high-status visitors, and often a successful tracker will be rewarded with gifts of boots, jeans, or sneakers from a grateful Earthwatch volunteer.

"The presence of volunteers galvanized the research efforts of Project staff," Biruté wrote in her Earthwatch field report in 1985. In December of that year, the Project logged 936 hours of orangutan observation—more than Biruté had achieved in her entire first year of study.

Ironically, during Camp Leakey's most productive decade of research, Western scientists' view of Biruté's work has considerably cooled.

The most frequent criticism is that she doesn't publish. "The fact of the matter is," says John Mitani, a respected primatologist who has studied all three of the great ape species, "she's pushing twenty years there, and she's published virtually nothing beyond her first few years of work. There's a big black hole out there. I'm very anxious to know what has happened in the last ten years."

"It's very infuriating not to have that information," says primatologist Alison Jolly. She deeply admires Biruté's courage and stamina and calls her early publications "exceptionally well documented, fascinating." Which is why, she says, she is frustrated that Biruté hasn't published her more recent findings. Though Jolly defends Biruté as a "top-notch researcher," she adds, "That she hasn't published is a valid criticism."

"The project just doesn't generate publications," said one anonymous reviewer. "It simply isn't scholarly enough." Another former supporter says Biruté did not deliver field reports on time; without this documentation the agency could not renew her grant, although the money had already been amassed and earmarked for her project.

In number of papers published, Biruté's vita compares favorably with Jane Goodall's, considering that Jane has spent almost twice as long in the field. Jane's 1988 vita lists forty articles, one scholarly book, and seven books for popular audiences. Biruté's 1986 vita lists forty-one articles and one scholarly book. But of her twenty-four articles published between 1980 and 1989, four are less than three pages long, and a handful of others are simply replies to articles by other authors. The remainder augment her first four years of data with a few recent observations.

New discoveries continue at Tanjung Puting, but the news from the Orangutan Project is about as quiet as the rain forest at noon. A few years ago Earthwatchers saw a male orangutan reach into a tree, then pop four baby flying squirrels into his mouth. No scientist had ever seen Bornean orangutans eat meat before. Twelve people witnessed the incident, including one biologist with a Ph.D. But more than five years later, that finding has not been published. Biruté says that ten years ago such an observation would have been considered important; today it is thought to have little theoretical significance. "I agree," she says, "it's something I should do, but it's number 302 on my list of priorities. I have half a dozen things like that on the back burner."

Lack of time is a common complaint among field scientists who must at once collect data, negotiate with foreign officials, and administer a large camp in a Third World country. Most field biologists, as Biruté has pointed out, spend a month or two in the field collecting data, then return to their comfortable labs and universities to spend nine or ten months writing it up. Jane Goodall and Dian Fossey both faced the same problems as Biruté; in Dian's case her backers essentially forced her to leave Rwanda for nearly three years to write up her findings in *Gorillas in the Mist.*

"To put things in perspective," says John Mitani, "when you look at Fossey and Goodall, it's helped them getting other scientists in there to kick their butts." In the scientific heyday of the research at Gombe, he points out, Jane's students and staff often outnumbered the study animals. Even when Jane couldn't find time to publish, her students kept a steady stream of publications flowing. Although Dian had fewer students, several who were respected in their field published widely and thus raised Karisoke's status as a research station.

Most of Biruté's students, though, are Indonesians; if they publish, they write in Bahasa Indonesia, a language inaccessible to most Western scientists. Biruté's only published book, describing orangutan adaptation, was also written in Indonesian and has not been translated into English.

Yet most of the data on the Tanjung Puting orangutans are gathered neither by Western nor Indonesian scientists but by

Dayak assistants and Earthwatch volunteers. "To be perfectly honest, I don't know how Galdikas will be using the data they collect," John Mitani said.

Earthwatch volunteers have assisted with many prestigious projects, including Alison Jolly's long-term lemur project in Madagascar and a cooperative American-Soviet study at Lake Baikal. But some scientists mistrust the quality of data gathered by volunteer laymen. "People at universities have purist attitudes — that a person can't do quality science who hasn't spent twenty-five years in education training for it," admits ornithologist Charles van Riper. He has used more than 150 Earthwatch volunteers on his biological projects and has been pleased with their data; but his colleagues, he recalls, were shocked. Biruté is aware of her colleagues' reservations. Once, in her early days of working with Earthwatch, she asked a science reporter to play down her connection with the organization.

But Earthwatch has been good to Biruté, and she is grateful. Its volunteers do more than just provide funds and collect data; by coming halfway around the world to Tanjung Puting, they demonstrate international support for her project to the Indonesian government, the provincial government, and the local people with whom she works.

She is equally quick to defend her choice of Dayaks and other Indonesians as staff. Indonesia is the only nation on earth where orangutans are found; the animals' fate rests in Indonesian hands, and it is appropriate that these people become their champions.

But the fact remains that Camp Leakey is not primarily a community of scientists. Her critics see it as little more than a Dayak village disrupted by constant tourists and overrun by tame orangutans.

Biruté's orangutan rehabilitation work has never had much scientific support. "It has been generally agreed that returning human-oriented animals . . . into healthy wild populations is not a useful exercise," states John MacKinnon. Biruté says Mac-Kinnon has told her privately that he was referring not to her project but to one at Sepilok; but such disapproval is echoed widely in scientific and conservation literature. This view is so well accepted that it has even found its way into popular animal encyclopedias.

Each wild adult orangutan needs a relatively large tract of land to find enough food, as Biruté amply demonstrated in her early work. The ex-captives she releases could potentially usurp the food resources of wild-born orangutans. There is no evidence to prove that they do not. It is clear, however, from Biruté's data that the well-fed ex-captives weigh more, mature faster, and give birth more frequently than do wild orangutans. At one time Biruté was quietly looking into implantable birth control devices for ex-captive females.

In response to colleagues' criticism, Biruté points out that the project serves to check the illegal trade in orangutans; without her center, local forestry officials would have nowhere to place confiscated pet orangutans. The project is also good public relations. In one year seven hundred Indonesian tourists visited Camp Leakey, mainly to see the ex-captive orangutans.

But beyond these justifications is this fact: if Biruté did not take in the ex-captives, they would live and die in captivity. And this is the ultimate reason she remains committed to the rehabilitation project: "These individual orangutans have a right to survive and a right to return to the forest," she says.

This is where Biruté's outlook diverges from that of most of her scientific colleagues. In every Earthwatch expedition briefing, she prints Camp Leakey's cardinal rule: "Remember that in camp the orangutans come FIRST, science second, local staff and people third, and we, the foreign researchers, LAST."

Early in her study, in 1974, Biruté started seeing wild orangutans suffering from a hideous skin disease. She wrote a friend in the States about one of the stricken babies: "Carl is absolutely disfigured. I can barely refrain from crying whenever I look at him." The afflicted animals lost huge patches of hair, and their skin became leathery and wrinkled; wounds opened where scratching broke the skin and the bloody flesh protruded.

Biruté and Rod retrieved the body of one infant who died of the disease and sent tissue and organ samples to American pathology labs. They tried offering the wild orangutans fruits with medicine hidden inside, but the wild animals would not accept the proffered foods; eventually the afflicted animals either died or spontaneously recovered on their own. But for Biruté and Rod, there was never any question about whether they should try to help the orangutans. Scientific integrity was not the issue. What mattered, said Biruté, was that orangutans were suffering, and she would try to help them if she could.

In 1979 a scientist working with Biruté suggested they try monitoring the orangutans' movements with radio tracking devices. He spoke enthusiastically of a colleague's project: he had tranquilized howler monkeys in Panama and put radio collars on them. The project worked well, and they had a "sacrifice" rate (the percentage of animals who died because of the capture and tranquilizer) of only 8 percent, which was considered very low.

Radio collars wouldn't work for orangutans; Biruté knew the animals would deftly remove the devices. So her colleague proposed surgically implanting radio tracking devices under the skin. "He was certain this could be done," Biruté remembers. "He was convinced we could do it." The idea was exciting. With such devices Biruté could conceivably keep track of every wild orangutan in the study area simultaneously — a scientific coup, beyond her wildest dreams. But she shelved the plans for the project.

Biruté takes a deep draw from her clove-flavored cigarette, as if to inhale the memory: "You know where we parted ways? It was very interesting, you know? Where we parted ways was, he was a scientist. His first priority was science. He was Harvard educated, very smart, quite brilliant, I would say. He was the smartest primatologist I've ever met, and a nice man, a very nice man. I said, OK, if we go through with this and one orangutan dies, that's it. We stop immediately. And he said, oh, no, no, no—our sample would be too small, from a scientific point of view. And if we had already got funding, we just couldn't stop at one dead orangutan. And I said, no, if just one dies, that's it, it's over. Because I, in full conscience, could not continue any project or any endeavor that was harmful to orangutans. I just wouldn't do it.

"This is where we parted ways. We had been good friends, we'd been collaborating, but it was like, all of a sudden, two worlds clashed. He put science first. And I was thinking, is that the difference between a man and a woman?"

"I have given up a lot for orangutans," Biruté once told an interviewer. "I'll never have a life with Rod, a house with a mortgage paid off, or tenure, or any of the trappings of success." She made these statements completely without remorse or self-pity; she was simply making an observation, as if she were describing the configuration of a leaf.

Today, she says, she is very happy. And now she does have a house with a mortgage paid off, or nearly paid off, in Canada. She does have tenure at Simon Fraser. She doesn't want a life with Rod. She is deeply in love with Pak Bohap; she says that despite their disparate backgrounds, he understands her better than Rod ever did. Pak Bohap is sitting beside her on a couch at his large wooden house in Pasir Panganj, a Dayak village near Pangkalanbuun. He smiles when she translates her words into Bahasa Indonesia for him.

Here, as the couple awaits the arrival of the next Earthwatch team, Biruté and Pak Bohap can enjoy the comforts of civilization: this is a spacious, welcoming home, decorated with hand-made Indonesian tapestries and tall earthen jars in the hall. They have electricity, thanks to her private generator, and even a color television. Their son Frederick will soon begin attending classes at a nearby school.

Camp Leakey has grown considerably. The government of Kalimantan Tengah province has built her a long wooden dock. There are now seven buildings, including a dining hall and guest house, all relatively orangutan-proof, with wire mesh over the windows to bar ex-captives from entering. Biruté's house and the guest dormitory both have bathrooms, with a tall, square *bak mandi* from which you dip water to pour over yourself for a bath. The camp also boasts a generator that usually powers lights until about nine at night. There is a small refrigerator. And the diet, though monotonous, is tasty: fish, rice, noodles, a variety of vegetables, tiny sweet bananas, pineapple, papaya, and, on special occasions, Coke and cakes.

In contrast to her earlier life, Biruté now enjoys relative luxury. She can reach Pangkalanbuun, the nearest large town, in two hours via a speedboat she bought from a French film company. But by the end of a trip to town, the Dayak assistant piloting the speedboat is nearly blinded by the insects that fly into his eyes, for the boat's windscreen was removed by orangutans, and he has no goggles.

A Javanese student mounting a study of proboscis monkeys here needed a quiet motorboat to observe the animals from the river. The camp had one once, but it sank. He went out in the camp's spare boat to try to retrieve and repair the sunken craft, but this boat was so leaky that it sank before he could find the other one.

More than half the donated drugs Biruté keeps in her medicine chest expired months or years ago. Pangkalanbuun has a doctor and a small hospital, but their drugs are even older, and the surgery's walls are splattered with blood. Biruté's diet, the heat, and disease have taken a toll on her health. Occasionally as she sits at the head of the dining hall table eating rice, she suddenly stops chewing. Another piece of a tooth has fallen out.

Sometimes it seems that even with a budget many researchers would consider large, the Orangutan Project is held together by pennies, masking tape, and string. Biruté knows full well that she could have traded this for a comfortable post at a university. In her first few years of study she proved she could do the science. Her methods were impeccable, her data were sound, her theories were innovative. Her scientific reputation was established.

Some field biologists would say that Biruté blew it. She could be working full-time at a university. She could be spending her time working up and publishing her data, collecting the admiration of her scientific peers. But no. She stays in the grip of the wet heat of Indonesia, mothering ex-captive orangutans, an activity that few scientists respect, and trekking through the forest with Dayaks.

One could argue that Biruté doesn't publish much because she doesn't have to; the popularity of her Earthwatch expeditions assures continued funding, releasing her from the pressures of "publish or perish." One could argue that she has put off publishing because she simply doesn't have time. One could argue that much of the recent criticism of her work, her orangutan rehabilitation, and her Dayak and volunteer staff stems from personal and professional jealousies—"because I stuck it out and [other primatologists] didn't, there must be something wrong with my work," as Biruté puts it.

But the bottom line, as with Jane and Dian, is that science is not her top priority. Science was the reason she first went into the field, but science is no longer what keeps her here.

III *Warriors*

8 Crusader: The Moral Dilemma of Jane Goodall

JANE GOODALL'S SMILE has vanished. She thinks I have looked away. The smile was there half a second ago; it had seemed as sincere and welcoming as the sunny back yard of The Birches, her family's country home in the seaside town of Bournemouth, England, where I stand; there were even dancing little wrinkles at the corners of her eyes. But the curve of her lips dropped faster than a ripe fruit from a tree, leaving no trace of amusement or pleasure. This smile was a monument to British courtesy—not only to produce a smile, but to make it look real. Had I not looked back, I could comfortably have thought she was not unhappy, at least for that moment.

Jane Goodall looks like a fifty-five-year-old woman who desperately needs to lie down with a wet cloth over her eyes; instead, she is springing up to bring a tray of hot tea to the back yard from the kitchen, trying to decide whether she should prune a dinner engagement down to just drinks so she has time to write a tribute to a National Geographic colleague, and rushing inside to answer the incessant telephone. ("Sit down and relax, Jane," exhorts her peppy octogenarian mother, only to have Jane volley back the same phrase moments later.)

Finally Jane does sit down in a lawn chair to share a lunch of hot macaroni and cheese with her family. They're all together now at The Birches, where Jane grew up: her Aunt Olly, a physiotherapist, who regularly massages the hind legs of her two elderly tortoises, Romeo and Juliet (Romeo apparently has arthritis, and Juliet's back leg was dislocated once when Romeo got amorous); the effervescent Vanne, her auburn hair done in motherly curls with stately white tufts at the temples; Jane's suntanned and sun-blond son, Hugo, who still goes by his nickname Grub; and a shaggy medium-sized dog named Cida. It's a glorious, hot late May day in 1989, and the garden is drenched in vanilla sunlight; fat bees bumble lazily between clovers, and tits crack nuts from a hanging feeder.

But on the beaches of the Canary Islands, drugged baby chimpanzees dressed in clothes are "performing" for tourists; in the laboratories of medical research facilities, AIDS-infected chimps are rocking autistically in unlit cages; and in the dwindling rain forests of Africa, chimpanzee mothers are shot, their babies stolen. These are the scenes that infect this lovely day with Jane's family, spreading like a bloodstain on a linen tablecloth.

Grub has just returned from a "secret mission" in Spain: the son of the world's most famous primatologist went undercover to document the beach chimps at the southern resorts. They're dressed up in baby clothes and diapers that are never changed, paraded around in the sun all day and in the nightclubs under blaring lights at night, their thumbed feet crammed into tight little shoes. The owners of these smuggled babies shove the chimps into the arms of tourists and take a picture that sells for ten dollars. A few of the chimps have been rescued; their bodies were covered with cigarette burns.

This cruelty recalls another: the fate of one of the four chimps who, wearing a twelve-ounce latex "gorilla suit," played the orphaned baby gorilla Pucker in the film based on Fossey's life, *Gorillas in the Mist.* Jane relates how after the working conditions had been carefully inspected and approved, one of the chimp actors, its job completed, ended up in a medical lab.

Jane relates these vignettes falteringly, like an exhausted walker who is tripping over stones. The images waft like ghosts wandering from one ring of hell to another: veal calves crammed into squalid pens on factory farms; drugs smuggled inside the bodies of animals; oil-soaked birds in Alaska after the Exxon oil spill.

And the medical labs. Their steel bars, it seems, are always clanging in her skull, like a lingering headache after a long fever. But it's all of a piece: man's arrogance. "To think that animals don't feel pain, or have emotions, or consciousness. Just monstrous. It's a nonsense."

But isn't the garden beautiful today?

"There used to be butterflies all over the garden," Jane remembers. "And turtles, wild turtles. Once I had a pet tortoise who escaped and returned the next day with a female. Now you don't see tortoises here anymore. And birds—the woodpeckers are all gone. The pesticides have poisoned them. If I leave the windows open at night, I find only one insect in the room." She then advises her mother to buy moth and butterfly eggs; the larvae will help feed the birds.

Talk turns to her schedule: fresh from opening the Jane Goodall Institute's London branch the previous Friday, she must go to Edinburgh for a speech tomorrow, then to Germany next week, and then, in late June, an emergency trip to the United States to testify on behalf of the Improved Standards for Laboratory Animals Act, an amendment to the Animal Welfare Act. The U.S. trip will delay her return to Gombe; a month ago she had hoped to arrive in early June, then mid-June, and now it looks as though she may get there after the hearings conclude on June 26. In the past four years she has spent no more than three weeks in one place.

"It's worth it for the chimps, I suppose," she says, her words a sigh. She excuses herself to work on the National Geographic tribute — even the pared-down plan for drinks with the family friend must be canceled — and evaporates into the house.

The Goodall parlor is generous, welcoming, and very English, with sagging velvet easy chairs in greens and golds, fringed lampshades, pots of blooming flowers, and a large blow-up plastic snake coiled into the strike position on a divan. A photograph of toads copulating adorns an end table, and crowning the TV is a black-and-white picture of Jane, beaming, with the white-bearded Konrad Lorenz. Over the tiled fireplace hangs an enormous photo of Jane at the Peak at Gombe: "Sun's Fading Glow Silhouettes Jane Goodall," reads the caption reprinted from *National Geographic*. Taken by Hugo, it is a portrait of soul-soothing solitude: seated on the ground, her limbs coiled comfortably as a cat's, Jane is surrounded by all she loves. The African night is about to enfold her, the last rays of the sun a lingering embrace. Here, especially in the early days, Jane would go to scan the rounded humps of fig trees below, voluptuous as moss, to listen for pant-hoots and watch for black shapes among the green. Here, with the stunted *msagamba* trees at her back, sitting on a stone the size of a Victorian plush chair seat, she offered her presence like a prayer: I am here, if you will show yourselves to me. I wait.

But no longer has she the luxury to watch and wait. This is a photo of what Jane has lost.

Today it is as if Jane is paying penance for her years of bliss at Gombe. As if for each night she slept to the rhythm of Lake Tanganyika's lapping waves, she must endure the drone of another airplane engine carrying her to Washington or London or New York. As if for each hour she watched Flo tickling a youngster, or juveniles circling a tree in play, she must now dissect the words of some medical researcher at a congressional hearing who's outlining the need for more lab chimps. Once she groomed the hair of chimps she knew as personally as her own name; now she mainly visits chimps in laboratories, who hug themselves, rocking themselves insane, behind glass walls in autistic anonymity. Each face is a litany of pain. She remembers one small chimp in a lab cage so dark technicians used a flashlight to peer inside. Its eyes reminded her of those of a Burundi refugee boy she once met, whose family had been massacred; his stare was devoid of life or meaning.

Jane spends only a few weeks a year at Gombe these days. And when she does visit, she says, the place is mobbed by tourists: "I almost dread going back there in the summertime." Cameras click as she washes her hair in the lake. "I felt as if I were in her bathroom," one tourist confessed.

Even Jane's beloved Birches has become a purgatory, taunted by memories of a garden once filled with butterflies, where trucks and cars now roar behind the hedges, and the occasional airplane drowns out back-yard conversation.

For years, and some claim even decades, animal rights activists and conservation groups begged Jane to throw her fame behind efforts to protect chimps around the world. For although the chimpanzees of Gombe seemed safe in a national park, thousands of other wild chimps were being killed as pests or for food or, more often, so their infants could be captured to serve as stand-ins for humans in laboratory experiments or to amuse people at zoos or TV viewers.

Geza Teleki, who worked with Jane at Gombe in the 1960s, later set up a national park in Sierra Leone, West Africa. Before the park protected them, chimpanzees there were routinely shot to supply meat markets in neighboring Liberia. Thousands more disappeared into medical research labs. Geza knows that for every chimp delivered to an overseas buyer, five to ten are killed or die in transit. Local poachers who cannot afford bullets sometimes make buckshot from metal shards; many times they kill the infant intended for capture as well as the mother holding it in her arms.

At Gombe Geza had seen Jane haggard, worrying over the fate of individual chimpanzees. He knew how she had suffered during the polio epidemic, and he'd seen her grieve over the deaths of chimps who used to frequent her camp. But she was strangely unmoved by the plight of the nameless chimps of Sierra Leone.

"The fact that she would not get involved really disappointed me," Geza confesses. "I thought it was her responsibility, given her visibility. But she was very oriented toward individuals and very narrow about understanding general chimp problems. She knew everything about Gombe and nothing about chimps anywhere else."

For the past thirty years, capturing live chimpanzees has been a source of quick cash in poor African nations. The export market began with the entertainment industry and escalated with the increasing investment in biomedical research, beginning in the 1950s. Then civil wars put machine guns into hunters' hands, and many of Goodall's colleagues lost their study sites. By the 1970s chimpanzees were extinct in four of the twenty-five countries where they once ranged. Concern was so high that in 1976 chimpanzees were placed on the CITES (Convention on International Trade in Endangered Species) threatened list—one rung below endangered in the hierarchy of protection.

Dr. Shirley McGreal was another conservation activist who tried to talk Jane into speaking out. "Jane Goodall was the most popular and powerful voice for animals possibly in the world, yet she wouldn't speak out," she said. "It was very frustrating to us."

In her 1971 classic, *In the Shadow of Man*, Jane acknowledged the problem of poaching in a five-page chapter of the nearly three-hundred-page book. But she would not lend her name or testimony to fund-raising or publicity efforts to slow international traffic in infant chimpanzees; she could not be persuaded to talk to influential senators or congressmen about better conditions for captive chimps. When wild-eyed Dian Fossey was hunting down poachers and pestering ambassadors with gruesome photos of headless gorillas, Jane Goodall, always cool and poised, simply would not raise an unseemly fuss, for the chimpanzees of Gombe were safe.

Even longtime friends like Alan Root, the Nairobi-based wildlife photographer, were perplexed. "I mean, she is enormously concerned about individual chimps, but can't see the overall picture at all," he told an interviewer in 1985. "She's got tremendous international clout and so on, but in fact, conservation-wise, she is absolutely above all and her idea of looking after chimps is making sure the individuals she knows are healthy. It's very weird. She doesn't seem to be able to see that even her own bloody park is under tremendous threat [from potential poaching]. She just doesn't see beyond the individual groups that she studies."

Then came the transformation. It happened at a conference organized by Dr. Paul Heltne, director of the Chicago Academy of Sciences, in November 1986. The symposium coincided with the publication of what Jane calls "the Big Book" (*The Chimpanzees of Gombe: Patterns of Behavior*—the scientific compilation of her study results of the previous twenty-six years). The conference was titled "Understanding Chimpanzees," but the participants were less concerned with new instances of warfare or tool use than with the question whether there would be any wild chimpanzees left to study at all. "Everyone was appalled at how bad the situation was for chimps everywhere in the world," said Geza Teleki. "And she suddenly threw herself into the issue of protecting chimps, to an exhausting degree. Once she herself decides on something, she throws herself into it."

Jane explained simply: "I owe it to the chimps."

"It was as if Jane suddenly got religion," one friend said. That weekend she and several other scientists organized the Committee for the Conservation and Care of Chimpanzees (the "Four C's" she calls it), of which Geza is now chairman. The committee, backed by Jane's impressive reputation and public appeal, was to document, in exhaustive scientific detail, that chimps should be listed as an endangered species and thus given more international protection, and that their psychological and physical well-being should be assured when they are incarcerated in labs and zoos.

The committee churned out powerful documentation. Jane lobbied legislators and bureaucrats in Washington, wrote opinion pieces for publications such as the *New York Times*, and toured medical laboratories where chimpanzees were being infected with human diseases. She called press conferences and made a spate of TV appearances focusing on the issue: "The Donahue Show," "Nightline," "Good Morning America," "National Geographic Explorer," "Nature Watch." Her lectures took up the new theme. Her trips to Washington from London and Dar es Salaam increased from one or two per year to eight or ten.

Meanwhile her visits to Gombe were repeatedly postponed; her summer 1989 trip was delayed three times in two months. Fifi's newest baby was more than a month old before she had a chance to name it, sight unseen, and more than two months old before her staff learned that the little male would be called Faustino. He was named after Princess Genevieve di San Faustino, who dreamed up the idea of the Jane Goodall Institute in the 1970s; but the name — "little Faust" — was an ominous one.

Some animal rights activists are still angry that Jane didn't jump into the fray earlier. Jane would rather not analyze the reasons for her previous silence. "I was very isolated in Tanzania, living my own little life, watching the chimps and writing about them; selfish in a way," she admits. "I've often thought, well, I should feel guilty that I wasn't in it long ago," she says.

After decades of studying chimps in the wild, Jane
now has taken on the task of bettering conditions for
chimpanzees held captive in laboratories and zoos.
Steve Matthews

For the happiness of animals had concerned Jane since her
early childhood. As a little girl, she would walk neighbors' dogs
when she considered they weren't getting enough exercise. She
formed a nature club with her sister and two other girls, then
organized a museum in the family greenhouse, to which she
charged admission; the fees were donated to a society that rescued old horses from butchers and put them out to graze. As
an adult, when Jane watched wildebeest kills on the Serengeti
with Hugo, tears would pour down her face.

Yet for decades Jane was haunted by her failure of courage
in an incident during her childhood. She was moved to confess
it in her 1988 children's book, *My Life with the Chimpanzees*:

> When I was about your age, I once saw four boys, much bigger
> than I was, pulling the legs off crabs. I was very upset. I asked
> them why they did it, and they said, "None of your business." I
> told them it was cruel. They laughed. And I went away. Now,

forty years later, I am still ashamed of myself. Why didn't I try harder to stop them from tormenting those crabs?

Her own son, at age five, was braver, she continued: when he saw a seven-year-old boy at a nursery school hosing a terrified rabbit in its cage, Grub tried to pull the hose from his hands. When the boy wouldn't let go, Grub fought him and won. The nursery school teacher, Jane remembered, punished Grub, not the other boy. "But Grub," Jane wrote, "even though he was punished, knew he had done the right thing. He had stopped the tormenting of the rabbit."

Should Jane have spoken out on behalf of chimpanzees earlier? Perhaps, she muses. "On the other hand, publishing [*The Chimpanzees of Gombe*] gave me the credibility that maybe I would have lacked in scientific circles. I think in fact that destiny determined the exact right moment to launch myself into it. I could not have done the book *and* this."

But one cannot help but wonder if she remained silent for so long because she knew what speaking out would cost her.

In the early days Jane and Hugo sometimes hid bananas under their shirts to feed their friends at a convenient time. Of course it took no time for the chimps to figure this out. Hugo once snapped a wonderful photo of Jane standing at the edge of the forest as a squatting chimp peers up her safari shirt. Jane, a few wisps of blond hair loose from her ponytail, in a balletic, casual posture — left knee bent, right arm angled behind her curved back — looks down at the ape with a faint smile, as it lifts the cloth of her shirt so gently, delicately, by the tip of the third finger of the left hand, more tenderly than a groom lifts the wedding veil from his bride's face. Such care, such grace, from a being confronted with her terrible human vulnerability.

If she then could have had a vision of her 1988 visit to the chimpanzees of IMMUNO, she would have dismissed it as a demented nightmare.

She looked as if she'd been swallowed by the Michelin Man. A movie camera filmed as she waddled down the antiseptic halls of the chimpanzee research lab run by the Austrian drug company IMMUNO, clad in a bulky white contamination suit, peering out through a rectangular plastic face mask the size of a small TV. The suit was equipped with its own purified air supply.

In hospitals and hospices, doctors and nurses care for infectious patients with only rubber gloves and cloth face masks between them and disease. But at IMMUNO the researchers insulate themselves from toes to fingers, from heart to head; in a ritual of awe in the face of horror, they assume the shape of monsters to even look upon the monstrosity they have created. They have infected these six chimps—each isolated from the others by cement and steel—with the human AIDS virus.

Jane's first visit to a medical research lab took place in March 1987, when she went to SEMA, in Rockville, Maryland, which is funded by the National Institutes of Health (NIH). She'd already seen a film of what was inside. An animal rights group called True Friends had broken into the lab with a hand-held video camera to tape the feces-spattered floor, the frantically circling monkeys, the sound of flesh hitting metal as the chimps rocked in their tiny isolation chambers—22 by 22 by 24 inches. A three-year-old female, a toddler, screamed in terror. An older male, tattooed on the chest with the number 1164, mumbled silently to himself, expressionless, his lips slack. Images like these permeate Jane's dreams. When she's awake, they lap at the edge of her consciousness as the waves of Lake Tanganyika lick the shores of Gombe.

Using the film as a basis, Jane wrote an affidavit deploring the conditions. When the director of the lab dismissed her criticisms as based on second-hand information, she went to see for herself. She asked to be shown the little female who was filmed screaming. The youngster was taken out, she said, "to show all her screaming was not for real."

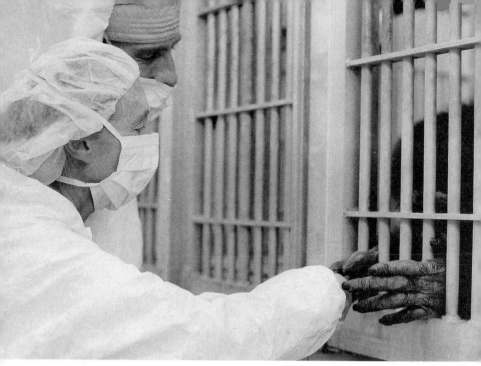

Jane reaches out to JoJo, an adult male chimpanzee captive at the Laboratory for Experimental Medicine and Surgery in Primates. *Susan Farley*

Jane relates this, crumpled in a chair by the curtained window of her room at the Mayflower Hotel on Central Park in New York. She suffers from insomnia. Her jaw still aches from recent dental work. She is exhausted from the morning's taping of the "20-20" show. She does not yet know she is coming down with pneumonia. Her brown eyes look distant, blank. "And it was far worse to see what did happen to her," Jane says quietly. "She was just lifted out by her keeper, she sat in his arms, and she was put back. There was no expression, no change, no fear, or pleasure at seeing her keeper. I shall be haunted forever by her eyes."

Not all the facilities that house research chimps are this awful. Jane is quick to credit the more humane labs. One of them is LEMSIP, New York University's Laboratory for Experimental

Medicine and Surgery in Primates, which she visited in 1988. Dr. James Mahoney, who is an advisory member of CCCC, works here, and he escorted Jane first to the nursery, where six diapered infant chimps played on a jungle gym. The floor has a carpet, the rooms have windows, and the babies enjoy constant human companionship.

Then they visited the bare windowless rooms where the adult experimental chimps live. "I got just inside the door," Jane wrote in the Fall/Winter 1988–89 newsletter of the Jane Goodall Institute. "The noise was deafening. The chimps, the appalling monotony of the day broken at an unexpected moment, were excited to see Jim, their friend. They called out and shook the bars of their prisons and beat on the floors and walls." Once they quieted down, Jim Mahoney introduced Jane to JoJo, a beautiful, gentle adult male. "In his eyes, I read gratitude because I had stopped to talk," Jane wrote. "It seemed to me there was no resentment, only puzzlement. Why was the world so strange and grim? Jim moved on to talk to the others . . . And there I was with JoJo, looking into his clear sad eyes."

With the bars between her and the chimp, into her mind seeped the images of the Gombe chimps she loved: their comfortable nests, the cool forest, their delight at finding a weaver ant nest or, with excited pant-hoots, announcing their discovery of a tree laden with beautiful fruit. Tears ran from her eyes into the face mask she had to wear to keep from infecting the research chimps with the wrong disease. JoJo stared at her intently. He reached a black hand through the bars. He touched the wetness on her cheek, sniffed its scent, and then licked her tears from his finger.

"When Jane is in the States, there's no release, ever," says Geza Teleki. "The world of chimpanzee promotion takes over. She has interviews at breakfast, and television interviews, and writing, and then a lecture, and then dinner. It's a horrible schedule. She's constantly inundated."

In one fifty-two-day visit to the United States in 1987, she passed through fourteen cities, delivered twelve lectures, visited six zoos and one lab, organized a major conference for the next spring, and gave seven big press conferences, seven major TV interviews, two seminars, and five dinner talks. All this was done without the help of even one private secretary.

"We set up fifteen senators for her to talk to on one trip," Geza continues. "Most people would take months to get an appointment with a senator. But we set this all up in two weeks. Because they want to talk to Jane Goodall. They want to hear stories about Flo."

After her transformation, Jane read everything available on chimpanzees in medical labs. She became an expert on the AIDS virus and the intricacies of hepatitis vaccine—another major use for lab chimps is in testing this vaccine, since they are the only animal besides man whose bodies can host the virus. Three years ago she knew nothing of any of this. Today she is an expert on virology, she can tell you the estimated number of chimps remaining in any African country, and she can quote chapter and verse from any law on the books dealing with animal welfare.

But this is not why she is so welcome in senators' offices when she comes to ask them a favor. This is not why 54,000 Americans wrote to the U.S. Fish and Wildlife Service in support of the petition to upgrade chimps' status to endangered in 1988—the most public participation in an endangered species issue ever. Her crusade is effective because she is a master storyteller, and the characters in her stories are so powerful and so real that they can move an audience to tears.

While politicians and biomedical researchers debate standards for "animal technicians" and how to "manage important breeding resources," Jane speaks from another perspective. People listen to her because she is talking about individuals: chimps with histories and motives, who have fantasies and dreams, who mourn their dead and enjoy a good joke.

Mary Smith, Jane's friend and editor at *National Geographic*, calls it "star quality": her terrific grace, her self-assurance, her soothing English voice.

Of course, Biruté and Dian told wonderful stories, too. Their study animals—Supinah and Digit, Ralph and Uncle Bert, Siswoyo and Macho, are individuals as steeped in character as Flo and Fifi and David Graybeard. But perhaps the reason that Jane's stories move us the most is that her stories are so intertwined with our own.

Jane's own family drama unfolded along with the chimps': on National Geographic specials, we watched the infant Flint take his first uncertain steps right along with Jane's toddling son, Grub. Dian lived out her lone life on the mountain; Biruté chose a life in Indonesia, forsaking Western custom and protocols. But Jane was always one of "us": her Westernness stands out like a porcelain teacup on a rough-hewn tree stump. Hers was the story with the familiar, fairy-tale elements: the intrepid blonde marries a baron and produces a golden-haired son. Hers was the choice we felt was most comfortable and, well, respectable. It is the weight of her whole life, and her persona, that she brings to bear on the plight of chimpanzees jammed into tiny cages. Their fate, she tells us, is in our hands.

It is impossible for even her most vocal critics to lump Jane with the "humaniacs"—those animal rights activists who often come off sounding shrill and moralistic. Jane is too reasoned for that. She is attuned to medicine's urgency in its quest to ease human suffering; after all, she lost her second husband to cancer and her mother owes her life to a bioplasticized pig valve in her heart. "If you stopped all animal research now— bang—that would lead to extra human suffering," she freely acknowledges. But she rejects any rationale that pits humans who have benefited from medical advances against the welfare of animals. "These are the people I want on my side," she says. "They owe animals their lives, and they're the very people, if you approach them right, who would push to get more money for the humane care of the animals who have given them their lives."

And Jane knows how to approach these people. Her opponents' statistics and abstractions crumple before the concrete, the immediate, the individual. Veterinarian Thomas Wolfle, formerly of the NIH, said it would cost too much to provide laboratory primates with the improvements — larger cages, comfortable bedding, compassionate care givers — that Jane suggests. Jane answered (with the voice of reason): "Look at your car. Look at your house. Look at your office, look at your administration building, look at the holidays you take — and then tell me that you want to deprive these animals, whom we use for our own good, of just a little bit more space, just a little bit more care and compassion."

The Jane Goodall Institute for Wildlife Research, Education and Conservation in Tucson organizes Jane's grueling schedule. The institute, incorporated in 1977, was at first a rather loosely organized collection of friends and admirers, a sort of fan club. If you joined, you got a handsome pin and a newsletter written largely by Jane, and you could buy her books. Now posters and T-shirts are available.

Today JGI, with more than 3,000 members, is a powerful force in promoting chimpanzee survival and welfare; the CCCC is a formidable lobbying arm. Jane's lectures alone generate about $150,000 a year, all of which goes to Gombe, the CCCC, and the running of the institute. The institute's stated purpose is to support the research center at Gombe and educate people about chimps and chimp conservation. Recently it has made available to schools sophisticated and well-organized teaching aids and information packets; and it has launched a research program called ChimpanZoo, in which captive chimps at zoos are studied using the same observation methods as are used in Jane's Gombe research.

But the institute's unstated purpose is to protect Jane. It seems that she has always inspired this emotion; in spite of her accomplishments, her poise before audiences, and her demonstrated physical stamina, she exudes an air of vulnerability: "I would always worry about her," said Emilie Bergman-Riss, the sturdy and kind Dutch girl who in December 1972, at age twenty-two, became Gombe's camp manager and worked there until July 1975. "Although I hardly ever see her now, I still have that feeling." Even Dian Fossey, nearly crippled with emphysema and nearly bankrupt, felt this way about her famous colleague. After picking Jane up at a New York airport, Dian wrote to Vanne: "I felt as if I were picking up a poor, wounded pigeon."

One reason people worry about Jane is her British reserve. "You never quite know: Is she sick? Is she tired? Does she have malaria?" said Emilie. "She never complains, and is a private person. Even if she becomes angry, she only becomes more quiet. She doesn't confront you."

There are other reasons to worry about Jane. For one thing, she doesn't eat. ("You don't want to be a guest in her house," warns Geza. "She doesn't eat and you don't either. If you're lucky, she might bring out a couple of boiled eggs for you after a couple of days.") She also gets sick a lot. Though there are few mosquitoes at Gombe, when they do bite they almost invariably transmit malaria. Jane cannot count the number of times she's had this disease. And, like the chimps, she often gets pneumonia.

Institute staff try to protect Jane, with a polite ferocity born of loyalty bordering on reverence. At least one and sometimes several institute members accompany her on all her lecture tours, staying in her hotel. (But seldom does a single staff member accompany her for a whole tour — "the long haul" the staff call it. It's simply too grueling. They switch off like a relay team. And though institute staffers are always excited at Jane's arrival, after she leaves the country, often for a similar tour in Europe, everyone in the office is physically and emotionally spent. "It takes us about a week to recover from one of Jane's visits," confides Judy Johnson, the institute's former executive director.)

Like policewomen, they inform interviewers before Jane appears that she is very tired; and they let you know in no uncertain terms when your time with Jane is up. They screen her telephone calls. Friends trying to reach Jane through the institute say it's like trying to get into Fort Knox. Nor is it easy to get Jane on the speaker's podium. The Massachusetts Society for the Prevention of Cruelty to Animals, which cosponsored animal welfare legislation she proposed and publicized her crusade, wanted to make Jane their 1989 Humanitarian of the Year; but they couldn't afford the $15,000 the institute told them she would have to charge to deliver the acceptance speech.

Since the institute was founded, Jane's public status has been elevated from celebrity to dignitary. Heather McGiffin, a longtime friend, recalls a reception held before a lecture Jane was delivering at the Smithsonian. It was like a private gallery showing, with Jane as the prized artwork, held "for people who had money."

The reception was held at the Castle, the Smithsonian's original Gothic brownstone building. "It was very plush. They had one of their high-backed thronelike chairs set up for Jane. Two men were standing on either side of her to protect her. And Jane walks in with this evening gown on, up to here [above the throat] down to there [tips of wrists] and down to there [over the shoes]. She walks to this chair, sits down, looks around here, and now people are allowed to go up and say how much they adore her. It was almost weird."

Jane's fame has engendered some resentment among academic and conservation groups, which are forever scrambling for publicity and scarce research and conservation dollars. The director of one conservation organization points out: "Dian's organization was named after an individual animal. Biruté's is named after the species she studies. Jane's organization is called the Jane

Goodall Institute. Don't you think that says something about her?"

Jane's recent crusade has pitted her directly against many of her colleagues—researchers who study primates and disease in medical laboratories or who explore their psychology in experiments using punishments like electric shocks or sensory or social deprivation. She cites many of these studies in the second chapter of the Big Book, and researchers have quoted her work extensively in their own published papers. Once they were on the same side, fellow explorers in pursuit of human knowledge. But today Jane sneers at that kind of science, "Science with a capital S."

Just when the Big Book, like a merit badge, had earned her the scientific credibility her popular articles lacked, Jane's opponents began to portray her as antiscience. "What Goodall is opposed to," says Frederick King, who heads the Yerkes Regional Primate Research Center in Atlanta, "is keeping animals in cages. If you want to study diseases, you must have periods of time when they are kept in isolation."

Jane needs no protection from these barbs; she says they only strengthen her resolve. The only thing that could really crush her is something neither her institute staff nor her mentors at National Geographic nor her closest friends or family can protect her from: the crusade that chose her. The enormity of her task stretches out before her like a yawning abyss.

"The feeling has been expressed that if Jane gets her way with chimps, that's the thin edge of the wedge," she told reporters gathered at a press conference. "Next, they say, she's going to want to improve conditions for monkeys and dogs and all the other animals.

"You bet I do."

It would be inaccurate to portray Jane's life now as a joyless string of meetings, lectures, and plane rides. The human species may be arrogant, but Jane finds great joy in its individuals.

"She makes friends with every taxi driver, every bellman, every maid," said Beverly Marker, a former institute staffer who has accompanied Jane on lecture tours. "And she always says, 'Those are such wonderful people. George's daughter just loves animals; so and so's son is sick; that cab driver sure cheered up.' "

Her son is a source of delight. In *My Life with the Chimpanzees*, she wrote, "Suppose someone else asks me: What have you contributed to the world?" The first of her answers was, "Well, I have raised a wonderful son."

Grub, at twenty-two, is healthy, handsome, intelligent. After his first adult appearance on TV, on "The Donahue Show" with his mother, the institute's switchboard was jammed with calls from teenage girls wanting to know his address. For Jane he's a lot of fun to be around. During a New York stop on a recent lecture tour, Grub and Jane couldn't get adjoining rooms at the Barbizon Hotel. To make light of the situation Grub ordered take-out food, and from his room on the thirteenth floor, directly above hers, he pieced together luggage straps to create a rope (he'd asked the maid for a real rope, but she refused to be party to a hanging) and lowered her lunch out his window down to dangle outside her room on the twelfth floor.

And there is Gombe to return to, waiting for her like a lover's promise.

"In that environment, with the chimps around me, I find the spiritual strength to battle in the States." She begins a National Geographic lecture with these words, like an incantation.

Each visit to Gombe is, for Jane, a family reunion. In the summer of 1988 her staff told her the chimps had been roaming to the north of their traditional range for the past three days. But her first day back she found them in the home valley, which takes its name and nourishment from Kakombe Stream, which Jane also drinks from. The chimps—the "big group," headed by alpha male Goblin, whom Jane first met the day after his birth in 1964—were plucking ripe figs from the trees near the waterfall, hooting and barking with excitement.

As her subject for the day's observations, Jane chose Fifi, the daughter of her beloved old Flo. Fifi, who as a youngster so loved babies she would try to steal them from their mothers' arms, now has her wish fulfilled: she has proved as gentle and playful a mother to her own two daughters, five-year-old Flossi and nine-year-old Fanni, as the venerable old Flo was to her children.

Flossi is playing a chasing game with Tita, Patti's young daughter. Fanni scraps with young Gimble, Melissa's surviving twin. Darbie, who was orphaned in the pneumonia epidemic of 1987, grooms with the big, sterile female, Gigi. Goblin grooms Kidevu as Kidevu's five-year-old son, Konrad, briefly suckles.

Soon Gigi comes to Jane's side; Evered, an adult male, joins her. The two chimps groom each other until Evered sleeps. Gigi stretches out beside Jane and closes her eyes. Everything is perfect; the midday heat, filtering through the forest canopy, bathes an Eden of tranquility, peace, and trust.

But for Jane, there is no escape. The sound of flesh hitting metal in a laboratory half a world away drowns out the birdsong. Where there is soft earth, she sees cold steel. As she pauses in her note taking, the images before her blur.

9 Sorceress: The Madness of Dian Fossey

THE headline read: DIAN FOSSEY ASKED FOR IT.

Shortly after Fossey's murder the *Philadelphia Daily News* ran this banner over an opinion piece by wildlife researcher Nina Stoyan. "Dian Fossey was murdered by an unknown assailant," she wrote, "but her story survives as a dramatic example of means which did not justify the end."

"Obsessed conservationists" who put animals' needs before humans', Stoyan wrote, alienate local people from their conservation projects and do more harm than good. Dian Fossey, she concluded, "certainly asked for it, because she alienated, insulted and injured the very object lesson to all she needed. . . . Not surprisingly, arrogance will get conservationists nowhere."

Like a Greek chorus, many in the wildlife conservation community echoed the opinion. "She got what she wanted," Kelly Stewart, a former student of Dian's, told a reporter. "She viewed herself as this warrior fighting an enemy that was out to get her. . . . It was a perfect ending. It was exactly how she would have ended the script."

Dian's antipoaching patrols confiscated and destroyed
thousands of poachers' snares, bows, and spears.
Bob Campbell © National Geographic

"It was only a matter of time," said Diana McMeekin of the
African Wildlife Foundation. "Dian's usefulness to the gorillas
stopped at least five years before her death. The woman lost it
very severely. She couldn't get away with that kind of behavior.
And she didn't."

"She got killed," said former student Bill Weber, "because she
was behaving like Dian Fossey."

Dian called her strategy "active conservation": it included
funding her own "army" of antipoaching scouts, torturing
poachers, burning their possessions, and kidnaping their children. At first when she corraled illegally grazing cattle and destroyed poachers' snares, she could argue that she was only
enforcing her host country's laws. But as poachers' spears and
snares claimed animals she knew by name, her war grew private and personal, fired by fury and a terrorist's zeal. She was

no longer simply thwarting the poachers; she was punishing them.

When Dian wrote to her friend Richard Wrangham in November 1976, her anger had congealed into hate. In the letter she described an "ordinary day" at Karisoke: at eleven A.M. five park guards brought her a Batwa poacher who specialized in killing gorillas and elephants. "We stripped him and spread eagled him outside my cabin and lashed the holy blue sweat out of him with nettle stalks and leaves, concentrating on the places where it might hurt a mite. Wow, I never knew such little fellows had such big things. . . . I then went through the ordinary 'sumu,' black magic routine of Mace, ether, needles and masks, ended with sleeping pills. . . . That is called 'conservation'—not talk."

Students' and colleagues' tales of her cruelty gather momentum with each telling, like ghost stories that grow more gruesome with each campfire: mock hangings, poachers injected with gorilla dung, Halloween-masked raids. One student says Dian administered mind-altering drugs to a poacher. When the man recovered, she allegedly said to him: "I have taken away your mind. Next time I won't give it back."

Not even Jane Goodall, who considered Dian a dear friend, could publicly defend such tactics. The best she could offer was an attempt at excusing them. Jane did not attend the memorial fund-raiser at National Geographic after Dian's death, but she did send a taped message: "It's probably true that Dian chose wrongly when she decided to take the law into her own hands, to try to fight the poachers by herself. And yet she felt this way was the only way to try to put right the terrible wrongs that she saw being done. But who are we to blame her? I don't know how I would react if there were poachers threatening the chimps at Gombe."

"I warned her," Jane later told a reporter. "Everybody who was fond of her did. But she didn't want to listen to things like that. She was a law unto herself."

Dian's death, as many see it, was the sum of a neat equation.

By imposing her own laws on a sovereign nation, by making enemies of local people instead of friends, by caring more about gorillas than people, Dian was just as responsible for her death as the person who wielded the panga that split her skull.

But Biruté Galdikas, as an anthropologist, offers a different explanation: "Dian was very, very African. That's the only reason she survived as a lone, white woman on the mountain for nineteen years. She was doing what an African would have done in the same situation.

"What killed Dian," says Biruté, "was Africa."

One day, only two years into her study, Dian's staff reported hearing the wailing of a cow in pain. Dian went to investigate and found an adult bull buffalo wedged in the forked trunk of a *Hagenia* tree. But poachers had heard the sound first. While the animal was still living, they had hacked off its hind legs for meat. They left it there, bellowing in agony, trying to stand on the stumps, drenched in blood and dung. When it saw her approaching, it snorted in defiance.

Dian, weeping, shot the bull in the head. She wept at the animal's pain. She wept at the Africans' cruelty in leaving it in this condition. She wept at the animal's courage in the face of its agony. But an African, unless his tribal heritage had been modified by Western education, would have laughed.

Here is an African joke: an epidemic swept through a village, and everyone who could move left. Two old, dying men, weak with disease, were left behind with the bodies of the dead, which attracted scavengers and predators. One day a leopard came. It walked up to one of the dying men, easy prey. The man's companion was too weak to chase the leopard away, but he did cry out, trying to deflect the attack.

The punchline of this joke is the victim's retort to his friend's effort to help. His dying words were "So what?"

The Ju/Wa San, or Bushmen, of Namibia told this story to

John Marshall—and it is true, they say—amid peals of laughter. Few Westerners would find this story funny. Yet many Africans think the futility of the man's effort to save a doomed companion is the height of wit.

A Belgian who has worked in Rwanda for twenty-five years once told me, "The Africans, they are very nice, they are very smart, but you must remember: we are not the same as them. They are not like you and me."

Once this man visited the area reputed to be the source of the Nile and found people there diving into a deep pool. One diver never came up; only bubbles rose where he had dived. After five minutes, the Belgian was alarmed and insisted on informing the authorities. He drove to the police station, but no one wanted to investigate. The police told him there was a whirlpool at the bottom of the spring, and that this was the tenth report of a person drowning there that day—and these were only the *reported* deaths. The Belgian asked if he should go back to retrieve the dead man's clothes, to return them to his relatives. The police asked, "How long ago did you leave?" And he replied, "Fifteen minutes ago." "Well," the police said, "you're about ten minutes too late." Nobody even looked for the missing diver—not even his companions, who minutes before had been diving there beside him.

From the struggles of a wounded animal trying to free itself from a snare, to the tragedy of a drowned diver, the African response is almost universally the same. Life is cruel, pain is rampant. "So what?"

"Our ideas about altruism are pretty far from these people's ideas," says Robinson McIlvaine, a former director of the African Wildlife Foundation, who lived in Africa for fifteen years. "It's a cruel life in the bush. They're used to the fact that everything can disappear in a storm or a coup, that famine can destroy everything. Life is cheap. So you grab what you can."

He recalls a conversation he once had with the president of

Guinea (who, says McIlvaine, "had some admirable qualities even though he was a dictator"). McIlvaine was discussing his ideas for helping polio victims and supplying medicines to the elderly. The president was incredulous. He replied to the American, "we can't devote any of our scant resources to take care of the old and handicapped."

"You put that into the light of [Americans] redoing buses so wheelchairs can board," says McIlvaine, "and you see it's a different world in Africa."

It is a world where one in ten babies dies before its first birthday and is likely to be buried in an unmarked grave, without ceremony. Among the Akamba people of Kenya, a newborn is considered not human but an object belonging to the spirits until it has survived for four days.

In Africa small children are made to guard cattle against lions, and the safety of the cattle—a form of currency among tribes like Rwanda's Tutsi and Kenya's Masai—is given greater emphasis than the safety of the children in the village's communal prayers. It is a world where teenagers are often subjected to days of brutal torture in initiation ceremonies. Among the Nandi of Kenya, if a girl cries or screams when her clitoris is ripped out during her initiation ceremony, her relatives may kill her for her cowardice. Merciless tribal wars erupt with the regularity and virulence of recurrent malaria, and each member of the tribe is taught from childhood to face pain and death with neither fear nor pity.

And Africa is a world of personal vengeance. Rosamond Carr, Dian's American friend in Gisenyi, tells how, less than a year before Dian's death, an African friend named Valentine—a driver for the American ambassador—exposed another driver for selling American embassy gasoline on the black market. When the man was fired, he yelled at Valentine, "I'll kill you! I'll kill you for this!"

A few weeks later Valentine was riding his motorcycle on a

Sunday morning when the man, driving a minibus, chased Valentine and struck him down at high speed. Valentine lay crumpled on the road; the man backed the van up and ran him over, crushing him to death.

Tried and convicted in a Kigali courtroom, the man was out of prison in eighteen months. But few Africans expect courtrooms to mete out justice, and according to the religious beliefs of most Africans, God does not punish in the afterlife. Justice can be a very personal affair.

Ian Redmond remembers a conversation he had with one of the Africans who worked at Karisoke: "He said to me that he didn't understand how Wazungu [whites] sorted out their differences with people. He said, 'If you get angry with someone, you can hit them, and if you really get angry with them, you can kill them. What about all the in-between? We can poison someone for a week; we can make them ill for a month; we can make them die a slowly lingering death. And there are all these different things we can do to someone with witchcraft. But the Europeans have only a simple-minded approach: hit someone or kill someone. There is no middle ground.' "

Dian was typically, even exaggeratedly Western in her attitude toward children and animals. She adored kids; she treated poachers' children, and even their dogs, with great tenderness. In a land where animals are valued only for food or skins, she sided with the gorillas and duiker and buffalo. But in her "active conservation," she adopted the tactics and philosophy of an African.

After she shot the mutilated buffalo, Dian wrote a friend that the experience had "done something to me that I didn't think possible. Now I am finding myself out to avenge the cruelty of the Tutsi," she wrote. Before that she would only try to scatter them, shooting above, below, or near the herds. Now she was crippling the cattle, pumping bullets into their hind legs.

"Obviously this makes me no better than the Tutsi who hacked off the hind legs of the buffalo," Dian realized. But her tactics, at least initially, worked—the cattle disappeared from the area.

Dian proved capable of matching African standards of vengeance. Her use of stinging nettles as implements of torture— a concept that particularly horrifies Westerners—was borrowed directly from African tradition. The Nandi use nettles to whip the breasts and genitals of female initiates the night before their circumcision. When Dian arrived in Rwanda, whipping prisoners with nettles was legally sanctioned as punishment throughout the country.

But she did not stop at inflicting physical punishment. As her fury smoldered, Dian incarnated a new persona: the avenging sorceress.

She painted hexes, cast spells, pronounced curses. She spent hundreds of dollars on realistic masks and carefully rehearsed her "raids" on Rosamond Carr's African staff before springing upon the poachers: "I am the Goddess of the Mountain," she would hiss in KiSwahili, "and I will avenge you for killing my children." It was a vow she later swore on the soul of Digit.

Faking the supernatural is an old colonial trick; to convince Africans of their mythical powers, early explorers would do everything from discharging firearms to pulling out their false teeth. But Dian's ventures into witchcraft were more than a trick; they became a sacred rite. She took to performing a private ritual, burning small amounts of money, the way Africans often burn meat to appease the spirits of their living dead.

Several times Dian was the target of spells and hexes. After she discovered that her hair was being systematically collected for such spells, she was frightened enough to assiduously clean her hairbrush daily, a habit she kept up even when in the United States. There is evidence that she knew, as Africans know, that witchcraft works. She had seen at least one man in her camp

die as a result of witchcraft. Her friend Rosamond Carr sometimes employs a Congolese-born Hutu tribesman to stop hail-
storms, using an animal horn and a spoon.

Westerners scoff at witchcraft, but in Africa it is considered
a force as powerful and immediate as wind and rain, as real as
the scars of tribal markings. Within the past fifteen years the
Kenyan government has hired rainmakers to end drought; after
a flood Tanzanian officials have jailed rainmakers. Rwandan
hospitals frequently refer patients to local witch doctors. But as
magic can bring rain and health, it can also bring death. Geza
Teleki, while working to set up a wildlife reserve in Sierra Leone,
was sentenced to death by a witch doctor who pointed the left
foreleg bone of an aardvark at him. "This meant I was to die
within twenty-four hours," Geza said. "It was the moral equivalent of murder. As far as they were concerned, I was a dead
man."

That Geza failed to die was considered a sort of miracle; it
was concluded that he must therefore be not man but spirit,
wielding an even more powerful witchcraft himself. "Anything
that happened was always believed the result of witchcraft," he
said. Geza carefully guarded this image. When he received the
news that his father had died, "one of my main concerns was
to show no sign of being troubled, because they would have said
immediately that this had been arranged by the local witch doctors."

Ian Redmond says Dian's war against poachers was, like
witchcraft, largely psychological. She would spit on them, rub
gorilla dung on their bodies, hurl threats and insults with the
force of a club. But Ian, who worked with Dian for more than
two years, says he never saw her strike anyone, though she never
stopped the Rwandan park guards from doing so.

Likewise, during the more than four hundred days that Bill
Weber and Amy Vedder worked at Karisoke, they never saw
any poacher physically abused. Kelly Stewart relates that Dian

forced barbiturates down the throats of poachers and injected them with gorilla dung, but they are events she admits she did not witness. She was told about them by Dian.

Dian often wrote letters to colleagues describing her methods of punishing poachers and spoke about them to friends over the phone. Former Leakey Foundation president Ned Munger says Dian told him that she woke in the night to boil water to pour on a poacher's binding ropes to tighten the knots; she described to him an interrogation in which she lent a knife to her men to hasten a confession.

But Dian also describes in her book scenes that eyewitnesses say were overdramatized. Her own affidavit counters her book's account of her "capture" in Zaire. In her diary excerpts, published in Farley Mowat's *Woman in the Mists*, former staff members find discrepancies — in names, dates, reported conversations — compared to their own field diaries. It is possible that many of the unwitnessed atrocities Dian described herself perpetrating never really happened. Diana McMeekin, of the African Wildlife Foundation, concedes that "there is an element of exaggeration in the stories about Dian. But the stories were exaggerations on the theme of truth."

The stories, well known in the villages below Karisoke, are almost universally believed — as Dian doubtless willed it. Giving voice and print to cruelties she never inflicted may well have been her attempt to give her hate a reality that she could not act out. There is no doubt that she wanted to: she wrote to her Louisville "family," the Schwartzels, about the Twa poacher whose T-shirt was splattered with Digit's blood: "I wanted so badly to torture him to death," she wrote.

Like the death curses uttered by witch doctors, like the punishments inflicted on effigies by practitioners of voodoo, Dian's voicing and printing of her wishes fed her hate with power. That the stories, true or not, were imbued with belief made them as potently fearful as pointing the left foreleg bone of an aardvark.

Whether Dian merely allowed or directed Rwandan park
guards to punish poachers in traditionally African ways, or
whether she herself regularly added knife and noose and nar-
cotics to the torture—still the question remains, as demanding
as a fist pounding a table: what right had this American woman
to frighten and torture Africans who had, legally or illegally,
lived on this land for hundreds of thousands of years? What did
she think she was doing?

"She was applying African justice to the situation," answers
Leonard J. Grant of the National Geographic Society.

Rwandan officials did not object particularly to Dian's treatment
of poachers. A former director of parks, Dismas Nsabimana,
enthusiastically applauded her setting fire to the matting inside
a poacher's hut. He said she should have burned down the entire
village. At a meeting with two of Rwandan President Juvenal
Habyarimana's top staffers, the Rwandans agreed with Dian
that Digit's killers, once found, should be put to death—though
they argued that hanging would be more appropriate than shooting. What angered some authorities, according to surviving rec-
ords of Dian's correspondence with them, were the occasions
when she deflected money from their pockets—by driving away
tourists, for example—or portrayed them in articles and films
as incompetent in protecting the gorillas.

But Western reaction to Dian's tactics came swift as a gag
reflex. Most of her students recoiled from the force of her rage.
One threw her pistol into the forest. Most refused to carry guns.
Many left within days of their arrival.

Many of them were Peace Corps volunteers, college students
whose older siblings had marched in civil rights protests. They
had come to Africa with Western, liberal ideals of equality,
human dignity, and the power of logical reasoning and good
will. One Peace Corps volunteer showed up with a marvelous
plan: he would teach the poachers, who had lived for centuries
by stealth and spear, to raise rabbits instead.

Dian, who was politically conservative, sneered at the "Peach Core types" and their "rose-colored glasses" view of the world. The match was wrong from the start. They were about people and peace. Dian was about animals and war.

Conservation fund-raising leaflets often liken conservation battles to war. But it has long been politely agreed that this is really only a war of words, fought with paperwork and policies and public relations. The "artillery" is launched by diplomatic pouch from one suit-and-tie capital to another: money and plans for development and education are the weapons these diplomats wield. The enemy is a faceless attitude or principle or a practice taking place far away; the "victims" are concepts—species, not individuals. Many in Nairobi and Washington privately admit they thought Dian was insane.

Dian's was a real war, hand-to-hand combat, with blood and bullets, hate and hostages. Poachers bearing spears and arrows were leaping over her tent pegs; they were killing gorillas she knew by name; they set fire to the wall of her kitchen, left hexes along her paths, speared one of her students, poisoned her parrots, kidnaped her dog. One visitor was nearly crushed to death by a poacher's log-drop trap, and Dian herself fell into a pit trap. She did not have time to craft "resource management plans" or wait patiently for diplomatic pressure to bring new laws to pass. Only 480 mountain gorillas were alive in the park when Dian arrived in Rwanda, and by 1985, according to her count, only 260 were left. Dian had come to know 88 of them personally and by name. Six had died at the hands of poachers, two had been captured for the Cologne Zoo. "It takes one bullet, one trap, one poacher to kill a duiker, a buffalo, a gorilla, an elephant," Dian wrote to Ian in 1983. Only well-equipped patrols, she wrote, could preserve the animals remaining in the park.

Her initial opposition to gorilla tourism—which she later reversed—was dismissed by other conservationists as shortsighted. Interestingly, this is a criticism often leveled at Africans.

The Ugandan philosopher and scholar John S. Mbiti carried out a study of East African languages; none of the languages he studied contained words or expressions to convey a future more than a few months away. The African concept of time, Mbiti explains, actually proceeds backward from the present — *sasa* in KiSwahili — to the past, or *zamani*, the time of the ancestors, to which the dead return. In a land with no winter, there has never been much need to plan far ahead for a future that, unlike the present or past, was never experienced. "You do not plan in Africa," says Geza Teleki. "You react."

The Mountain Gorilla Project began largely as a reaction. In 1978, only months after the murder of Digit, Amy Vedder and Bill Weber learned that Rwanda planned to take over 5,000 hectares of the Parc des Volcans for cattle ranching. Forty percent of the original park had already been taken in 1969 for a European-backed scheme for farming pyrethrum, the daisylike flower that yields a natural insecticide. This new plan, Bill and Amy knew, was as immediate a threat to the gorillas as poachers' spears: it would effectively eliminate most of the park's bamboo zone and split the gorilla habitat into three small islands.

"The situation was too urgent for us to go back and write up our dissertations," said Amy. They had to come up with a lucrative alternative to the cattle-grazing scheme, one that would show the worth of saving the gorillas in dollars and cents: gorilla tourism.

"We had considerable reservations about tourists," said Bill, "but a thousand head of cattle in the park was much worse. The Mountain Gorilla Project's first priority was antipoaching, but along with the stick we needed the carrot. This was a compromise with the devil, we knew. We were faced with overwhelming decimation of the forest. If tourism was to come, it had to be done right."

After eighteen months of research, backed by the Fauna and

Flora Preservation Society and the African Wildlife Foundation, Bill and Amy, with J. P. von der Becke, set up the Mountain Gorilla Project in September 1979. It was a three-pronged approach: beefed-up antipoaching patrols, gorilla tourism, and education.

At first Rwandan park officials pressured Bill to take more than a dozen tourists at a time to visit the two gorilla groups that were habituated to observers. Only after an unwieldy tourist group of sixteen provoked a silverback attack—resulting in two deep puncture wounds millimeters from Bill's spinal cord—did park officials agree to limit the tourists to six per group.

The tourism program is carefully controlled. Only a one-hour visit with each gorilla group is allowed each day. Before the tourists undertake the climb to see the apes, they are given a short course in gorilla etiquette: always defer to the animals. Stay quiet and low. Do not touch the gorillas. If an infant gorilla approaches you, back away.

In 1981 the park paid for itself for the first time in its history. Foreign tourists paid forty-five dollars each for an hour with the gorillas; native Rwandans were charged the equivalent of only a couple of dollars. By 1988, with four gorilla groups habituated to tourists, gorilla tourism had become the highest foreign exchange earner in Rwanda, ahead of coffee, copper, and tea. Funds generated from the tourism project allowed the MGP to double its staff, reclaim sixty-two hectares of cattle pasture for gorilla habitat, and fund wide-ranging antipoaching patrols. In 1984, for the first time in Rwandan history, not a single gorilla died at the hands of poachers, and this record remained intact until 1988, when a subadult in Group 5 died from wounds from a snare.

The educational component of the project generated impressive results as well. Bill's initial surveys, before the project began, showed that more than half of Rwandans living in rural areas wanted to convert the tiny park to agriculture. Today more than 70 percent wish to preserve the forest. The gorillas' image now appears on Rwandan postage stamps and money; they have even made it into a popular Rwandan song: "Where can the gorillas go? They are part of our country. They have no other home."

In *Gorillas in the Mist* Dian Fossey lauded the idea, in theory, of properly controlled tourism, but called it a low priority — one of the "Z's of theoretical conservation." In the book's epilogue she couldn't resist a swipe at the Mountain Gorilla Project, writing that "the survival chances of these species are little improved by tourism compared with more expedient actions." She feared the encroachment of strangers on an area she had come to consider as hers and the gorillas' alone. She loathed the idea of Rwandan officials making money off the animals she considered sacred. She did not trust the then director of parks, Laurent Habiyaremye, who she believed wanted to take over her research station to house tourists. She told people she would burn her camp to the ground before she would allow it to be overtaken.

Amy recalls Dian's prediction: "I'm going to die and the gorillas will all die around me. They'll be gone within ten years."

And many believed, after Dian's murder, that this would indeed be the gorillas' fate. When I first visited the gorillas of Parc National des Volcans in 1986, the year after the death of their avenging sorceress, I expected to catch a last, fleeting glimpse of Dian's majestic gorillas before they faded into the *zamani* of the dodo and the passenger pigeon. To my surprise and delight, the gorilla population was instead increasing. "The gorillas aren't dying," MGP staffer Mark Condiotti assured me. "Nothing could be further from the truth."

There is an old military adage all generals know well: "Don't name the chickens." Just as a farmer can't consider his chickens pets if he is raising them for meat, a commander cannot become too friendly with individual soldiers, for he may well have to send them to death to win a battle.

The trouble with Dian's conservation strategy, some say, is that she named the chickens. (Quite literally: she kept chickens as pets and gave them fanciful names like Lucy and Dezi and Madoughadougha.) Diana McMeekin told me, "Dian wanted only *her* gorillas protected from poachers. We wanted to extend protection to all the gorillas of the Virunga Volcanoes. That's where we had trouble."

"Good conservationists can't afford to be that emotionally involved with the populations they're trying to save," says Michael Hutchins, a conservation biologist with the New York Zoological Society. "Individuals can't mean that much when you have to do large-scale manipulations of populations, as a conservationist sometimes must." A few years back the zoological society sponsored a study: "Wildlife Conservation and Animal Rights: Are They Compatible?" The answer was no.

With Dian dead and the Mountain Gorilla Project a resounding success, it appeared that the Greek chorus's verdict had proved to be correct: Dian Fossey had been wrong.

Today Kigali sports several European-style hotels and handsome Dutch-style homes for Western immigrants. The hotel Mille Collines, where Dian used to stay when she came to town, is carpeted and mirrored, and black high heels click down the semispiral staircase from the reception area to the tiled terrace and swimming pool. Coffee costs a dollar for a tiny *tasse.*

Just off the main streets of the capital, where chickens and goats crowd the roads, people in filthy, ill-fitting rags stained with red dirt and sweat live in rusted, tin-sided shacks, sometimes no more than sheets of discarded metal propped over dirt floors. The tin shacks magnify the sound of coughing, mucous rattling in the throat. Polio victims lean on old pipes for canes, with a leg shriveled to bone, or walk with crude crutches, a limb twisted absurdly like a bent pipe cleaner or missing entirely. By the Episcopalian church's guest house, an old man without front teeth coughs and rattles and laughs as he tries to sell some flowers he is carrying. One madman walks in a circle in the street; people do not respond to a French greeting.

The Rwandan office of parks and tourism is located on a major street, away from most of the beggars and cripples, along with the banks and the American embassy. Outside the one-story building in a glass case is a large photo of Uncle Bert—the cover of *Gorillas in the Mist*—and a poster from movie box offices advertising the film of the same name. Every Westerner who comes to town is automatically asked, by immigration staff, by taxi drivers, by hotel personnel: "Vous venez voir les gorilles?" And the answer, almost invariably, is yes.

More than four thousand tourists a year now make the steep, nettle-strewn climb to the Virungas to see the gorillas of Rwanda. It now costs $180 for a one-hour visit. The special price for Rwandans has been discontinued.

The movie—the rights to which Dian sold in 1985 for $150,000 (had her mother and stepfather not contested her will, the money would have gone to the Digit Fund)—was a smash success. From the publicity it generated for gorilla tourism, Rwandan parks officials saw new opportunities to make money. They wanted to habituate two more groups of wild gorillas to tourists and to increase the number of tourists allowed to visit each group from six to eight and then ten.

Only a year before this plan was announced, an outbreak of respiratory disease that a Mountain Gorilla Project report called "catastrophic" killed six gorillas between February and May; twenty-seven other cases were treated or monitored. One illness—three-year-old Kato of Group 13, who was abandoned by her group and died—was diagnosed as probably measles by four independent research facilities. In June workers began delivering measles vaccine to the gorillas by blowgun.

Early 1988 had been exceptionally cold and wet; that May forty people died in flood-induced mudslides in Ruhengeri. The Mountain Gorilla Project report for that year does not answer whether the disease was carried to the gorillas by tourists or brought on by the weather alone. But a 1985 MGP report, written after an autopsy revealed that the silverback Nunkie had been heavily parasitized by human hookworm, warned:

> The gorilla populations of the Virunga Volcanoes have been subjected to increasing human encroachment. . . . Common human infections like influenza, the common cold and herpes simplex could easily be transmitted to the gorillas . . . with potentially devastating results. Habituation of gorilla groups to human proximity carries a very serious risk to the continued existence of the small surviving mountain gorilla populations.

And as early as 1987, the director of Rwanda's parks proposed to David Watts, then the director of Karisoke, that Dian's house be turned into a museum. "Thousands of tourists tramping through camp!" Watts wrote in dismay to a World Wildlife Fund colleague. Habiyaremye "hastily modified it to 'a national monument' — charging tourists for the opportunity to see where The Great Person lived, died, and is buried. From there a short step to turning this place into a deluxe tourist center. Stay at Fossey's camp, gawk at her grave, go to see 'her' gorillas."

International pressure has, for the moment, staved off both plans. In the summer of 1989 it was rumored that the Mountain Gorilla Project would pull out, along with its supporting funds, if parks officials threatened the gorillas with too many tourists or the research center with extinction. But, commented one American embassy official, "Once the goose has laid the golden egg, it will be impossible to go back to the way it was. Dian must be turning in her grave."

Dian's old tracker, Nemeye, says that her grave has moved one meter to the left since she was buried on New Year's Eve in 1985. People seldom visit the gorilla graveyard where she is buried. The boot-worn trail from the camp to the study area passes to the left of Dian's green, corrugated tin cabin, and you

Dian's marker became the sixteenth in the gorilla
graveyard she created near her cabin. Her stone reads:
"No one loved gorillas more . . ." *Sy Montgomery*

can easily miss seeing that the graveyard is there. But when you
catch sight of it, it takes your breath away.

The graveyard covers an area half as wide as a tennis court,
a breadth of grief unimaginable. From almost every angle it
seems to be embraced by the muscular arms of the great *Hagenia*
trees, weeping with ferns and moss and trailing wizardly beards
of light-green lichen. The grass and herbs are cropped close
around the graves; here the blades bear the tooth marks of
grazing duikers, where only a hundred yards away the grass
swallows your knees.

Dian watched the graves fill. Fifteen carved wooden markers
bear the names of the gorillas she loved: Uncle Bert, Kweli,
Macho, Digit, Tiger, Lee, Frito, Nunkie. Her own marker, directly in back of Digit's, Uncle Bert's, and Macho's, bears the

name she loved, which was never hers: Nyiramachabelli. It is almost a relief to find her buried here, to believe her anguish is finally quelled under the wet, black Rwandan earth. It is like a reunion. And in the jewel-like sunshine, it is so peaceful; it seems that nothing bad could happen here.

A new bronze marker, installed with money raised through an international effort after her death, reads:

Dian Fossey
1932–1985
No one loved gorillas more
Rest in peace, dear friend
eternally protected
in this sacred ground
for you are home
where you belong

Camp researchers still talk about Dian, and even the youngest students, who never met her, swap stories: the torture of poachers, attempted seductions of visiting Western men, the whiskey bottles under her bed. When I returned to the camp in 1989, I asked the students what they thought of the new marker. "It's in English, for God's sake," a fresh-faced young student replied in disgust. "This is a country that speaks Kinyarwanda."

10 *Diplomat: The Politics of Biruté Galdikas*

BIRUTÉ GALDIKAS often dreams about orangutans; for her this is as natural as dreaming about people. She doesn't set much store by dreams and usually forgets them. But one dream stays with her. She recalls it breathlessly, its terror intact, hurrying her usually soft, well-chosen words:

"There was a cheek-padded male orangutan, and the forest was being cut down, and there were trucks, and there was a highway, and he was running, and somebody, some people, were trying to find him and kill him. Concrete and huge megaton trucks, like you find on a California freeway—a huge urban center right next to the orangutan habitat. I was running . . ."

In the dream Biruté is running through the forest, trying to get to the orangutan before the people and their megaton trucks overrun him. But the orangutan keeps disappearing—"He'd be over here, and then the next minute he'd be over there." He is long-calling, bellowing the ear-splitting, soul-shattering call that adult males use to announce their territories—"and I kept wishing he would stop, thinking, he's giving himself away! If only he would be quiet, and I could get to him first. These people were trying to kill him."

She pauses, as if to recover. Then, composed, she says: "I still have dreams like that."

The dream is so terrifying because it is chillingly close to reality. Near the village of Kumai, where Biruté sometimes stops for supplies, is a shallow, bulldozed soil mine, white and sterile as sun-bleached bone. Huge trucks like those in her dream have taken the topsoil away for sale. Without the top six inches of living earth, a layer seething with bacteria, viruses, lichens, and humus, only pale clay remains. And here are roads where two years ago was forest, gaping raw wounds flanked by severed tree trunks.

Like the mountain gorilla and the chimpanzee, the orangutan is an endangered species; only about 20,000 of the orange apes remain, confined to the islands of Borneo and Sumatra. When Biruté and Rod first arrived in Borneo, orangutan females were routinely shot so that their babies could be taken as pets. Orangutans are still killed in fear or for food sometimes. But today it is human encroachment — concrete and huge trucks — that threatens orangutans with extinction.

An Indonesian resettlement scheme, begun in 1979 and financed with World Bank loans, moved nearly a million Javanese to Indonesian Borneo, or Kalimantan, and encouraged the immigrants to clear tropical forest and create new cropland. Government plans to make roads throughout the province of Kalimantan Tengah are proceeding remarkably on schedule. Areas that a year ago required a two-week journey by boat to reach are accessible to loggers and farmers in two days by truck. Logging is officially allowed in 45 percent of Indonesia's rain forests; but unofficially, which is how most things are done in Indonesia, almost any tract of forest can be clear-cut for the right price.

Biruté wakes to these realities with the urgency of a nightmare. But Indonesia defies conventional conservation solutions; it is a notoriously difficult place for biologists and conservationists to work.

Tom Struthsaker, a primatologist who worked in Uganda through the reign of Idi Amin, says he could never work in Indonesia; the bureaucracy is tangled and slow, the government notoriously corrupt, and the social etiquette so subtle and layered it is nearly impossible to figure out how to work with the officials. (Said one anthropologist who worked there: "I don't mind paying bribes, but in Indonesia, I couldn't even get a straight answer on who to pay or how much.") Hank Reichart was appointed World Wildlife International representative in Indonesia in 1986, but he left after a year and a half. "I couldn't take it anymore," he said. "You cannot work with these people on the same level you work with any other people in the world."

Even getting the right research permits is a nearly insurmountable hurdle: primatologist John Mitani has run field expeditions there for the past eleven years; his last research permit took seventeen months to secure. He once counted the offices from which he had to get permits, from the time he left America to the time he arrived at his camp. They numbered seventeen. Tanzania, he said, required only two.

Yet Biruté Galdikas has virtually eliminated trade in captive orangutans in her province. At her bidding two entire villages were moved from a nature reserve and relocated. Her work at Tanjung Puting is the reason the 250,000-hectare area was declared a national park in 1982, for which she wrote the management plan.

"As a guest here in Indonesia, public criticism and activism is not my place," Biruté once told an interviewer. Indonesian culture sculpts her conservation strategy: its shadowy politics, primitive ritual, and elaborate protocols. After nearly two decades in the Bornean jungle, this white-skinned Canadian of

To reach Biruté's camp at Tanjung Puting requires a five-hour journey up the Sekoyner-Cannon River by motorized kelotok, so named for the sound it makes: *klo-TOK, klo-TOK, klo-TOK. Harold Walker*

Lithuanian heritage has become not only an insider in Indonesia but one who, slowly and subtly, wields a profound influence.

The remote Dayak village of Kanepan is decked with ceremonial banners and long woven baskets hanging from bamboo poles. The wide dirt streets, bordered with bamboo and ironwood houses on stilts, are alive with people, the women in sarongs, the men in T-shirts and pants. They are waiting for the celebration to begin.

A shout goes up when a boat appears upriver. At its prow stands a man bearing a sword, wearing only a yellow loincloth and a ceremonial hat tipped with a hornbill feather. Music throbs like a fever dream: men strike drums and wooden xylophones, *kelenangan,* the high notes like chimes, the low ones like gongs calling from the underworld. The rhythm is irregular but fluid, like the muscles of an animal stalking its prey: briefly hushed and crouching here, quickening there, then slowing again.

Now begins the main event of the *tewa,* an occasion of great import in the life of a Dayak village. The three-day ceremony celebrates the rejoining of the two halves of the soul, which part at death. Half of the soul journeys to rest in the palm of the goddess of the underworld; the other half stays with the body. Only many years later, when the body is exhumed at the *tewa,* does the soul again become whole.

Biruté has traveled for two days, over excruciatingly bad roads and up rapids deep in Kalimantan's interior, to attend the ceremony, which few whites have ever witnessed. It is the body of the vice governor's mother, who died twenty-eight years ago, that is to be exhumed. The vice governor, Pak Victor, personally invited Biruté to attend, to add honor to the occasion.

Because we have arrived late, we have missed the exhumation of the body. Even the woman's bones have been consumed by the earth; only six pieces of the skeleton remained, and the top crescent of her skull, tiny as a child's. The bones, we are told, were then packed up in a suitcase—a new element in the tradition, presumably—and reburied rather quietly. But the main drama is yet to take place.

Pak Robin, the man with the sword, disembarks from the wooden boat and hacks through each of the three barkless logs of a ceremonial gate fringed with palm leaves. The crowd shouts, voices swelling to a frenzied "Wwhooo!" with each strike of the blade. A white and gray spotted pig, its trotters bound with rope, lies screaming on the other side of the gate. It is slaughtered slowly, the sword slicing a cross down its back and shoulders, as the pig screams and screams. Pak Robin climbs a coconut tree; he hacks off the top fronds, the lower fronds, the coconuts, and finally fells the tree itself; he slices through decorative bam-

At a traditional Dayak *tewa,* celebrating the joining of the two halves of the soul after exhumation of the decades-buried body, a pig is ceremonially slaughtered with the *mandau,* or headhunting sword. *Dianne Taylor-Snow*

boo poles holding baskets and flowers and hanging parcels of
betelnut wrapped in leaves.

The crowd shouts its frenzy. An elder turns to Biruté and
smiles widely; his gums glisten with dark red fluid, his teeth are
black. When he spits the juice of the betelnut, it stains the dirt
like a clot of blood. Finally the sword's work is done. While the
elder men dance—the slow-motion movements precisely mus-
cled, joints angled like a sculptured crane's—the slaughtered
animal's blood, mixed with water, is spewed over the crowd,
like rice thrown at a wedding.

That night there is a feast and rice wine and dancing. Then
at three A.M. the celebrants are awakened. By lamplight the
mandau, or headhunting sword, is unsheathed. The celebrants,
one by one, are made to kiss the blade. Holding the *mandau*
over their own head, they are passed the ceremonial rice wine,
called *tuac*. The bowl they cup to their lips is a human skull.

Indonesians, Biruté says, are exquisitely generous, gentle, courteous people—"probably the nicest people on this planet." Passing another on a path, an Indonesian will duck his head and
stoop his back, extending one arm forward and requesting *per-
misi*, permission, please, to pass. Indonesians do not point their
feet, the lowliest part of the body, at others; to do so would be
an insult. Any conversation begins with an inquiry about your
well-being and that of your relatives; your arrival or departure
from any village is likely to be marked with a ceremony honoring
the occasion. The people are always smiling.

Biruté explains, "For an individual Indonesian, the most important thing is that he or she be in harmony with his or her
family, with his or her group, with his or her universe.

"You'll never know if some Indonesian absolutely hates you,"
Biruté says. "They would smile. There's nothing in their body
language or their eyes or the way they speak that reveals themselves."

But beneath this serene surface, hidden like a crocodile submerged in a tea-colored river, is another aspect of these charming, gracious, gentle people.

"You couldn't have a worse enemy in the world than an Indonesian," says World Wildlife's Hank Reichart, now working in Surinam. He remembers the story circulating in Java while he was posted in Djakarta: an American woman with a small child was driving along the street when an Indonesian child darted in front of her car. Though she tried to swerve, she hit the child, killing it instantly. The villagers pulled her own child out of the car and killed it in front of her eyes.

Indonesians, as Biruté puts it, do not tolerate disharmony well. She once heard of an auto accident in Sumatra. At first the drivers seemed to be discussing the situation quietly. "Then all of a sudden, the face of one of the drivers—it was like a mask fell over it. There's a name for it: 'the face gets dark.' He pulled out a knife and killed the other person on the spot." In Indonesia killing a person for an insult is not considered a major offense. Killing a person in a robbery may carry a twenty-year jail term, but the penalty for murder provoked by insult is usually only a year and a half in jail.

This is the culture from which the term "to run amok" arose. It is a land of headhunters who did not spare women or children. The Dayaks were eating Dutch people until the 1900s, and there are reports that headhunting still occurs. German anthropologists recently reported that the Sea Dayaks, of northern Borneo, took several heads to celebrate a *tewa*.

"But still," says Biruté, "the Indonesians are gracious, gentle people—as long as the universe is at equilibrium."

Preserving equilibrium is the foundation of Biruté's conservation strategy, from which all else proceeds. Immersed in a culture delicately balanced between courtesy and violence, she works, carefully and subtly, within this equilibrium.

"I'm amazed she's been able to stick it out under such tough bureaucratic conditions," said John Mitani. What she's been able to accomplish "reflects her incredible degree of rapport with the officials there. It is a remarkable feat."

"She has earned the respect of almost everybody there," said Gary Shapiro, who worked with Biruté at Tanjung Puting for two years. There he met and married an Indonesian; now he lives in California and serves as vice president and treasurer of Biruté's Orangutan Foundation, which helps fund her work. "That's how you effect change over there; you work within the system, you need to be very astute about the ebb and flow of political life, you need to know the importance of paying the right calls, observing the rituals. Everything she is doing is to consolidate her position."

In Western conservation circles, Biruté's name is not widely known. She isn't called upon to help draft American policy statements or legislation affecting Southeast Asian rain forests or animals. Some of her colleagues were alarmed by her marriage to Pak Bohap. Former Leakey Foundation director Ned Munger comments, sounding distressed, that she has "gone native." But this is precisely her strength.

For it is here in Indonesia that the wild orangutans live. Here, in the hands of her neighbors, their fate will be decided. So it is here, over cups of hot, sweet tea, in conversations about weather and children, that she exerts her influence. In fluorescent-lit offices of town officials and in the shadows of lamp-lit long houses, she augments her status. Though it is almost imperceptible to the Western eye, Biruté is constantly lobbying, influencing, building, and consolidating her power.

Biruté goes nowhere in public without an entourage of Dayak assistants. In Indonesia respectable people do not walk alone; status is read in the size of one's entourage. When the director of nature protection once visited her at Camp Leakey, he brought two hundred people with him; Biruté's assistants had to move out of their quarters and sleep in hammocks in the forest to accommodate them.

Biruté's entourage for the journey to the *tewa* is modest in comparison, but still, with their gear and gifts, they fill three large speedboats: three Dayak assistants, three visiting German officials, Biruté's Californian volunteer, Dianne Taylor-Snow, myself, a middle-aged American tourist who heard about the *tewa* where she was vacationing in Palangka Raya, a journalist from Java, and two policemen.

The Indonesian government insists on police escorts for whites traveling to the interior. One reason is that the Malayu suspect that the Dayaks poison people. The accusation seems verified by the fact that almost every Westerner who visits the interior becomes ill afterward. But Biruté assures us that these illnesses are not the result of intentional poisoning. Water for drinking and cooking comes from the river, which in remote villages also serves as bath and latrine; when you lift a plastic scoop of water out of the river to rinse shampooed hair, it's important to preview the contents for globs of fecal matter. And at the *tewa* everyone shares communal glasses of the urine-colored ceremonial rice wine. *Tuac* is often flavored with the corpse of a fetal barking deer, which pickles like the worm in a bottle of tequila. You don't need to be deliberately poisoned to become ill.

Biruté, however, will not become ill. The vice governor has set aside for her a private bathroom—a bark-walled room of the guest house on stilts above the river. The toilet is two slats missing from the floor. Her Dayak assistants will bring boiled water for her bath. And she, alone among the few whites to attend the celebration, can politely refuse the *tuac* without offending the vice governor. He reserves for her a seat of honor near himself and his wife at the nighttime ceremonies at the long house.

*

When she was a graduate student at UCLA in 1979, Biruté's first expedition outside of the United States was a summer archeological dig in rural Serbia, in Yugoslavia. "I was absolutely shocked," she remembers. "The American anthropologists could not deal with the Yugoslavs. It was the equivalent of moral warfare."

The Yugoslavian archeologists wanted to unearth cities, discover the whole pattern, make bold, quick brushstrokes of discovery. The Americans, on the other hand, wanted to painstakingly examine every sliver of bone, every preserved scrap of food.

The Americans, said Biruté, treated their hosts "as if the Yugoslavs didn't know anything, you know, like they were stupid? They made absolutely no concessions to the Yugoslavian way of doing things. To me it was unbelievable—I was trained as an anthropologist, right? And we weren't in the United States, we were guests in their country. I was appalled to watch this."

The polite, reserved Indonesians couldn't be more different from the boisterous, open Yugoslavs. But, says Biruté, "the lessons were the same."

"One thing I learned is you can never, never, never make assumptions about people unless you totally understand them. And I began to learn this possibly as a child, and certainly in Yugoslavia, and in Indonesia. And that is, if you see somebody act in a certain way, maybe it makes no sense to you, but for that person it makes perfect sense. I always try to figure out how it makes perfect sense."

When Biruté and Rod first met with Indonesian conservation officials in Djakarta to get their scientific permits, the officials wanted the couple to change the only solid plan they had: their study site. When the officials suggested they go to Borneo instead of Sumatra, Biruté and Rod agreed without hesitation.

"They liked us, and I don't know why they liked us," Biruté says today. "I think the thing was," she says, "we listened."

Unlike Dian Fossey, whose study animals were being slaughtered in front of her eyes, Biruté had time to listen. But although orangutans were protected by law, the law was not enforced; the local pet trade in orangutans was openly flourishing. To protect her study animals, she and Rod quickly realized they would have to stop the trade.

Dian took up her machete in defense of her gorillas. To defend chimpanzees, Jane Goodall took up the microphone. Biruté's strategy was far less direct: she pulled up a chair and sipped tea.

In Indonesia, "if there's a problem, you can't just rush in and solve it," Biruté says. There is first the labyrinthine etiquette to be observed, relationships built, harmony established. "You establish that you're not going to make troubles," said Biruté. "I am careful about what I ask for. I don't impose myself on them. My gut feeling is that when I walk through somebody's door, they don't say, 'Ah, here comes a problem.' They say, 'Ah, here comes my friend.' "

Biruté and Rod began not by citing a problem but by agreeing to a favor: they'd be happy, they said, to provide the forestry's nature protection agency with a place where ex-captive orangutans could be rehabilitated and released. This gave the agency a reason to confiscate illegally owned orangutans. Biruté and Rod often relieved these officials of the embarrassing task of actually confiscating the animals. They would show up at the owner's house and try to persuade him that the best place for an orangutan was the forest. Usually they succeeded.

Biruté and Rod spent hours "harmonizing" with the local officials; often conservation was not even a topic of discussion. "We in America think that people are most themselves when they are frank and honest," says Mount Holyoke anthropologist Frederick Errington. "But in Indonesia the cultural value is on indirectness. To be refined is to be indirect, and this is carried to elaborate extremes. The real self, the valued self, is the self that has mastered these elaborate forms of etiquette."

So between the talk of weather and grandchildren and the latest news of the progress of ex-captive orangutans, Biruté and Rod gradually, subtly, began to hint at the topic that bothered them. An hour's journey upriver from Camp Leakey, within the borders of Tanjung Puting, was a Malayu village of two hundred people. They were cutting trees and trapping forest animals. Their fishing disturbed the river. Biruté and Rod intoned to the head of forestry: "This village isn't allowed. This is a nature reserve, and you can't have a village in a nature reserve."

Actually, Tanjung Puting was not a nature reserve. Everyone involved in these discussions knew it was a game reserve, and villages are allowed within its boundaries. In fact, a game reserve carries no restrictions on what can be done to the land; only killing the animals is outlawed. "But we pretended it was a nature reserve," said Biruté. "And when I look back at how we did it, it's incredible to me that we persuaded them to move the village, when in reality the village had every right to be there. But again, remember: this is Indonesia; you're dealing with people who if you talk to them long enough, you can persuade them."

"Remember, this is Indonesia," Biruté often says. A nation that runs on both courtesy and corruption, it is riddled with paradox and protocol, a land where words and actions are layered with obscure meaning.

Among the Minangkabau of western Sumatra, the Indonesian tribe that anthropologist Errington worked with in 1975, every word, every movement, down to the angle of the knees, carried meaning. Attending one formal ceremony at which the celebrants sat cross-legged with both knees to the floor, Errington inadvertently let his knees rise. Members of the tribe thought the anthropologist had become so seriously upset that he had forgotten where he was — the only explanation they could think of for this serious breach of protocol. Within such an elaborate social system, said Errington, "it was difficult for me to function as a competent human being. I found it a struggle."

"There are so many things you need to know," said Gary Shapiro. "You can say something with good intentions and it may haunt you later on." A few years ago he came up with what he thought was a good idea: on a trip to Palangka Raya he thought he'd visit Pak Binti, a former government official and Biruté's "adopted father." Even in retirement, Pak Binti still had Djakarta's ear. Gary wanted to suggest to Pak Binti that the government help fund Biruté's work. The ex-captive orangutans consumed enormous amounts of bananas, sugar cane, and rice; money for their food would be appreciated.

Biruté advised Gary against this plan, but he went ahead anyway. Within weeks Biruté was shocked to see an article in the local newspaper claiming that the orangutans at Tanjung Puting were starving. She was summoned to the administration center at Bogor; government officials were angry. "If you can't feed these orangutans," they said, "maybe you shouldn't be there."

Biruté straightened out the mess, and today the province's governor donates part of his discretionary fund toward the ex-captives' food at her camp. But for Gary it was a painful lesson: in Indonesia the words matter less than the way in which they are spoken.

The village of Tanjung Harapan, by decree of the forestry department, was evicted in 1977; later a second village was moved at Biruté's request. Today Tanjung Harapan is officially a park headquarters. A visitor's center was being erected in 1988. The building under construction bore the graffiti *Di Sini Ada Hantu*: There are ghosts here. The forest has overtaken the remains of the houses. Only the cemetery, its ironwood headboards obscured by tall grass, recalls that people once lived, and died, here.

That same year, 1977, was the first in history that a resident of Indonesia was fined for illegally keeping a pet orangutan. The amount of the fine—fifty dollars—wasn't as important as the fact that by having to appear in court the owners were publicly shamed. Word got around. Today the orangutan trade in Biruté's province is virtually nil. In 1986 she persuaded the commander of the air force base at Pangkalanbuun to hand over his pet orangutan to her. The exchange was honored with a half-day ceremony, tea, and speeches, with government officials, the military, even Boy Scouts and Girl Scouts in attendance.

For today Biruté is not just a persuasive young researcher with tattered jeans and an open mind. Her name and her status are known throughout Indonesia. In 1982 she was nominated by the governor of Kalimantan Tengah as the province's candidate for the National Hero of the Environment award. She has presented addresses at the palace of the vice president of the Republic of Indonesia.

But Biruté is careful about whom she will align herself with. "She's always warned me, you don't want to get too close to the top," Gary said. Once he suggested publicizing her project by having her photo taken with a certain high Indonesian official. She rejected the suggestion; if the official fell from power, she could fall too. "You want to watch the powerful people who are coming into play in the lower echelons," Gary remembers she told him. "These are the people you need to work with."

Biruté serves as professor extraordinaire on the faculty of biology at Indonesia's leading university, Universitas National in Djakarta, and she has always made the training of Indonesian students a top priority at her camp. (Dian Fossey never hosted a Rwandan student until the last year of her life; Jane Goodall's students were mainly Westerners until politics prohibited long-term studies by Western students.) More than thirty Indonesian students have completed their *Sajana* degrees (roughly equivalent to a master's) from data gathered at Tanjung Puting; after such prestigious training they often rise to positions of power. Several of her former students now serve in the Indonesian government; others are teaching at local universities; one served as an adviser to a cabinet minister and founded a prominent Indonesian nature conservation foundation.

Biruté is no longer merely a guest in Indonesia. Since her marriage to Pak Bohap and the births of their two children, she is assured permanent residency. This is a culture that affirms nepotism, and Pak Bohap's status—many have tried to recruit him for local political office, but he has refused—enhances Biruté's power. When she is asked to reflect on her status in this society, she recalls the words of Prince Charles: "I have absolutely no authority; I just have influence."

Expert at concealing their own emotions and intents, Indonesians seem almost prescient about reading the feelings and motives of others. Once Pak Bohap, who understands no English, watched two Earthwatchers talking together in the dining hall. After dinner he said to Biruté, "They are boyfriend and girlfriend." Neither Biruté nor the other Western volunteers detected a hint of romance between the two. But after the team had left camp, a postcard arrived announcing their marriage.

"Westerners are like an open book to Indonesians," says Biruté. But what an Indonesian and a Westerner read from the book may be very different.

Biruté speaks with a questioning lilt in the middle of her sentences ("I was trained as an anthropologist, right?") as if requesting the listener's permission to continue. In her lectures to Earthwatch volunteers she prefaces many statements with a self-effacing, "Well, I don't know, but I suspect . . ." She listens intently to others, and seldom interrupts someone who is speaking. Biruté also does you the honor of remembering what you say to her: she often will repeat, almost verbatim, something you said many days earlier.

Yet many Westerners come away with the impression that she is arrogant. One of her former long-term volunteers says Biruté exudes an aura of "entitlement." She is notorious for keeping people waiting. Biruté arrived late at the air force commander's orangutan exchange ceremony; a London *Times* reporter was kept waiting for four days in Pangkalanbuun for an interview with her. Earthwatchers have complained that they have waited till nightfall for a lecture she had scheduled for noon. One of her American volunteers was kept waiting in a hotel room for three days. Biruté was in town the whole time. When the volunteer finally ventured out for a restaurant meal, one of Biruté's assistants tracked the woman down. "The professor is very angry," he told her. "She has been waiting for you for an hour."

Other visitors to camp are dismayed by Biruté's control over the lives of her Indonesian staff. If Earthwatchers donate items to camp, Biruté strictly controls who gets to keep what. Leaving a gift of boots or pants or a backpack to a specific staff person is discouraged. And no one, Indonesian or white, calls her Biruté. It is always "Professor" or "Dr. Biruté." Even American volunteers use one of these terms. Two Western women her own age call her "Ibu," a term of respect that means "mother."

Some visitors—usually older men—have come away with the complaint: "She's running a little empire out there."

But Indonesians apparently see the situation differently. Once Biruté was visiting Djakarta with Rod when the police there confiscated a captive orangutan from Sumatra. A Swiss woman who worked with a rehabilitation and release program in Sumatra planned to take the animal back to its country of origin.

The next time Rod and Biruté were in Djakarta, they saw the animal in the Djakarta zoo. "We asked the Indonesian police chief what had happened, why didn't you turn the orangutan over to the Swiss woman?" Biruté remembered. "And he said, 'She was conceited. She was proud. She was arrogant. I refused to meet with her.' He said, 'I heard her ask for me at the door, and I didn't like the way she asked for me. I don't have any dealings with people who are conceited or arrogant.' "

But the police chief's anger softened as he talked to Biruté.

Biruté and her second husband, Pak Bohap bin Jalan. Pak Bohap holds the blowpipe with which he sometimes hunts fruit bats, a Dayak delicacy.
Noel Rowe

He told her, "From the moment I saw you, I felt a kinship with you."

"It's very interesting that some foreign people in Indonesia think I am arrogant, that I deal with Indonesians not in the right way," Biruté muses. "The foreigners don't understand what is happening. I have never had trouble with Indonesians. The relationship is difficult to understand if you haven't experienced it."

One winter while Biruté was teaching in Canada, she received a letter from an American graduate student she had left in charge at camp. "The Indonesians say I no longer have the *pusaka*," the student wrote. This was grave news. It meant that the student no longer was perceived as having control of the camp.

A *pusaka*, as an item, is an embodiment of power. In Kanepan the *pusaka* of four villages, a Buddha-like figurine, was enshrined in the five-hundred-year-old long house; visitors paid their respects by sprinkling rice over its head, dropping coins inside it, and placing a cigarette—a popular gift to both living and dead—in its mouth. The *pusaka* of the Republic of Indonesia is the red and white flag made by former president Sukarno's wife that flew at the republic's declaration of independence.

A *pusaka* may be stolen. But if you steal it and you don't have the power, the *pusaka*, it is said, will return to the person who has the power.

When not represented by an item, *pusaka* is the power itself. And once the graduate student lost that, she was unworthy of the respect accorded to either an employer or a leader.

One must understand two things about the Indonesian concept of power. First, explains Biruté, power, like the light from a light bulb, is finite. There is only so much of it in the universe. Biruté once had a problem with the former acting head of national parks. "Whenever something good would happen to me, he would become very upset," she said. She couldn't understand this at first; she had thought they were friends, and he should be happy at her good fortune. But one day she had a talk with him. "I sat him down and I said, 'My power and your power come from different sources. My power has nothing to do with your power.' And after I explained that to him, it was like he saw the light, you see?"

Second, once the power begins to slip away, it cannot be retrieved. Indonesians are always watching, monitoring, waiting for signs of weakness in their leaders, signs that the power has begun to slip.

"If somebody stands up in the dining hall and says 'No' to me, in America it is seen as insubordination. But in this context it is seen as a sign that the power may begin to slip away," Biruté says. "Everybody is watching to see if indeed the power is slipping away. And I would have to fire the person on the spot."

One day I went out on an orangutan follow at Tanjung Puting with two Dayak assistants and an Earthwatch volunteer, a fit, fortyish American teacher. From five A.M. until about one P.M., through clawing thorns and boot-sucking swamp, through heat that the sweat pouring from our bodies could not cool, we followed the dark shape moving through the canopy above us. Our target animal was a female erroneously named Pete who was due to give birth any day.

Then Pete came to the edge of a shallow lake. The Dayaks insisted that Pete was leaving the study area and that we couldn't follow her farther.

The teacher and I thought it odd that we should turn our backs on an orangutan about to give birth, a crucial event for the study. For about ten minutes, in fractured English and Bahasa Indonesia, we argued with the assistants. Couldn't we follow at least a little farther? Wouldn't the Professor be mad if we left? Finally, as Pete faded, like a whisper, into the trees, we acquiesced. We concluded that there must be some security reason for our not being able to go beyond the lake.

On the two-and-a-half-hour walk back to camp, the teacher was hit in the eye with a thorn from a thread-thin rattan, which pained her enormously. When we arrived back at camp, drenched in sweat, plastered with mud, covered with insect welts and bleeding from leech bites, our first thought was to dive into the Sekoyner-Cannon River. But Biruté was giving a lecture in the dining hall to some Indonesian visitors, and we waited for her to finish. When she saw us back so early, she was surprised. "The assistants told us Pete had left the study area, and we had to come back," we told her.

"Pete did *not* leave the study area," she said to us. "You'll have to go back and find her."

"Professor," said the teacher, "I have a thorn in my eye, and I would really rather not go back."

The teacher, I told Biruté, needed to lie down and rest. I would be happy to go back without her, in the company of the assistants, to try to relocate Pete. I knew, as Biruté surely knew, that our chances of finding the orangutan, wary before her impending birth, were virtually nil. Because we had turned our backs on her, we would probably not see her again until after the birth. We were being sent out again to punish the Dayak assistants with our slow but overeager presence.

Biruté addressed her reply to the Earthwatch volunteer. She did not raise her voice. Her face, smooth as a calm lake, betrayed no feeling, but something in her flashed like a knife blade. "If you have a thorn in your eye," Biruté said, slow and controlled, "then you should put some antibiotic cream on it. But I think you really should go back and find Pete."

While crossing the swamp on the way back to the lake, the teacher began to cry. And five hours later, when dark had come and we still hadn't found the orangutan, one of the Dayak assistants was sobbing. He was sure he'd be fired.

But there is another twist to the Indonesian concept of power. Biruté has fired assistants many times, then hired them back.

"One assistant I have fired three times—and nobody respects me more than he does," Biruté says.

On the way to the *tewa* in Kanepan, we spent a night in the Dayak village of Panopa on the river LeMondu. Told that the Professor was coming, the whole village turned out in the dark for Biruté's arrival.

In the village long house, a fifty-foot-long wooden hall built on stilts over the river, we sat, listing with exhaustion, trying to stay awake in the flickering shadows. Biruté sat in one of the few chairs, erect and regal, talking with the headman.

Hot, sweet tea appeared on trays, and later a feast of *ladang* rice and meat and seaweedlike vegetables. It was well past midnight when the headman informed Biruté, "Now we have to have a ceremony."

"Oh, no," she said, "do we have to have a ceremony?"

"Yes, we're tired too," he replied, one elder speaking frankly to another, "but we must have a ceremony."

"Yes, I suppose so."

We filed wearily into another long house with the other villagers. The *kelenangan* was already being played.

Biruté was directed to sit on a cloth-covered series of wooden blocks, like a shallow throne. Behind her two women draped her shoulders with narrow golden scarves. Carefully and with reverence, they draped her head in a sarong.

A priest knelt in front of her. He held a knife-shaped wooden blade and touched it slowly to her temples, her neck, her lips —points of power. And finally, as is done with a *pusaka*, dry rice was sprinkled over her head.

Epilogue: Shamans

FEW SCIENTISTS TODAY would fail to concede their admiration for the wealth of data on the great apes that Jane Goodall, Dian Fossey, and Biruté Galdikas have collected. Most would also agree that the women's efforts to conserve these endangered species are important. Both these pursuits are considered reasonable, and their accomplishments praiseworthy. Yet still, some people find something disturbing about these three women, something out of place. What propels their pursuits, what powers their convictions? These questions give some scientists pause.

It is one thing to name your study animals. It is now considered important to be able to recognize each animal for proper record keeping. But it is another thing to relate to the animals as individuals, to establish singular relationships with them. Some people dismiss the very notion of a relationship with an animal as a dangerous delusion. The very idea of such a relationship skews priorities: from the *real* world—the world of people—

to an imaginary world, one in which animals as well as people think and feel, in which animals' thoughts and feelings matter. Really, to spend your whole career living with apes! Something must be wrong with these women. Surely they have missed the point of their endeavors. The point, of course, is to serve and to live among and to uphold the world of men.

Yet many people—respectable people, *normal* people—intuitively feel they have a relationship with animals, such as their pet dogs, and believe that this relationship is worth nurturing. Why would such a feeling for animals be so widespread if it were not natural, not normal, not true?

Human behavioral scientists have come up with an explanation: the animals we have positive feelings about are "baby releasers." The idea is that the very sight of an animal that shares certain visible characteristics of a human baby (and theorists have catalogued these characteristics: large eyes, round head, short snout, round body) automatically releases a misdirected flood of maternal feelings. This is why people tend to inherently "like" animals such as chimps and dogs and owls, which tend to look more like human babies than do, say, spiders or snakes or crabs. This reaction is said to be particularly pronounced in women, who are "programmed" to respond to childlike visual stimuli. It's all just a big mistake, this feeling of kinship, of friendship, with animals—the result of a glitch in the wiring of the human psyche.

"Oh yes," said one Harvard-educated ethologist, "this is a common reaction. There are people I know who think they have relationships with their *cats*! But if you know anything about cat brains, you can see this isn't possible."

Her words recall those of the cosmonauts who, on their first voyage into space, saw nothing but stars and sky and proclaimed there was no God. The ethologist knows much about cat brains; she has dissected them, observed the cells under a microscope, compared the brains of cats with the brains of humans; she has doubtless read the literature on electrical stimulation of cat brains and the recordings such experiments yield; but she knows very little about cats.

In other, older cultures than our own, in which people live closer to the earth, humans do not look down on animals from an imaginary pinnacle. Life is not divided between animals and people, nonhuman and human; life is a continuum, interactive, interdependent. Humans and animals are considered companions and coplayers in the drama of life. Animals' lives, their motives and thoughts and feelings, deserve human attention and respect; dismissing their importance is a grave error, akin to the modern Western concept of sin. To these peoples, "the animals are great shamans and great teachers," wrote Joseph Campbell in *The Masks of God*. "And any beast that may pass, whether flying as a bird, trotting as a quadruped, or wriggling in the way of a snake, may be a messenger signaling some wonder — perhaps the transformation of a shaman, or one's personal guardian come to bestow its warning or protection." Animals, like people living and dead, are teachers, protectors, destroyers, bearers of extraordinary perceptions, bringers of rain and drought, providers of meat and clothing. Animals, like people, are endowed with souls, and they are respected, imitated, sought, and consulted.

Among the North American Oglala Indians, a person on a vision quest would often seek an animal. Perhaps it would be a turtle, who, as tribespeople told anthropologist James Walker, is like a wisewoman who "hears many things and says nothing." Perhaps it would be a bear, the chief of animals in regard to herbal medicine. Or a spider, the namer of all people and animals, or an eagle, who sees all that happens on earth.

Many of the original inhabitants of the Americas selected a particular animal as a personal patron or tribal totem — a source of strength, wisdom, inspiration.

And this is why today the great American biologist E. O.

Wilson, the founder of sociobiology, keeps 10,000 Amazonian leaf-cutting ants in an aquarium in his Harvard office. His speciality is ants, and upon ant society he has largely founded his theories. Certainly he studies these ants in his office: sometimes he looks at them under the microscope, and he says that when they are thus enlarged, he can see individual differences between them. But this is not why he keeps them there. To him the ants as a species are his inspiration, his "personal muse": "The ants give me everything," he wrote in his chapter of a book about scientists who study animals, "and to them I will always return, like a shaman reconsecrating the tribal totem."

To the ants Wilson owes a large part of his understanding of the world. Such an understanding is a time-honored relationship, one that cuts across many cultures. The book of Job exhorts: "But ask now the beasts, and they shall teach thee; and the fowls of the air, and they shall tell thee." To the Oglala, the tutelary spirit of the animal would actually enter the body of the seeker on a vision quest; the animal would become part of his *waken*, or strength.

For a person to partake of animal knowledge, animal power, it is often necessary to *become* the animal. Some cultures in East Africa have a secret society known as the Leopard Society. Anthropologist Colin Turnbull, visiting Zaire, briefly investigated one manifestation of the Leopard Society. No one in the Bantu-speaking tribe, other than initiates, knows who the Leopard Men are. But one Leopard Man revealed himself to Turnbull and explained the extraordinary transformation that the initiate undergoes. When called upon, a Leopard Man must act exactly as a leopard would. At night he hides in the tall grass beside a path to a waterhole, where leopards, notorious people hunters, are most likely to lie in wait. When the first person passes by, the Leopard Man's hands form into claws, his lips pull away from his teeth, and he kills, with leopard claws and leopard teeth, his victim.

The victim could be the Leopard Man's wife or his child or

his father—whoever passes by first. The kill is exceptionally gruesome: the bodies left by Leopard Men are mutilated by claw marks and puncture wounds. No human in this society would normally attack a relative, nor would they kill even an enemy in this dreadful manner. But when the kill is made, said Turnbull, the Leopard Man is no longer a man. He has become a leopard.

Powerful shamans in some cultures say they can transform themselves at will. The ethnobotanist Mark Plotkin, visiting the Yanomamo Indians of Peru, once asked to see a certain witch doctor, but he was denied. That night Plotkin dreamed of a jaguar. In the morning he told a villager to fetch the witch doctor: "Tell him that I have seen the jaguar." Came the reply from the witch doctor: "Yes, that was me."

The concept of beings part animal, part human is an ancient one, as old and intimate as our human lineage, reflecting beliefs of paleolithic antiquity. In the caves known as Trois Frères in the Pyrenees, among the more than four hundred paleolithic rock paintings and engravings is one image that dominates all the others. At the far end of the cave's sanctuary, some fifteen feet above the floor, is the image of the Sorcerer, with antlered head, the pricked ears of a stag, the round eyes of an owl, the full beard of a man, the tail of a wolf, the paws of a bear, and the legs and feet of a person. This powerful image recurs throughout human history: from the sphinxes and bird-men of archaic Egypt and Mesopotamia to the animal garb donned by the shamans of aboriginal cultures from the Americas to Australia.

For millennia it was not only desirable for a person to become an animal, it was necessary. In totemistically conceived cultures, not only are animals great shamans and teachers, wrote Campbell, they are also "co-descendants of the totem ancestors." The various clans or groups are regarded as "having semi-animal, semi-human ancestors." To become an animal is to be one with the ancestors, to return to the source of our lineage, to join in the mystery of the original creations of the gods.

This insight was precisely what Louis Leakey, the son of an Anglican missionary, had in mind in his search for the ancestors of Adam. He, too, looked to animals—our closest living relatives, the great apes—to tell us about ourselves. In the great apes rested the story of our creation, our lineage, our place in the world. Sending forth Jane Goodall, Dian Fossey, and Biruté Galdikas not only to watch but to live among these apes must have been, to this deeply religious man, more than a scientific exploration; it must have been a sort of vision quest. Theirs was a profoundly sacred journey to the brink of the chasm that modern man has carved between himself and the animals; and once there, to peer over its edge and perhaps, if they dared, to cross.

At first, of course, the three young women approached their task as a great adventure, not a sacred quest. There were logistics to be worked out, goals to be named and achieved; it was an exercise in problem solving, which is, after all, what scientists do.

But it didn't work out that neatly. Each woman's first few months in the field were marked by despair, as the study subjects either could not be located at all or fled at first sight. The women couldn't *make* it work—not by extra stealth, not by better equipment, not by new techniques. One can manipulate an experiment to hasten it, but one cannot force or hurry a revelation.

The people of cultures older than ours know this well. On any vision quest the seeker must first achieve a purification, an altered state. The Yanomamo court the spirits by imbibing mind-altering drugs; the Oglala fast for many days, as did the Jew Jesus during His forty days in the wilderness; in other cultures sacrifices must be prepared, pilgrimages made. Only after such ritual purification is the seeker prepared to see what ordinary people cannot normally see.

For Jane, Dian, and Biruté, purification was achieved through loneliness and despair and, particularly in Dian's and Biruté's cases, deprivation. Their waiting, their despair was their sacrifice. Only afterward were they permitted to see, to understand, what ordinary people could not: the individuality of the apes, each animal as clearly unique as is each person.

The women learned to approach the animals' world with the reverence of a priestess approaching an altar. Biruté thinks of the forest at Tanjung Puting as "a great cathedral." At the dining hall her staff cooks and serves her food and washes and folds her clothes; but when Biruté walks in the forest, she bends down to gather up the tiniest scrap of cigarette paper, any trace of human litter; this is desecration, she considers, of a sacred place that must be kept pure. She often compares the tropical rain forest to a holy place, calling it "the original Garden of Eden" — the place of creation, where once man walked with the gods and spoke with the animals.

At Gombe, too, Jane feels a holiness; for her it is a place of spiritual transformation. "At Gombe, I could wander in the timeless forest and touch the bark of ancient trees," she wrote in a chapter contributed to the inspirational book *The Courage of Conviction.* "I could sit on the beach and watch the moonlight glinting as the waves tumbled, one after the other, onto the sands. There I felt part of the harmony of all life, and that, for me, was to know God again."

In these holy places the women walked in the apes' footsteps or under their aerial pathways. They sampled the foods the apes ate. Sometimes they slept in the forests with the animals, Jane at the Peak, Dian in her tent, Biruté in her hammock hung under the treetop nest of a sleeping orangutan. Daily they made the pilgrimage into the animals' universe, not only to probe and record, but to enter, to join.

Whether it was voiced or subconscious, sustained or abandoned, each woman had to have felt the ancient longing to become one with the animals.

*

To become one with another. It is the promise of marriage: that the two shall become one. It is the glory of pregnancy: to carry another life within you. It is the goal of religion: to become one with God. So deep is our spiritual and emotional need to join with another, to become part of another, that it remains a centerpiece of modern Western religious practice. In the sacrament of Holy Communion, Christians reiterate what we once played out in the ancient ritual of cannibalism: in drinking the blood and eating the flesh, we take in the power and spirit of another. We achieve, in this way, oneness with the dead, oneness with the sacrificed Christ.

But to modern Western notions, the chasm between man and animal yawns wider than the gulf between male and female, between man and deity, between living and dead. We have largely lost the knowledge possessed by the shamans. We have created a God in our own image; our priests have rejected the animal gods, and our scientists deny that animals have souls. In the Garden of Eden man knew how to speak with the animals. But today we have mostly forgotten—or perhaps unlearned— how to do this.

There may be another reason why Louis Leakey selected women as the shamans to reapproach the world of animals. Traditionally men have been aligned with the world of culture; women, "coded dark," as Donna Harraway puts it, implicit and hidden, are aligned with the world of nature, with the wild, the ethereal. It is no coincidence that in much of the modern Western world, we worship a male god and that our priests are men; but most of our modern shamans, whom we call mediums, who slip between the worlds of the living and the dead, are women.

Until recently women have largely shared the status of animals in male-dominated culture: like animals, women were considered unpredictable creatures who responded to hidden impulses and required taming by a possessing male "master," as in "master of the house." In psychology, Carol Gilligan has pointed out, the human archetype has been the male. Women, so mysterious that Freud couldn't figure them out (even though most of his patients were women) were the exception to the human "norm"; like wild animals, they did not adhere to man's civilizing rules.

In many cultures a female deity presides over the world of wild animals. Among the Caribou Eskimo, this deity is named Pinga, and to her realm the shamans must go to request a successful hunt; Pinga alone looks after and understands the souls of animals, and it is said that she does not like to see too many of them killed. Somewhere in the collective human psyche we seem to know that women are best equipped to approach the world of the animals.

For millennia there have been legends of women who turn into animals, and animals that turn into women. In the Fox Woman tale of the Labrador Eskimo, a man follows the tracks of a fox to his house and inside discovers a beautiful woman who has hung a fox cloak up on his wall. They live together happily until he complains of a musky odor in the lodge. Thereupon she throws off her clothes, resumes her fox skin, and slips away, never to be seen again.

The story is similar to the Crane Wife tale of the Japanese, the Buffalo Woman myth of the Plains Indians, and the Wild Goose Woman legend common from Greenland to Asia. These tales bespeak old knowledge: a woman's talent for transformation. And indeed, Louis Leakey's three primates — a religious term in his Anglican church — transformed our views of man and ape, human and animal.

At first some scientists thought the findings too incredible to believe: when Jane Goodall reported that the chimpanzees of Gombe used tools, some people privately whispered that Jane had taught them to do this. Dian insisted that some gorillas, combining learning with reasoning and great manual dexterity, could remove tight wire nooses from the wrists of snare victims. Some of her coworkers at Karisoke doubt that this is true.

Even today some findings about the Gombe chimps have gone unpublished simply because no one would believe them. Once, in the 1960s, Patrick McGinnis called Geza Teleki over to see something. Fifi had injured her foot and was lying on her back. "Just watch this, and don't say anything," Patrick told Geza.

Geza remembers: "He started talking to me in a real normal tone: 'Geza, blah-blah-blah-blah, and Fifi show me your foot.' He was careful not to change the tone or quality of his voice. And Fifi lies there and sticks her foot up in the air. And then he does it again, and she does the same thing. And these are chimps that have never been coached in any language. It was seen by five other people."

The findings that were deemed believable enough to be published, however, revolutionized ethologists' thinking. Ethologists began to speak less often of a chasm between man and ape; they began to speak instead of a dividing "line." And it was a line which, in the words of Harvard primatologist Irven De Vore, was "a good deal less clear than one would ever have expected."

What comprises this line between us and our fellow primates? No longer can it be claimed to be tool use. Is it the ability to reason? Wolfgang Kohler once tested captive chimps' reasoning ability by placing several boxes and a stick in an enclosure and hanging a banana from the high ceiling by a string. The animals quickly figured out that they could get to the banana by stacking the boxes one atop the other and then reaching to swat at the banana with a stick. (Once Geza Teleki found himself in exactly this position at Gombe. He had followed the chimpanzees down into a valley and around noon discovered he had forgotten to bring his lunch. The chimps were feeding on fruit in the trees at the time, and he decided to try to knock some fruit from nearby vines with a stick. For about ten minutes he leaped and swatted with his stick but didn't manage to knock down any fruit. Finally an adolescent male named Sniff collected a handful of fruit, came down the tree, and dropped the fruit into Geza's hands.)

Some say language is the line that separates man from ape. But this, too, is being questioned. Captive chimpanzees, gorillas, and orangutans have been taught not only to comprehend, but also to produce language. They have been taught American Sign Language (ASL), the language of the deaf, as well as languages that use plastic chips in place of words and computer languages. One signing chimp, Washoe, often combined known signs in novel and creative ways: she had not been taught the word for swan, but upon seeing one, she signed "water-bird." Another signing chimp, Lucy, seeing and tasting a watermelon for the first time, called it a "candy-drink"; the acidic radish she named "hurt-cry-food." Lucy would play with toys and sign to them, much as human children talk to their dolls. Koko, the gorilla protégée of Penny Patterson, used sign language to make jokes, escape blame, describe her surroundings, tell stories, even tell lies.

One of Biruté's ex-captives, a female orangutan named Princess, was taught a number of ASL signs by Gary Shapiro. Princess used only the signs she knew would bring her food; because she was not a captive, she could not be coerced into using sign language to any ends other than those she found personally useful. Today dolphins, sea lions, harbor seals, and even pigeons are being taught artificial languages, complete with a primitive grammar or syntax. One leading researcher, Ronald Schusterman, is convinced that "the components for language are present probably in all vertebrates, certainly in mammals and birds."

Arguing over semantics and syntax, psychologists and ethologists and linguists are still debating the definitions of the line. Louis Leakey remarked about Jane's discovery of chimps' use of tools that we must "change the definition of man, the definition of tool, or accept chimps as man." Now some linguists have actually proposed, in the face of the ape language experiments, changing the definition of language to exclude the apes from a domain we had considered uniquely ours.

The line separating man from the apes may well be defined less by human measurement than by the limits of Western imagination. It may be less like a boundary between land and water and more like the lines we draw on maps separating the domains of nations.

Henry Beston, in *The Outermost House*, wrote:

> The animal shall not be measured by man. In a world older and more complete than ours, they move finished and complete, gifted with extensions of the senses we have lost or never attained, living by voices we shall never hear. They are not brethren, they are not underlings; they are *other nations*, caught with ourselves in the net of life, fellow prisoners of the splendor and travail of the earth. (italics mine)

The dividing line between nations may well be invisible; but it is no less real. How does one cross that line to travel in the nation of animals? Having traveled in their nation, where lies your allegiance? What do you become?

One is struck, when talking with people who have known Jane or Dian or Biruté, at the frequency with which, unprompted, the analogies arise: Jane, the most socially poised of the three, is often compared to the social chimpanzee. Biruté, serene, quiet, and auburn-haired like the solitary orange apes she studies, is likened to the orangutan. And towering, dark-haired Dian, so often blustering with threat, intensely loyal to her group, is often described in the same terms as the mountain gorilla.

Jane used to joke about this once in a while. "I'm becoming increasingly arboreal," she once quipped to a reporter. She and Hugo used to kid each other about Grub "keeping up with the chimpanzees." In a recent magazine article on Jane, the lead illustration portrayed her thus: the left half of the face was her image, the right half that of a chimpanzee.

Yet Jane does not consider that she has actually crossed the line from man to ape. She refers instead to having seen "Through a Window"—as she titled her most recent book. We have many windows through which to view the world, she points out; some are "opened up by science, their panes polished by a succession of brilliant penetrating minds." There are windows "unshuttered by the logic of philosophers; windows through which the mystics seek their visions of truth; windows from which the leaders of the great religions have peered." Too often, she argues, these windows are "misted over by the breath of our finite humanity." Jane's was a window from which she wiped away that mist, a window opened through the power of her relationships with individual chimps like Flo, David Graybeard, Mr. McGregor, and Fifi.

Once Jane called this relationship friendship. She titled one book *My Friends the Wild Chimpanzees*. But since then she has changed her mind. She considers "friendship" inaccurate, for her relationship with the chimpanzees is not predicated upon the usual bonds between humans or even the usual bonds between people and animals.

Friendship, says Jane, "is different from what I have with the chimpanzees. Friendship is shared goals, aims, helping one another through life, depending on one another—and that's what I don't have with the chimps."

To David Graybeard Jane owes the first two major discoveries of her career, tool use and meat eating by the chimpanzees. To Flo, from whom she learned the joy and wonder and skills of mothering, she owes the debt of an initiate to her wisewoman. She owes much to the chimpanzees, but they do not participate in her debt.

Jane made offerings to the chimps. She left out piles of bananas for them, she administered medicines to those who were sick. Her first offering to a chimp—the palm nut she held out to David Graybeard—was rejected. He did not want or need the fruit from her hand. And this was the nature of the chimpanzees' relationship with her: they might choose her company, they might sometimes accept her offerings, but they never *needed* her. They refused to participate in the debts that tie humans together. "There's no way the chimps depend on me for anything. What I feel with the chimps is something rather different. It's a closeness, an awareness, an empathy with, a respect for, love of," says Jane today. "But to me that isn't friendship. Friendship must be reciprocal."

Jane has carefully nurtured her relationships with the chimps: she has kept her promises to them, to remain harmless, waiting, receptive. She has codified the knowledge they have handed over to her, less a scientist than an initiate, a scribe at the oracle. She has become a warrior in the cause.

Yet Jane is not one with these animals; the chimpanzees have never considered her one of their own. "Perhaps they think of me as another inferior creature like a baboon," she muses. She cannot cloak her Otherness from them. She is permitted to travel in their nation as a visitor, not a citizen; she lives only at the edge of their world. "They know they can get away from me if they want to," Jane told me, "because I, as a human, can't keep up with them. They would have more trouble getting away from another chimp."

And perhaps, suggests Geza Teleki, this is why a chimp may sometimes choose to keep company with a human for a while instead of another chimp: "He knows he can get away from you whenever he wants." A chimpanzee's relationship with another chimpanzee is reciprocal. But a chimpanzee's relationship with a human is always on the chimpanzee's terms.

"For the first ten years I was here," Biruté told me at Camp Leakey, "I wanted to be an orangutan."

Biruté had always been drawn to orangutans, more so than to any other being. When her departure for Indonesia was delayed again and again, Louis Leakey offered her the opportunity to study other animals in other places—pygmy chimps, for example. But she held out for orangutans. Even before she saw a wild orangutan, she felt both awed by and connected to them. It was as if the orangutan—serene, solitary, self-contained—was her personal totem, an animal whose power and knowledge she wished, like the Oglala Indians, to gather into her personal *waken.*

"We Westerners," she says in her thoughtful, quiet voice, "aspire to be orangutans. If you look at the end goal of our culture, it's to be an orangutan, to be totally independent of everybody—spouses, parents, children."

And indeed, during the first ten years of her study, Biruté questioned her own independence. She loved her husband Rod, but she did not depend on him. She loved her child Binti, but she did not need him with her to make her life worthwhile. But she was not, she realized, totally independent. She needed the orangutans. She wanted them to need her. "For the first ten years, I was totally immersed in them. You can get sucked in, if you want to be sucked in. I got sucked in. But they don't need that. If you want to get sucked in, you have to do it yourself. They don't do it to you.

"The difference is, if you're honest with yourself, orangutans never let you hold the delusion that they need you. They can just walk by you and never look back. They're very engaging animals. But you have to push yourself on them. The relationship is like seventy percent you, thirty percent them, not fifty-fifty. And what that means is, you have to push harder.

"Watching them, I realized I could never be an orangutan. Maybe you can be a chimpanzee; maybe you can be a gorilla. But you can't be an orangutan. If you step back you realize you're fooling yourself. But that's what gives them their majesty, their nobility—they don't need anybody."

Biruté, so thoughtful and seemingly self-contained, has realized her human needs: to raise a family, to love and depend upon a husband. Yet at times Gary Shapiro catches her staring into space with a peculiar expression. It is a gaze he has seen on the faces of the orangutans. He calls it "the fruit stare," the slow-motion gaze used by a slow-moving, intelligent ape to search the canopy for fruit. It is unlike the expression found on the face of any other animal. In this, he says, Biruté is "very much orangutan."

Biruté draws on a clove-flavored cigarette and says thoughtfully: "I am probably more of an orangutan than a lot of other things."

By the time I began work on this book, Dian Fossey had been murdered. To learn about her findings and methods, I could consult her book, her scientific and popular articles, her Ph.D. thesis. But scientists are often loath to write about their feelings for the animals they study or about what they consider to be their place among them. I would not have a chance to talk with the living Dian about these things.

A friend of mine who is a medium — a sort of modern shaman — offered to try to contact Dian for me. Gretchen Vogel Poisson farms near our house. She had never read Dian's book and had not read anything about her recently in the popular media. Nearly two years after Dian's death, alone in her home on a Saturday in March 1987, Gretchen narrated her vision into a tape recorder. This is what she saw:

"My impression is of Dian in a cavelike structure. She has on light-colored clothes, and she is still surrounded by some gorillas, not very numerous. But she's in a place of so little light that the only way I can even perceive her is because of her clothing. And this seems very odd. I ask for my angels to take me right up to her."

Here Gretchen pauses. On the tape you can hear her suck in her breath: "She is actually a gorilla in the suit of clothes."

"When I look at a gorilla," Dian once told a reporter, "I feel like I'm looking at the better part of myself."

"I talk to the gorillas in their language," she said during an appearance on "The Johnny Carson Show." She leaned forward on her left forearm on Carson's wood-grained desk, lifted her chin, and stated: "Naoom, m-nwowm, manauum-naoumm, naooum?" And then she turned toward another guest and repeated: "Naoom, m-nwowm, manauum-naoumm, naooum?" At this point she was more relaxed than at any other time on the show.

Dian often stated to reporters that she would rather answer their questions in this way—to answer as a gorilla would. When Robinson McIlvaine last visited Dian at Karisoke, he said, "she was talking nothing but gorilla. Grunting and making all sorts of noises, for an hour. It was a little off-putting."

She was affected more deeply by the death of Digit than most people are by the death of a sibling or a spouse. Friends recall that after Digit's death, Dian could not so much as speak his name without a catch in her husky voice. "In reality," Biruté said after the murder, "this was Dian's second death. In reality, Dian died the first time with Digit."

To Dian, Digit was no "baby-releaser" stimulus. Digit "was the son she never had, the sibling she never had, the father she never had," said Diana McMeekin. "But the gorillas were far more than her children. They were her surrogate race."

It was during a visit with her in Sacramento a decade before Dian's death that Biruté first realized that "in some ways, Dian had become a gorilla." Dian was doing the comforting "naoom, m-nwowm, manauum-naoumm, naooum?" gorilla vocalizations. Biruté spoke about this at a memorial benefit for Dian's Digit Fund at National Geographic in March 1986: "I realized then," she said, "that Dian's soul was already tinged and had already merged with the gorillas'."

Some say that Dian's relationship with the gorillas, her feeling of oneness with them, bespoke a kind of psychological sickness. "A lot, I think, of her inexplicable sourness and unhappiness was accelerated [by the fact that] all the touchy-feely stuff with the gorillas was a need to substitute gorillas for the people in her life," said one American conservation official who knew her. Again the voice of the skeptic: Dian had lost touch with *reality*, the world of people, rather than attaining a new reality, the world of nonhuman minds. "I think she entertained the thought that gorillas cared for her and were more worth her love than human beings were," this person said. "The gorillas certainly tolerated her, but they certainly had no positive emotions with her. They were complete in their gorillahood, they had their own relationships. They had no need for her. They *didn't need* her."

Another scientist, one of Dian's former students, said, "Some of the gorillas may have real affection for us; nonetheless they don't like us as much as we like them, and they don't understand us as well as we understand them."

But perhaps, in a world "older and more complete" than ours, there is a love that does not demand a reciprocal debt of need. Certainly Dian needed the gorillas. But perhaps the gorillas understood Dian better than any human ever did.

Ian Redmond told a story at the National Geographic memorial benefit to Dian. He hadn't planned to tell it; it was prompted by a question: how did the gorillas react to Dian's death?

"This goes beyond the bounds of strict science," Ian said. "Just after Dian's death, three gorilla groups who had been at some distance from Visoke suddenly homed in on the mountain. One group traveled almost continually for two days to arrive in the vicinity." Ian is a scientist and would not want to volunteer the interpretation implicit in the gorillas' sudden, purposeful movement toward the mountain that was Dian's home: that they had come, in her hour of death, to be near to her.

In all of the ancient legends about women who become animals — the Fox Woman tale, the Buffalo Woman legend, the

Crane Wife story—the women all return to their animal form in the end. And there is yet another common thread: the men they leave become angry. In many of the tales, after the woman's final transformation into an animal, she is hunted down and killed by men.

This is what happened to Dian Fossey. And perhaps this names the unease some people feel about Biruté and Jane as well: that these women—and women are our most domesticated beings—would become transformed and then leave us to go wild.

Both Biruté and Jane are firmly rooted in the world of human endeavor. Jane has not become a chimp; Biruté has not become an orangutan. Yet the lives of all three women have been transformed by their visions; they are inexorably linked to the other nations through which they have traveled. In a sense they are, in the words of Henry Beston, living by voices we shall never hear; they are gifted with extensions of the senses we have lost or never attained. You need only listen to Jane's excitement at seeing "a tree laden with *luscious* fruit"—fruit that to human senses is so tart it prompts a grimace. You need only remember how Dian would sing to the gorillas a gorilla song—praising the taste of rotting wood. You need only imagine what goes through Biruté's mind when she does the "fruit stare" of the orangutan.

Western scientists do not like to talk about these things, for to do so is to voice what for so long has been considered unspeakable. The bonds between human and animal and the psychic tools of empathy and intuition have been "coded dark" by Western science—labeled as hidden, implicit, unspoken. The truths through which we once explained our world, the truths spoken by the ancient myths, have been hushed by the louder voice of passionless scientific objectivity.

But perhaps we are rediscovering the ancient truths. In his book *Life of the Japanese Monkeys*, the renowned Japanese primate researcher Kawai Masao outlines a new concept, upon which his research is built: he calls it *kyokan*, which translates as "feel-one." He struck upon the concept after observing a female researcher on his team interacting with female Japanese macaques. "We [males] had always found it more difficult to distinguish among female [macaques]," he wrote. "However, a female researcher who joined our study could recognize individual females easily and understood their behavior, personality and emotional life better. . . . I had never before thought that female monkeys and women could immediately understand each other," he wrote. "This revelation made me feel I had touched upon the essence of the feel-one method."

Masao's book, unavailable to Western readers until translated into English by Pamela Asquith in 1981, explains that *kyokan* means "becoming fused with the monkeys' lives where, through an intuitive channel, feelings are mutually exchanged." Embodied in the *kyokan* approach is the idea that it is not only desirable to establish a feeling of shared life and mutual attachment with the study animals—to "feel one" with them—but that this feeling is *necessary* for proper science, for discovering truth. "It is our view that by positively entering the group, by making contact at some level, objectivity can be established," Masao wrote.

Masao is making a call for the scientist to return to the role of the ancient shaman: to "feel one" with the animals, to travel within their nations, to allow oneself to become transformed, to see what ordinary people cannot normally see. And this, far more than the tables of data, far more than the publications and awards, is the pioneering achievement of Jane Goodall, Biruté Galdikas, and Dian Fossey: they have dared to reapproach the Other and to sanctify the unity we share with those other nations that are, in Beston's words, "caught with ourselves in the net of life and time, fellow prisoners of the splendor and travail of the earth."

SELECTED BIBLIOGRAPHY

Chimpanzees

Ghiglieri, Michael P. *East of the Mountains of the Moon: Chimpanzee Society in the African Rain Forest.* New York: Free Press, 1988.
Goodall, Jane. *Through a Window.* Boston: Houghton Mifflin, 1990.
———. *My Life with the Wild Chimpanzees.* New York: Minstrel Books, 1988.
———. *The Chimpanzees of Gombe: Patterns of Behavior.* Cambridge, Mass: Harvard University Press, 1986.
———. *In the Shadow of Man.* Boston: Houghton Mifflin, 1971.
Premack, David, and Ann James Premack. *The Mind of an Ape.* New York: W. W. Norton, 1983.

Gorillas

Fossey, Dian. *Gorillas in the Mist.* Boston: Houghton Mifflin, 1983.
Fossey, Dian. "The Behavior of the Mountain Gorilla." Ph.D. dissertation, Cambridge University, Darwin College, 1976.
Goodall, Allan. *The Wandering Gorillas.* London: William Collins Sons, 1979.
Mowat, Farley. *Woman in the Mists.* New York: Warner Books, 1987.
Nichols, Michael. *Gorilla: Struggle for Survival in the Virungas.* New York: Aperture, 1989.

Schaller, George. *The Year of the Gorilla.* Chicago: University of Chicago Press, 1964.

Orangutans and Borneo

Galdikas, Biruté M. F. "Orangutan Adaptation at Tanjung Puting Reserve, Central Borneo." Ph.D. dissertation, University of California, 1978.
MacKinnon, John. *In Search of the Red Ape.* New York: Holt, Rinehart & Winston, 1974.
Schwartz, Jeffrey. *The Red Ape.* Boston: Houghton Mifflin, 1987.
Wallace, Alfred Russel. *The Malay Archipelago.* London: Macmillan, 1869.

Primatology

De Waal, Frans. *Peacemaking among Primates.* Cambridge, Mass.: Harvard University Press, 1989.
De Waal, Frans. *Chimpanzee Politics: Power and Sex among Apes.* New York: Harper & Row, 1982.
Hamburg, D. A., and E. R. McCown, eds. *The Great Apes.* Menlo Park, Calif.: Benjamin-Cummings, 1979.
Harraway, Donna. *Primate Visions.* New York: Routledge, 1989.
Linden, Eugene. *Silent Partner: The Legacy of the Ape Language Experiments.* New York: Times Books, 1986.
———. *Apes, Men and Language.* New York: Penguin Books, 1974.
Smuts, Barbara, et al., eds. *Primate Societies.* Chicago: University of Chicago Press, 1987.

Human Evolution and Paleoanthropology

Cole, Sonia. *Leakey's Luck.* New York: Harcourt Brace Jovanovich, 1975.
Hrdy, Sarah Blaffer. *The Woman Who Never Evolved.* Cambridge, Mass.: Harvard University Press, 1983.
Leakey, L. S. B. *By the Evidence.* New York: Harcourt Brace Jovanovich, 1974.
Leakey, L. S. B. *White African: An Early Autobiography.* Rochester, Vt.: Schenkman Books, 1966.
Leakey, Mary. *Disclosing the Past.* New York: Doubleday, 1984.
Leakey, Richard, and Roger Lewin. *People of the Lake: Mankind and Its Beginnings.* New York: Avon, 1978.

Ethology

Gould, James L. *Ethology: The Mechanisms and Evolution of Behavior.* New York: W. W. Norton, 1982.

Hinde, Robert A. *Ethology: Its Nature and Relations with Other Sciences.* Oxford: Oxford University Press, 1982.

Lorenz, Konrad. *The Foundations of Ethology.* New York: Simon and Schuster, 1981.

Africa

du Chaillu, P. B. *Adventures in Equatorial Africa.* New York: Harper Brothers, 1868.

Knappert, Jan. *Myths and Legends of the Swahili.* Nairobi: Heinemann Kenya, 1970.

Mbiti, John S. *African Religions and Philosophy.* Nairobi: Heinemann, 1969.

Other

Campbell, Joseph. *The Masks of God: Primitive Mythology.* New York: Penguin Books, 1976.

Gilligan, Carol. *In a Different Voice.* Cambridge, Mass.: Harvard University Press, 1982.

Hearne, Vicki. *Adam's Task: Calling Animals by Name.* New York: Alfred A. Knopf, 1986.

ORGANIZATIONS

The following organizations support the continuing conservation, education, and field research of Jane Goodall and Biruté
Galdikas, and carry on the work of Dian Fossey. All would
welcome contributions sent to these addresses:

The Jane Goodall Institute
P.O. Box 41720
Tucson, Ariz. 85717-1720
Phone: 1-800-999-CHIMP
*Contributions may be earmarked for specific projects, such as the Com-
mittee for the Conservation and Care of Chimpanzees.*

The Digit Fund
45 Inverness Drive East
Englewood, Colo. 80112-5480

The Orangutan Foundation
822 South Wellesley Avenue
Los Angeles, Calif. 90049

International Primate Protection League
P.O. Box 766
Summerville, S.C. 29484

Paying laypeople may assist with Biruté Galdikas's fieldwork in Kalimantan Tengah, Borneo. Contact:
Earthwatch
680 Mount Auburn Street
Watertown, Mass. 02172